Gilles Aycelin
THE SERVANT OF TWO MASTERS

Gilles Aycelin

THE SERVANT OF TWO MASTERS

Jo Ann McNamara

Syracuse University Press   1973

Library of Congress Cataloging in Publication Data

McNamara, Jo Ann, 1931–
  Gilles Aycelin; the servant of two masters.

  An expanded and rev. version of the author's thesis,
Columbia University.
  Bibliography: p.
  1. Aycelin, Gilles, ca. 1250–1318.   I. Title.
DC94.A9M3 1973   327'.2'0924 [B]   73–6575
ISBN 0–8156–0094–1

*Publication of this book
was assisted by the*
American Council of Learned Societies
under a grant from the
Andrew W. Mellon Foundation

Manufactured in the United States of America

for Evelyn
who knows what friends are for

Preface

Gilles Aycelin, lawyer, councillor to Philip the Fair and two of his sons, president of the Parlement of Paris, diplomat, Archbishop of Narbonne and of Rouen, presiding officer of the papal commission to investigate the Templars, was one of the most influential men of his age. Yet, over the centuries since his death in 1318, he has so completely preserved the discretion which characterized his career that he has escaped the thorough investigation to which scholars have subjected so many of his contemporaries. My own acquaintance with him was initially accidental, arising out of an interest in the political activities of the French cardinals in the pontificates of Celestine V and Boniface VIII. In tracing the relations of Hugh Aycelin, his brother Gilles was brought to my attention. Thereafter, I began to find his unobtrusive hand in so many of the great affairs of the period that he soon crowded his brother to the fringes of my attention and came to overshadow, in my mind, even his famous partner and relative by marriage, Pierre Flote. To dislodge him from the obscurity which he preferred and trace the singularly comprehensive career which has been hidden behind his many titles soon became my chief object.

The reign of Philip the Fair has interested so many historians for so long, that a most extraordinary collection of material has reached the printed page. For this, I am grateful to all my predecessors over the centuries. I have drawn heavily upon their work since the conditions of my own life prevented research abroad. Despite this deficiency, so vast an amount of material from different areas of concentration proved to be available that it was possible to piece together the fascinating jigsaw of Aycelin's career—a career which has hitherto received only the piecemeal attention that the blind men gave the elephant.

For the most part, I have given my characters the modern

counterparts of their Christian names, as they occur in their own native languages, rather than the Latin names they carry in most of the original references. Exceptions have been made for such common usages as "Philip the Fair." Surnames presented a more difficult problem. Hugh Aycelin, for example, is more commonly called Hugh de Billon, but I preferred to emphasize his family name. Spelling, in every case, tends to be erratic in the texts. I have generally followed the spellings most commonly used by modern scholars. Aycelin himself is found under a variety of spellings, "Aicelin" and "Aiscelin" being the most common alternatives to the spelling which I have employed.

An earlier version of this work was accepted by the Department of History of Columbia University as a doctoral dissertation. It has since been expanded and revised. I wish to express my gratitude to Professor John H. Mundy and Professor Donald Watt for their helpful suggestions and criticisms. They saved me from many errors. Those that remain, of course, are my own. I wish also to thank the City University of New York for providing me with a summer research grant during the period of revision.

Hunter College   Jo Ann McNamara
Spring 1973

Contents

Gilles Aycelin

THE SERVANT OF
TWO MASTERS

I

Introduction

Silent and staring upon his throne, Philip the Fair has remained an enigma for over six centuries. No less mysterious are his councillors: Flote, the "one-eyed Belial," whom Boniface VIII saw as his nemesis; Nogaret, surrounded by the sinister shadows of Anagni and the prisons that engulfed the Templars; Marigny, suspended at last upon his own gibbet. Romanticized by Michelet as "the destroyers of the middle ages, the papacy feudalism and chivalry,"[1] they have compelled the attention of generations of historians who have attempted to pierce the obscurity with which they surrounded their own achievements. The councillors of Philip the Fair did not share the modern mania to "tell all" in countless memoirs. They remained faithful to the end: what was said or done in the king's secret council remained a secret. The great pioneer scholar of the period's documents finally despaired of discussing the councillors in individual detail:

> One will never know who these men were, for the archival documents give only their names, their titles, their comings and goings, and their salaries and grants.[2]

Pegues has recently attempted a new approach to the problem by studying the lawyers as a group:

> . . . if all these lawyers were studied together and their origins,

1. *Histoire de France,* III, 34.
2. Langlois, "Geoffroi du Plessis," *Revue historiç :e,* LXVII, 70. Despite this conclusion, a few attempts have been made to provi :e individual studies: Favier, *Un conseiller de Philippe le Bel: Enguerran de Marigny;* Holtzmann, *Wilhelm von Nogaret.* Nogaret and Pierre Dubois were treated at length by Renan, *Etudes sur la politique religieuse du règne de Philippe le Bel.* Short studies of some of the councillors are included in the *Histoire littéraire de la France,* particularly Delisle, "Gilles Aicelin, Archevêque de Narbonne et de Rouen," XXXII, 474–502, which is the only individual treatment ever undertaken of his career.

1

careers and conduct compared one with another, the individual might acquire a personality where he had none before.[3]

This study drew into some prominence the activities of Gilles Aycelin, as a lawyer and member of the royal council. Being focused upon the councillors as lawyers, however, it put little emphasis on his equally important responsibilities as archbishop of Narbonne and of Rouen. It is this dualism which provides the texture of Aycelin's career. Moreover, Pegues' study, with its necessary generalizations, led to the conclusion that Aycelin was a rare exemplar of moral integrity among his aggressive fellow councillors. This notion appears to be in the process of receiving general acceptance, having recently been reiterated by Favier who states unequivocally that Aycelin's conservatism undermined his influence with the king.[4]

A detailed examination of Aycelin's involvement in the great crises of the realm, particularly his role in the attacks on Bernard Saisset and the Templars, will disclose serious flaws in this image of rectitude. On the other hand, his achievements on many other occasions will demonstrate that he was far too important to be relegated to a subsidiary position as the impotent voice of conscience among the lawyers of Philip the Fair. However obscure they may frequently appear to be, the concrete acts of individuals are the only possible basis on which we can judge them. Even a bare record of the comings and goings of the Archbishop of Narbonne justifies the reiterated statements of his contemporaries that he was one of the chief councillors of the king of France. His deeds confront us in the records of all the great events of the time and many of the lesser ones. Though he remained as silent as his master about his personal thoughts, loyalties, and ambitions, much of what he was and what he wanted is betrayed by what he did.

3. *The Lawyers of the Last Capetians*, 35. His introductory chapter provides a thorough historiographical introduction on the general problem of the personalities and responsibilities of the councillors. A similar survey recently appeared in Favier, "Les légistes et le gouvernement de Philippe le Bel," *Journal des Savants*, 1969, pt. 2, pp. 92–108.

4. "Les légistes et le gouvernment de Philippe le Bel," 99: "The case of Gilles Aiscelin ought to be put to one side. We can see that the archbishop's moderation was checked in the end. The king did not condemn his too favorable attitude to Bernard Saisset and to the Templars but he passed over his counsels of moderation."

Although he has been largely overlooked by historians, partially due to his talent for hiding his actions behind the smoke screen created by his flamboyant partner, Pierre Flote, it is clear from an account of his work between 1293 and 1301 that Aycelin was one of the most active and talented of Philip the Fair's agents in foreign affairs. He was named head of innumerable missions to Rome, to Flanders, to the King of England, and to the Emperor. The treaties he negotiated set the standard for French policy for years to come.

But important as these activities were in maintaining the territorial integrity of the lands ruled by the French and substantially increasing their influence, the diplomatic and military successes of the reign constituted little more than a consolidation of the status quo established by Saint Louis. The major problems of Flanders and Aquitaine would require more than a century of war before a final settlement was reached. Indeed, the marriage treaty arranged by Aycelin to end the conflict with England would ultimately involve the two countries in a far more serious conflict over the disposition of the crown of France itself. If the reign of Philip the Fair were to be judged in this context alone, it would amount to little more than a prelude to the Hundred Years' War.

That king reigned for nearly thirty years, and his government was extraordinarily active domestically and internationally throughout every one of them. Much attention has been paid to the spectacular crises of the reign, but it is the quieter years of steady development of institutions and policies that deserve more consideration in a serious evaluation of the work of his officials. Aycelin was one of the very few councillors who held a position of confidence in the court throughout the reign—indeed, his activities continued unabated through the succeeding reign of Louis X and the early years of Philip V. His career lay in many areas, combining offices and responsibilities often thought to be totally incompatible with one another by the polemic-minded commentator. No one served Philip the Fair better as a lawyer and as a diplomat. He played an active and important role in each of the king's audacious attacks on his fellow sovereigns, the Templars and the pope himself.

On the other hand, he never neglected his duties as a prelate and showed a remarkable independence in domestic affairs. As an ecclesiastic, as a feudal lord, and as presiding official of the Parlement of Paris, he personally helped to maintain the balance between the central government and the holders of local rights and privileges in France. As Archbishop of Narbonne and then of Rouen, he left his churches in better financial condition than he found them. As a result of his labors, both churches were more firmly established in possession of their customary privileges and were endowed with new liberties. This feat was accomplished not despite the king but with his full cooperation and favor. Aycelin's domestic activities demonstrate that the French clergy was neither servile toward the king nor, in general, victimized by him. Nor did his loyalty to Philip the Fair prevent the archbishop from enjoying a fruitful relationship with the papacy throughout most of his career. He systematically built the structure of his church's privileges by complementing royal charters with papal grants.

In this respect, our study of Aycelin's achievements supports the modern tendency to modify the classic view of Philip the Fair as the aggressive enemy of the medieval church and medieval feudalism as exemplified by Boutaric[5] and his contemporary de Vidaillon, who argued that Philip used his council and his law courts to mount an all-out attack on the system of privileges and feudal liberties that had characterized the realm of Saint Louis.[6] Aycelin's successful defense of both his feudal and ecclesiastical rights in Narbonne and in Rouen, carried on within the context of his role on the council and in the Parlement, tends to support the interpretation of Philip's policies recently advanced by Strayer.[7]

5. *La France sous Philippe le Bel*, 3: "France then touched one of those solemn moments in the lives of nations when people decide their destinies. . . . The vigor and addresse of Philip would turn the balance to the side of the crown: with him began the absolute feudal monarchy which would subsist until the reign of King John without the counterweight of the clergy, nobility, or bourgeosie."
6. *Histoire des Conseils du Roi*, 87–90.
7. "Philip the Fair—A 'Constitutional' King," in *Medieval Statecraft and the Perspectives of History*, 209: "Philip tried to conform to the traditions of the French monarchy and the practices of the French government. As far as possible, he governed his realm through a well-established system of courts and administrative officials. He always asked the advice of responsible men; he was in-

Where Philip did undertake practical intervention in the affairs of his subjects, it was principally through his expanded use of the Parlement of Paris, a court whose functions and methods took clear shape during his reign. Here, if anywhere, the notorious legist spirit and its legendary expressions of violent opposition to the old principles of feudal law should be found. That this spirit existed was given the weighty support of Langlois,[8] who cited texts drawn from the work of Pierre Dubois[9] to illustrate the idea that the king's courts should abandon the old concept of their function as guardians of feudal customs in favor of a new role as defenders of royal rights against all comers.

The ideas of Pierre Dubois, however, cannot be taken as typical of the spirit dominating the royal council, since that lawyer apparently never participated in its deliberations and there is no evidence that his propositions ever received a serious hearing in Paris. Langlois ascribed the purported change in the direction of the Parlement to the invasion of such "violent men" as Pierre Flote. But there is no evidence that Flote was a lawyer at all, and his death at Courtrai excluded him from participation in most of the important administrative innovations of the period. Far more typical of the lawyers of the Parlement was Aycelin, who was specifically named in the ordinance of 1305 as one of the men whose presence at its deliberations was most desirable.[10]

Philip's goal, and that of the lawyers he employed, was unquestionably the centralization of the government. This is a natural aim of any government and by no means necessarily an unpopular or tyrannical one. There was no tangible opposition from the prelates and barons—who were supposedly its victims—until the very end of the reign. Even then, they apparently aimed at little more than the dismissal of a few councillors whom they believed to have been too greedy with the royal treasure, and a restatement of the ordinances of 1302–1304 guaranteeing their

---

fluenced by that advice in working out the details of his general policy. He tried to stay at least within the letter of the law; he tried to observe the customs of the kingdom."

8. Langlois, "Les origines du Parlement de Paris, *Revue historique*, LXII, 74–114.

9. "Summaria Brevis," 435–94.

10. *Ordonnances des roys de France*, I, 547.

various rights, clarified by a series of local charters. The failure of a more extensive opposition to form would be remarkable if the two leading estates of the realm had indeed been under violent attack. This, however, was not the case.

The traditional view of Philip's domestic policies has recently been altered, and it is now clear that the real end of his reforms and reorganizations was the creation of a government resting on the cooperation of the magnates of the realm.[11] From their seats on the royal council, nobles and prelates helped to formulate the policies of which they were once believed to have been the victims. The charters issued by the king, and the decisions of the royal courts based upon them, aimed at clarifying the relative positions of the king and his subjects and establishing a clear statement of the privileges of all.

Accordingly, Philip the Fair rarely sought to deprive his subjects of their cherished liberties. Rather, he attempted—with their active cooperation—to make himself and his court the arbiter of their disputes and guardian of their privileges. This is not to deprive the lawyers of their role in the government. Like Gilles Aycelin, most of the prelates who participated in the deliberations of the court were trained lawyers who represented, better than Nogaret, the real role of the jurist. In this respect, a detailed study of Aycelin's career is particularly valuable. As one of the most astute lawyers in France and an active and influential member of the royal council throughout the reign, he was incessantly involved in the formulation and execution of the royal program. Simultaneously, he was energetic in pursuit of all the advantages for his church in Narbonne which could be procured through his influence. He was persistent in stubborn defense of his rights as a feudal lord, even against the king. Yet he was able to pursue aims which would once have seemed hopelessly contradictory with indisputable success.

This aspect of Aycelin's history strongly suggests that Philip the Fair was far less aggressive in his policies toward his magnates than has sometimes been supposed. A desire to reorganize and clarify the machinery of the monarchy, which Aycelin shared,

11. Lot and Fawtier, *Histoire des institutions*, II, *passim*.

need not be defined as a drive to destroy the customary rights of the feudal classes. The tale of his involvement in the great quarrels with Boniface VIII demonstrates that, whatever aggressive stance he took against the pope, Philip handled the clergy of France with consummate tact. Opposition to a reigning pope did not constitute a generalized anticlerical stance.

On several occasions, Aycelin was forced to choose between the two masters to whom he owed loyalty. No doubt the decision was painful. But, like his fellow councillors and most of the prelates of the Gallican church, he found himself able to reconcile his conscience with his allegiance to the king.

Three kings placed their confidence in Gilles Aycelin and they were not mistaken. In the daily routine of the courts, in foreign affairs, and in the great conflicts between his spiritual and temporal superiors he played an invaluable role in the growth of the French monarchy. The human personality of this great councillor remains hidden from us, buried with his secret hopes and dreams. But the barebones record of his service discloses much about the dedication of the lawyers who served this most enigmatic of rulers.

II

Men of Auvergne

Throughout the thirteenth century, the kings of France had pursued a policy of territorial expansion with steady success. From the accession of Philip Augustus until the last years of the reign of Philip III, French arms and French prestige had been everywhere in the ascendant. Not France alone but all of Europe had paid homage to the resplendent character of the saintly King Louis IX. A French pope, Martin IV, put the power of his office almost exclusively at the disposal of his countrymen. Saint Louis' brother, Charles of Anjou, had carved a French kingdom out of the Hohenstaufen inheritance in Sicily. Of all the vast lands once held by the King of England on the Continent only the Duchy of Aquitaine remained, due to the generous wish of Louis to secure a peace without bitterness. In the north, Flanders had been reduced to vassalage and, in 1271, the great inheritance Languedoc had reverted to the French crown.

It was a brilliantly impressive achievement—but an unstable one. There is, perhaps, no peace without bitterness. The King of England chafed against his vassal status. In Aquitaine, in Flanders, in Languedoc, and along the imperial frontiers the hearts of all too many of these new subjects nursed residual loyalties to ancient lords that combined readily with present discontents and peristent hopes of a more promising future for the ambitious.

Their hour seemed to have come with the massacre of French forces in Sicily in 1282. The rebellion, named the "Sicilian Vespers," was followed by the offer of the Sicilian crown to the King of Aragon, heir of the Hohenstaufen claim. His acceptance was swiftly followed by retaliation. The French pope excommunicated the King of Aragon and offered his crown to Charles of Valois, younger son of Philip III. But by 1285 the French armies were being driven from Sicily. Philip III's attempted invasion of Aragon

was repelled. Charles of Anjou died in despair while his heir,
Charles of Salerno, was being carried as a prisoner to Aragon. In
France, the retreating army of Philip III paused at Perpignan.
There the king died of fever. A sixteen-year-old boy, Philip the
Fair, was left with a heritage of sudden disaster and long-standing
confusion.

Within France itself, royal authority had been nominally extended in every direction. But the great vassal of England had
never fully accepted his position in Aquitaine. The Flemings
sought continually to escape the restrictions laid on them by royal
policies. In the south, great lords like the Viscount of Narbonne
had not forgotten their old connection with the crown of Aragon.
Hundreds of enclaves within France were ruled by secular or
ecclesiastical lords with only the flimsiest ties to the crown. There
were too many lands and classes of men who owed allegiance to
someone other than the King of France, or who lived in virtual
independence from any outside interference. In many sensitive
areas, especially along the ill-defined frontiers, vassals were prone
to seek the assistance of rival sovereigns to defend their claims and
privileges against the efforts of the crown to consolidate its own
authority.

If the young king were to hold what his ancestors had gained
and create a stable monarchy, he would need all the support and
assistance he could attract to supplement his own considerable
talents. He would need men of wit and ability whose ambitions
would be tied to the fortunes of the crown. For such men he could
look, as his ancestors had done before him, to that class of men
peculiar to a society where wealth and status still attached primarily to the land: the younger sons of lesser noblemen whose
family domains could be expected only to support the heir. Such
men customarily sought to live by their native talents, advancing
through the influence their relatives could command with greater
lords. Ordinarily, in the south, they had sought careers in the
Church or in the service of great local magnates. After 1271, men
of this area could also look for advancement in the growing
bureaucracy of the monarchy.[1]

1. Carolus-Barré, "Les baillis de Philippe III," 123ff. has shown that the

Gilles Aycelin came from such a family. Their estates were in or near the town of Billon in Auvergne, an area dominated by the great seigneurial family of La Tour du Pin. The jurisdictional differences between the two branches of the family, between the head of the family and the Bishop of Clermont (himself a La Tour more often than not) and between them and other families of the area, provided ample occupation for officials serving that member of the family who bore the title of Count of the Auvergne.[2]

The Aycelins have generally been called a great family on the basis of Duchesne's unelaborated statement that Gilles' brother, Hugh Aycelin, came from "one of the most distinguished families of Auvergne." Duchesne's purpose was simply to establish Hugh's relationship to his brothers and to a family which was to become very distinguished in the following century.[3] He did not necessarily intend his statement to apply to the status of the family before Hugh achieved prominence as a cardinal. The early careers of both Hugh and Gilles Aycelin have been misrepresented by the assumption of Duchesne's successors that the family was already a powerful one in the thirteenth century.[4]

The first appearance of any member of the family yet discovered is that of "P. Anselinus," whose signature was appended as a witness to an agreement between the Bishop of Clermont and the Count of Auvergne and submitted to Innocent III in February 1207.[5] His fellow witnesses included two important local noble-

---

majority of the administrative officials of the crown in the thirteenth century were drawn from the families of the lesser nobility, complemented by a smaller number of bourgeois.

2. A. Bossuat, in Lot and Fawtier, *Histoire des institutions*, I, ch. 4, has traced the early history of the area and the complex jurisdictional arrangements of the La Tour family.

3. Duchesne, *Histoire des cardinaux français*, II, 230, was the first to notice that the cardinal generally called Hugh of Billon (or a variant spelling) in contemporary sources and, for unknown reasons, named "Seguin" by later authors, was in fact an Aycelin.

4. For example, Chapotin, *Histoire des dominicains de la province de France*, 685, assumed that Hugh's entry into the Dominican order was an act of pure piety: "To the career of ecclesiastical functions and dignities which would conduct one of his brothers to the see of Clermont and the other to Narbonne, he preferred the poor and laborious career opened at Clermont among the children of Saint Dominic." Hugh's later career and those of his brothers can be better understood if it is assumed that such a choice was not available to them in their youth.

5. Baluze, *Histoire généalogique de la maison d'Auvergne*, II, 79, could find no earlier mention of the family in local records. In his will, Hugh Aycelin stated

men, Hugh de La Tour and Robert of Oliergues, but the name of
Anselinus appeared only near the end of the list, among a group
of lesser men undistinguished by any titles.

No further record of the family has been found before 1257,
when Albert Aycelin, chanter of the church of Billon, helped
arbitrate a compromise of differences between Count Robert of
Auvergne and Hugh, Abbot of Monlieu.[6] In 1261 Robert Aycelin
sold a tithe he held at La Peschadoire,[7] which may suggest that his
need for ready money was pressing enough to induce him to sell a
source of assured income. When Alphonse of Poitiers brought the
area into his great southern appanage, he compiled a list of his
vassals and the dues they owed.[8] No Aycelin appeared in their
number. On the other hand, in 1269, "Magister Petrus Aycelini" is
named as procurator in the defense of several of Alphonse's vassals
against the claims of the Count of Rouergue.[9] It is therefore not
clear whether or not we are as yet dealing with a knightly family.
But Master Pierre was already moving in the upward direction
which would assure the family's position. He had formed a connection to the service of the royal family and must have gained
invaluable experience in Alphonse de Poitiers' administration.
There he could participate in the count's work of introducing
administrative and judicial procedures modeled on those of Saint
Louis and designed to facilitate the crown's ultimate absorption of
the country. This work was frequently supervised by persons
drawn from the royal administration itself. And men who made
themselves useful on this local level, often moved out into the
service of the crown, as Pierre Aycelin may have done.[10] Thus, by
1271, when Auvergne reverted to the crown of France, the Aycelins
were an old and well-established family, though there is no evidence that their position was particularly exalted.

---

that his ancestors had been educated for over two hundred years in the church of
Saint-Sirène in Billon: Duchesne, *Histoire des cardinaux,* II, 231–46.

6. Père Anselme, *Histoire généalogique de la maison royale de France,* 302.

7. *Ibid.,* 274.

8. Chassaing, *Spicilegium Brivatense,* 43ff.

9. Molinier (ed.), *Correspondence administrative d'Alphonse de Poitiers. Collection de documents inédits.* V², no. 1650.

10. This process is demonstrated by Bossuat, *Histoire des institutions,* I, 107–
108.

Pierre Aycelin seems to have achieved a few other modest distinctions. In 1280 he appears in residence in Paris, styling himself "Lord of Bressolie."[11] Though there is some confusion as to the actual possessor of the title, there seems no doubt that by that time it was held in the family. During these years Master Pierre married, bringing his family into a relationship which would play a central role in the career of Gilles Aycelin. In 1280 he was living in Paris with his wife "N. Flote."[12] The relationship between this woman and the future chancellor, Pierre Flote, is unknown. Later historians have so persistently assumed she was his sister that it has come to be treated as an established fact, but even her relationship to the children of Pierre Aycelin is somewhat unclear. The eldest son was presumably William, but the confusion over when he became Lord of Bressolie makes both his age and his relationship to Pierre's wife of 1280 unclear. There was a wide gap in age between Hugh Aycelin and Gilles, who was just beginning his professional life when Hugh had reached the summit of his, so it is not impossible that the brothers had different mothers. There was therefore some relationship—if only by marriage—to the Flote family. Aycelin may have been the nephew of Pierre Flote, but the matter is not yet susceptible of proof.

It has been claimed that the Aycelin marriage was the basis of the Flote fortunes.[13] However, the great men of both families emerged only after that event had been concluded: Hugh as cardinal in 1288, Gilles as Archbishop of Narbonne in 1290, and Pierre Flote at a subsequent date. There is no reason to suppose that the Flote family was inferior in station to the Aycelins, though their background is even more obscure to us.

Digard[14] believed that Pierre was the younger son of Arnaldus

11. Père Anselme, *Histoire généalogique*, 275. This evidence is seemingly contradicted by another document published by Duchesne, *Histoire des chanceliers et gardes des sceaux*, 305, who mentions "Guillelmi Aycelini" as Lord of Bressolie, in 1277. William is there listed as the eldest son of Pierre Aycelin. In 1294 "domini Guillelmi Aycelini" (presumably the same man) is named without any title in the account book of Jean de Trie, bailli of Auvergne: Chassaing, *Spicilegium Brivatense*, 226.

12. Père Anselme, 275.

13. Pegues, *The Lawyers of the Last Capetians*, 90.

14. Digard, *Philippe le Bel et le Saint Siège de 1285 à 1304*, I, 110.

Flota, Lord of Rupa, who figured in an act cited by Valbonnais[15] as the owner of fiefs in the Gapençois at Roches des Arnauds. Valbonnais himself favored that section of Vivarais held by the Dauphin, citing an act of March 1296 in which the Count of Forez was ceded lordship of the fief and castle of Torent held by "dominus" Pierre Flote, though he conceded that this fief could well have been a gift of the Dauphin for Flote's earlier services.

Alternatively, tradition calls him an Auvergnat. His own title was Lord of Revel, a fief in Auvergne only a few miles from Billon. There is, however, no proof that Flote held this title before 1294,[16] and Digard[17] suggests that the fief was a gift from the King of France and therefore does not indicate the location of the family holdings. This is conjecture, however, and the fact of the Aycelin marriage would seem to constitute a strong argument in favor of some proximity of the estates of the two families.

Pierre Aycelin had nine children. The eldest, William, whether or not he was "Lord of Bressolie and Billon" in 1277, did not acquire the greater estate of Montaigu until 1295, well after his brothers were solidly established and after he had himself performed some services for the king.[18]

The younger children began their careers modestly. Hugh joined the Dominican order, perhaps to benefit from the patronage of the Dominican Bishop of Clermont, Guy de La Tour. Gilles went to law school. Jean became a clergyman, receiving only modest benefices until Hugh and Gilles were in a position to help his advancement (to Bishop of Clermont in 1298). Of the five girls, four were placed in convents, probably to economize on their dowries. The youngest married a local nobleman, Evrard de Chalançon, in 1297, when her elder brothers had achieved their great positions and could contribute to her marriage settlement.[19]

Hugh pursued a successful scholarly career in the Dominican

---

15. Valbonnais, *Histoire des dauphins de la troisième race*, II, 389.

16. The designation appears for the first time in the *Comptes royaux*, R. Fawtier, ed., pt. 2, p. 43.

17. Digard, *Philippe le Bel*, I, 110.

18. 27 May 1294, he was compensated for having seized "certain lands" and placed them in the king's hand. Chassaing, *Spicilegium Brivatensis*, 226.

19. Duchesne, *Histoire des chanceliers*, 305.

order, gaining his doctorate in theology and acting as regent in the Convent of Saint James in Paris from 1282 to 1284.[20] He was then sent to teach in the order's Italian convents and by 1287 he was working in the convent of Saint Sabina at Rome.

On the death of Honorius IV, the cardinals met in this convent to elect his successor. Hugh may have known some or all of them previously but if not this event gave him his opportunity.[21] The conclave was interrupted by an outbreak of the plague which drove most of the frightened cardinals from the city. Only Jerome of Ascoli, a Franciscan cardinal, stayed behind at Saint Sabina, bravely observing the letter of the law of Gregory X forbidding cardinals to leave the conclave before the election of a new pope. With him was Hugh Aycelin. Even if the two had not been acquainted previously, it is not hard to imagine the two friars forming a friendship at this time of mutual peril. When the cardinals returned and elected Jerome pope, one of his first acts was to appoint Hugh Aycelin as cardinal priest of Saint Sabina.[22] In

20. Hugh's early career is traced primarily from references in his will. His later career is given in more detail by Quétif and Echard, Scriptores Ordinis Praedicatorum, I, pt. 1, 450–53; Mortier, Histoire des Maîtres Généraux de l'Ordre des Frères Prêcheurs, and, more recently, Lajard, "Le Cardinal Hugues Aicelin de Billiom," Histoire Littéraire, XXI, 71–79. Discussions of his probable literary output can be found in Forte, "A Late Thirteenth Century Collection of Quaestiones," Archivum Fratrum Praedicatorum, XVIII, 95–121; Glorieux, "Les Premières Polémiques Thomistes," Bibliothèque Thomiste, IX, 7–56, and XXXI, 7–29; Glorieux, Répertoire des maîtres en théologie de Paris au XIIIᵉ siècle, 152; and Mandonnet, "Premiers travaux de polémique thomiste," Revue des sciences philosophiques et théologiques, VII (1913), 46–70; 245–62.

21. For centuries the belief that Hugh Aycelin held the office of Master of the Sacred Palace was the sole support for the tradition that the office existed and was held by Dominicans from the time of their founder. Loenertz, "Saint Dominique, écrivain, maître en théologie, professeur à Rome, et Maître du Sacré Palais," Arch. Frat. Praedic., XII, 84–97, and Creytens, "Le Studium Romanae Curiae et le Maître du Sacré Palais," Arch. Frat. Praedic., XII, 5–83, have effectively disproven the claim with evidence from contemporary authors showing that the office was first created by Clement V in 1306. Ptolemy of Lucca, Hugh's contemporary and fellow Dominican, says that at the time of his elevation he was "legentem in curia," Historia Ecclesiastica, in Muratori, Rerum Italicarum Scriptores, XI, 1295.

22. The only account of Hugh's appointment was given nearly fifty years later by Galvano Fiamma: "La Cronaca Maggiore," Arch. Frat. Praedic., X, 361: "Cum autem summus pontifex alium de ordine predicatorum cardinalem substituere disponeret, illi de Columna pro magistro ordinis fr. Munione, quod cardinalis fieret, procurabant. Dominus autem frater Latinus cardinalis pro fr. Hugone de Bilomio, sacri palatii magistro ac Parisius magistro licentiato, stabat, allegans quod

the years that followed, Nicholas IV was to keep Hugh constantly at his side in the Curia and to grant him and his family a multitude of favors.

Hugh's brother, Gilles, did not at first seek to follow an ecclesiastical career: rather, he chose to study law. The time and place of his studies are unknown, but the most famous and readily available school at the time was the University of Montpellier, where Guillaume de Nogaret was teaching. Later in their lives, there is some suggestion that Nogaret and Aycelin knew one another before their acquaintance on the royal council—when Nogaret first appeared in Paris in 1299, he was associated with Aycelin in sponsoring the appeal of Arnald of Villanova to Boniface VIII. It is possible that Gilles had completed his studies by 1274. At that time he accompanied Bishop Guy de La Tour to the Council of Lyon. As assistant to the Bishop of Clermont, he participated in the task of arbitrating a dispute between the Archbishop of Vienne and the cathedral chapter.[23]

This slight connection with the affairs of Vienne might conceivably have brought Aycelin into contact with Pierre Flote, who entered the service of Humbert de La Tour at some period before the latter's marriage of 1282 made him Dauphin of Vienne. It is not clear whether Flote made this connection because he was known to Humbert in Auvergne or because he was recommended as the son of a noble of Dauphiné.[24]

---

ex eo quod regi Francorum amicissimus erat, ipsi regi rem gratissimam faceret et ordini satisfactum esset. Cui pontifex annuens, excluso fr. Munione, fecit presbyterum cardinalem tituli sancte Sabine prefatum fr. Hugonem." As the reference to Hugh as Master of the Sacred Palace attests, Fiamma was not a very reliable chronicler. There is no evidence that at this time in his life Hugh had the slightest connection with the King of France, except that he happened to be one of his subjects.

23. Digard, *Philippe le Bel*, I, 56. Gilles was not involved at this time in the affairs of the city of Lyon. Pegues' implication that he was (*Lawyers of the Last Capetians*, 92) is apparently the result of a misreading of Digard in which he substituted the name of the Archbishop of Lyon for the Archbishop of Vienne as a party to the quarrel.

24. In June 1277 Arnaud Flote, knight, son of Ossaseiche, Lord of La-Baume des Arnauds, gave homage to the Dauphin for the chateau of Montclus: Chevalier, *Régeste dauphinois*, III, 8, n.11719. On July 1 the same man gave homage to Aymar, Count of Valentinois for La-Roche des Arnauds: *Ibid.*, 10, n.11728. This double homage suggests that Arnaud was a young man just entering upon his inheritance. If Pierre Flote was his younger brother, he may have been recommended to the new Dauphin on Humbert's arrival.

Although he is invariably listed among the lawyers of Philip the Fair, no one has ever proferred any evidence that Flote undertook any legal study. His law degree apparently was awarded him by nineteenth century historians, who appear to have assumed that any layman who achieved an important position at the royal court must have been a lawyer. There is nothing in Flote's recorded career that required any special legal training and no contemporary document seems to have awarded him any legal title. His first recorded act occurred in 1281. As "Petrus Flote, Damoiseau," he witnessed a donation of land by Beatrice de La Tour.[25] Since he was continuously employed thereafter, any training he received would have had to precede 1281. But had he already earned a more distinguished title—such as "jurist," "magister," or "doctor of laws"—it seems strange that he never used it, especially in preference to so simple a designation as "damoiseau." In all the records of his work in Dauphiné he remained simply a "knight," although fellow witnesses occasionally are designated as lawyers.[26]

For nearly ten years, Flote was employed in various capacities by the Dauphin. In 1283, he acted as guarantor of the marriage contract of Humbert's daughter.[27] In the same year he helped settle the Dauphin's differences with the Archbishop of Vienne through a military alliance.[28] In 1287 he was charged with arranging the Dauphin's settlement of land on his wife.[29]

In 1286–1287, he undertook the interesting and difficult assignment of negotiating on the Dauphin's behalf with Amadeus, Count of Savoy, for a settlement of a whole series of conflicting claims resulting from the confusion of their borders. After a year's work a blanket agreement was finally reached in November 1287, and

25. Chevalier, *Régeste dauphinois*, 91, n.12235.
26. For example, in a document settling a dispute between the Dauphin and the Duke of Burgundy, 8 December 1285, the chateaux, towns, lands, and possessions of the Dauphin from which annual revenues were to be given were to be selected by "Pierrre Flote, knight, and Jacques Burgarelli, Professor of Civil Law." *Ibid.*, 208, n.12914.
27. Valbonnais, *Histoire des dauphins,* II, 26. By that time he had been knighted, and was listed as "Dominus Petrus Flota, miles."
28. Chevalier, 158, n.12603.
29. Valbonnais, 134.

sealed by a double marriage between the sons and daughters of the principals.[30]

In these years, affairs in Dauphiné—as in so many other places —were becoming ever more entangled with the greater conflict developing between the Kings of France and England. All of the great nobles eventually found it necessary to ally with one or the other. The Count of Savoy, for example, was already related to Edward I by marriage. In 1294 Dauphin Humbert and his son were to give homage to the King of France, agreeing to supply him with two hundred armed knights against the King of England in exchange for an annual stipend. Flote may well have been instrumental in arranging that agreement, for by 1294 he was firmly established in the royal service with Gilles Aycelin.

Gilles Aycelin had continued to profit from the patronage of Guy de la Tour in the years that followed his employment at Lyon. By 1287 he was provost of the church of Clermont,[31] an appointment he probably received before the death of Bishop Guy in 1286. The position was an important one, involving the administration of the temporal goods of the church. At the same time, he undertook additional services for the La Tour family.[32] By 1288 he had become an archdeacon, but as late as 1289—when Nicholas IV presented him with additional prebends "which do not require sacerdotal dignity"—there is no indication that he ever intended to become a priest.[33]

In 1287–1288, Gilles made another important contact which would prove valuable in his later career. Simon de Beaulieu, then Archbishop of Bourges, was accompanied by the provost of Clermont during his tour of visitation in the diocese of Clermont.[34]

30. Chevalier, 221, n.12990; 253, n.13180.

31. The documents published by Baluze, *Miscellanea*, I, 267–310, relating to Aycelin's tenure of this office employ the word "praepositor," an obscure form which was conceivably customary at Clermont.

32. 21 June 1288, he appeared with his brother Jean, then a canon of Clermont, as a witness to the marriage contract between the Count of Clermont and the daughter of the Count of Rouergue, and was entrusted with the arrangement of the dowry and inheritance provisions, Baluze, *Histoire généalogique*, II, 291.

33. *Les registres de Nicholas IV*, 980–81. These letters also credit him with canonries and prebends in Bayeux, Rouen, le Puy, Billon, and elsewhere. They confirm his status as "Professor of Civil Law."

34. The tour was part of a larger series of visitations begun in the reign of

The records are not precise as to the length of time Aycelin spent
with Beaulieu, but his presence is specifically mentioned in late
September and early October of 1287. His continued presence at
Clermont can be established in the summer of 1288,[35] and the following December he entered for the first time into the service of
the King of France.

Philip III, in whose councils Beaulieu frequently appeared. 26 June 1284, Philip
III ordered his sergeants to give the visitors whatever protection they needed.
Langlois, *La règne de Philippe III*, app. I, 158. The record of the visits is in
Baluze, *Miscellanea*, I, and was interpreted by Digard, *Philippe le Bel*, I, 247, n.1,
as a move in the process of annexation to the crown.

35. In addition to his presence at the signing of the marriage contract in
June (see above), he was among the witnesses at Easter to the homage given
by Count Robert to the Bishop of Clermont for his holdings in Camaleria: Baluze,
Histoire généalogique, II, 291.

III

The Archbishopric of Narbonne

Between 1285 and 1288 there had been a breathing space in the actual fighting between France and Aragon as both countries sought to adjust to a change in sovereigns. But there was no halt to their diplomatic maneuvering. Instead, the conflict spread. Edward of England moved from his original position as arbiter between the two kings to an open alliance with Aragon. With his assistance, Alfonso of Aragon succeeded in forcing French agreement to the Treaty of Canfranc in 1288, which set the price of Charles of Salerno's freedom as his renunciation of the Sicilian crown.[1]

This blow to French interests was counterbalanced by the newly elected Pope Nicholas IV, who wrote to Alfonso in March 1288 demanding an unconditional and immediate release of the Angevin heir.[2] In a second letter the same month[3] he commanded the King of Aragon to appear in Rome to discuss the entire Sicilian question within six months. Meanwhile, he was ordered to give no assistance to his brother James, who was fighting for the crown of Sicily.

Anxious to derive the fullest advantage from papal support, Philip the Fair prepared a mission to accompany Charles of Salerno to Rome. The young man's sojourn at the court of France after his release had greatly weakened his original determination to abdicate in accord with the terms of Canfranc. He left for Rome on 26 December 1288, accompanied by a group of Frenchmen with various commissions to assist the revival of the French offensive. Among these was "Egidio Acclini," provost of Clermont, who, with Jean de Wassoignia, Archdeacon of Bruges, was em-

---

1. Rymer, *Foedera*, I, pt. 3, pp. 27–33.
2. Dumont, *Corps universel dipolmatique*, 266.
3. *Reg. Nich.* 560–65.

powered to negotiate for funds from the pope to support the prosecution of the Aragonese war.[4]

For the day-to-day activities of an ambassador, relaying information about conditions abroad to the government at home and pursuing the interests of that government at the center of Christendom, the French ordinarily depended on cardinals resident at the Curia. Permanent diplomatic residents were not unknown in the last years of the thirteenth century, and the King of Aragon, particularly, maintained such a mission which reported to him regularly.[5] But there can be little doubt that a representative whose expenses were paid by the Church was preferable. This is probably the explanation for James II's constant negotiations to procure the appointment of an Aragonese cardinal.

The French were always well represented in the Curia, and the history of papal policy in these years consistently reflects the influence of the French party, working in support of the policies of their king. From 1288 until his death in 1297, one of the most influential of these cardinals was the brother of Gilles Aycelin, Hugh of Billon.

This relationship would seem to be the obvious explanation for Gilles' appointment to the mission of 1288. Digard believed that, although his name did not previously appear in the lists of the royal hotel, Aycelin must have been employed by the king at some earlier period to have earned his trust in such an important task.[6] However, there is no reason to consider this a necessary prerequisite. By 1288 Gilles Aycelin was certainly qualified for a responsible position by his administrative experience in Clermont and by his legal background. The king could have received further testimony as to his abilities from Simon de Beaulieu, who had often participated in his father's council.[7] Above all, Gilles' close

4. Baluze, *Vitae Paparum Avenionensium*, III, 6, n.4.

5. Studies in the Aragonese diplomatic archives for this period were the special interest of H. Finke. In addition to his three-volume collection, *Acta Aragonensia* (1291-1327), he included a generous supply of documents from this source in his books, *Aus den Tagen Bonifaz VIII*, and *Papsttum und Untergang des Templerordens*.

6. Digard, *Philippe le Bel*, I, 56.

7. Favier, "Les légistes et le gouvernement de Philippe le Bel," 103, believes that the joint recommendation of Hugh Aycelin and Pierre Flote might have

relationship to a newly created cardinal, reputedly close to the pope, should have been qualification enough to include his name in a commission intended to win favors from Nicholas IV.

At the end of May 1289, the ambassadors found the pope at Rieti, where he had taken refuge from the insurgent Ghibellines supporting the Aragonese effort. French troops under Amaury of Narbonne were immediately put to work restoring the papal position in Italy. In return, the pope absolved Charles of Salerno from the oaths he had taken "under duress" in Aragon. He was crowned Charles II of Sicily on Pentecost of the same year.

On 22 June Aycelin and his companion received from Nicholas IV a subsidy for the French prosecution of the war amounting to a tenth of the revenues of the French clergy for three years. Aycelin succeeded in having the grant extended to include not only the traditional dioceses of France but the sees of Lyon and Embrun as well, which had previously been exempt from royal exactions.[8]

After 1288 the Aragonese problem receded to a subsidiary position in French affairs. Charles II began to show himself well fitted to maintain his position in Italy, adroitly assuring continued papal support by a variety of maneuvers. French interests at the Curia could be left for a time to the French cardinals, whose position reached unprecedented heights during the brief pontificate of Celestine V in 1294. One of the closest confidants of the hermit pope was Hugh Aycelin, who was appointed to the highest office in the college: Cardinal-bishop of Ostia.

At the time of Celestine's coronation Aycelin, as well as his friends, the two Colonna cardinals, was called "Lord of the Curia," by a contemporary chronicler.[9] In the months that followed he accumulated such an excessive series of money grants that even

---

brought Gilles into the government. But in 1288 Flote was not yet in royal service.

8. *Reg. Nich. IV*, 1005. On the same day, the pope issued a series of grants to Aycelin personally: *Ibid.*, 980–81.

9. Ptolemy of Lucca, *Acta Sanctorum*, 429: "Interim autem Dominus Jacobus de Columna et Dominus Petrus [Colonna] et Dominus Hugo de Belliomo, Aquilam venit, factique sunt Domini Curiae; quod alii Cardinales videntes Aquilam properant."

Celestine, whose indifference to the financial business of the curia was notorious, requested him to cut some of his revenues in half.[10]

In the years that followed, as Gilles Aycelin rose to power in France and became increasingly involved in the growing strife between the king of France and his two great vassals of Aquitaine and Flanders, he could depend on an attentive ear in Rome through the influence of Cardinal Hugh.

After this successful debut in the royal service, Gilles Aycelin occupied a secure place in government. In the fall of 1289, following his return from Rome, he began to attend the meetings of the Parlement of Paris where he was able to put his legal training to use.[11] A few months later he was named to the important and sensitive place of Archbishop of Narbonne, and in 1290 returned to Rome to receive his pallium.

The appointment to Narbonne was a crucial one. The city occupied a key position in the great area of Languedoc which had reverted to the crown only twenty years earlier. The actual power exercised there by the king was still severely limited, however. In the city of Narbonne, no rights of ecclesiastical patronage, practice of regalian rights, or ownership of private property gave the king a foothold from which to intervene in its affairs. It was therefore a necessity for him to take steps to ensure that the local lords remain loyal, especially while Aragon remained a threat.

In his first message to Rome in 1285, Philip had sought assurances from Honorius IV that if the sees of Narbonne, Bordeaux, Lyon, or Carcassonne should fall vacant, the pope would recognize the election only of persons who loved the king and could be trusted by him.[12] It is reasonable to suppose that the king desired to ensure that of the two lords who divided the jurisdiction of the city between them, one at least should be firmly tied to royal interests.

For his holdings within the walls of the city, the Viscount of Narbonne unwillingly submitted to the overlordship of the arch-

---

10. Lajard, "Hugh Aicelin," 74.

11. Beugnot, *Les Olim*, II, 288, with the bailli of Amiens and others, he was assigned to investigate the complaints of the people of Pyceio that their lord was transgressing against their rights to high justice.

12. This mission is fully discussed by Digard, *Philippe le Bel*, I, 20–32.

bishop. In addition, the archbishop received the homage of the burghers, who had established a consular government of their own. The viscounts had long contested the archiepiscopal claim to supremacy, seeking to transfer their homage from him to some more distant lord and to supplant him as lord of the bourg.

In pursuance of this ambition the viscounts, like many of the nobles of the south, had alternated their approaches to the King of France with offers to the King of Aragon. This had been the case as recently as the reign of Philip III, although in the final crisis of 1285 the viscount had held firmly to his loyalty to Philip the Fair's father. In return for this show of faith in so dark an hour, the young king had confirmed the viscount's fiefs in 1286 and provided him with letters forbidding him to do homage to the archbishop.[13] Nevertheless, it is apparent that the king did not feel that his friendship with the viscount was sufficient to constitute a secure royal position in the city.

When the anticipated vacancy at Narbonne opened in 1286, disputes within the chapter caused the election of a new archbishop to be referred to Rome. The pope first suggested Adenulph of Anagni for the post, but he declined for unknown reasons.[14] The see remained vacant until 1290. In November of that year, Nicholas IV took up the question and decided on the appointment of Gilles Aycelin. The move was probably prompted by the pope's desire to gratify Hugh Aycelin, since his letter to King Philip suggests that the king had no prior knowledge of Gilles' candidacy.[15] But Aycelin's success in 1288, when he had undertaken negotiations for the king in Rome, must have reassured the pope that the appointment would find favor at the French court.

Aycelin was not a priest at the time he received this high

13. These letters have not been preserved, and the act is only recorded in a later act of the Parlement of Paris, 1 November 1291, in which it was annulled and the viscount ordered to give homage to the archbishop saving only the rights of the king over anything which he held from the crown, Les Olim, II, 325.
14. Presumably Adenulph's candidacy was acceptable to the king since he was bishop-elect of Paris at his death in May 1290, Reg. Nich. IV, 4282.
15. Reg. Nich. IV, 3709–24, relates the prior history of the vacancy. To the people of Narbonne, the pope praised their new prelate's learning and virtue. To the King of France, he added ". . . hortatur ut eundem electum, germanum Hugonis, titula Sanctae Sabinae presbyter cardinalis, regio favore prosequatur."

ecclesiastical appointment, although he had probably taken minor orders when at school. He had, however, had useful experience in church administration through his work at Clermont and had already held several benefices without care of souls. Nevertheless, he must have intended to pursue a career as a secular lawyer when his prospects were changed by the advancement of his brother. There can be little doubt that he was diverted to the clerical life not by a priestly vocation but by the possibility of advancement it offered.

Receiving notification of his appointment, Gilles sent a vicar to act for him in Narbonne and began to make arrangements for his installation. On 27 March 1291 he arrived at Navis in the diocese of Limoges, where Simon de Beaulieu was continuing his visitations. On that day the Archbishop of Bourges ordained the Archbishop-elect of Narbonne to the priesthood.[16] On 18 March Aycelin left for Italy to receive his pallium, reaching the Curia at Orvieto on 23 May, where he was consecrated with the assistance of his brother Hugh.[17]

It is apparent that Aycelin had lost no time in acquainting himself with the condition of his archdiocese. As he would do so often in the future, he took advantage of his presence at Rome to secure a series of privileges which would ensure his control over the clergy of his province. His first aim was to put benefices within the patronage of the cathedral under his sole control. Accordingly, he requested papal investigation of the actions of the cathedral chapter in disposing of vacancies during the absence of an archbishop. He claimed that they had usurped his rights by filling benefices and reserving the first fruits to themselves rather than to the archiepiscopal treasury. Nicholas IV agreed to appoint a commission to investigate the situation and ensure the archbishop his due.[18]

At the same time, Aycelin presented a more specific complaint that the abbot and monks of Fontfroid had taken advantage of conditions during the vacancy to steal two mules loaded with archiepiscopal wine, killing and injuring some of his men. On

16. Baluze, *Miscellanea*, 304.
17. *Reg. Nich. IV*, 4843.
18. *Ibid.*, 5200.

20 June the pope appointed a second commission to investigate that question.[19]

Aycelin's efforts to establish control over his chapter were strengthened by a further series of papal privileges given by Nicholas IV and Boniface VIII. Indeed, the program was fully in conformity with the Bonifacian policy of clarifying the hierarchy of administration. It is well known that the pope was eager to strengthen his own control over the Church. From his legislation, it is clear that he was equally anxious to affirm the rights of bishops over their chapters and benefices and to defend clerical privileges and immunities at the local level.[20] Thus Aycelin's program of privileges can be seen as a translation at the local level of general papal policy. Moreover, it conformed with the general aims of the King of France, who was also interested in the creation of clear lines of authority and must have been glad to see the position of a prelate he trusted thus enhanced.

These privileges of 1291 clearly define the terms in which Aycelin intended to operate. Apparently, the initial set of bulls he obtained from Nicholas IV were rare enough and important enough to warrant a reissue from Boniface VIII during the general housecleaning which occupied the first months of his pontificate.[21]

In addition to the general bulls regarding his position in the see, Aycelin received a series of bulls to ease his personal situation. To ensure his income, he was confirmed in the possession of six of the benefices he already held on an absentee basis. And he was dispensed from the normal requirement of residence in his see itself for five years, without prejudice to his right to collect its full revenues.[22]

There is no indication that Aycelin visited his see at all during the first years of his tenure. He was increasingly active in royal service, which required nearly constant attendance on the council.

19. *Ibid.*, 5769.
20. See the article by Lefebvre in Lebras *et al.*, *L'age classique*, 153.
21. *Les registres de Boniface VIII*, 930ff.
22. *Reg. Nich. IV*, 5181–82.

In 1293 this growing intimacy with the crown was confirmed by his standing godfather to Philip's newborn son, Charles (later Charles IV). In the years before Boniface VIII became pope, Aycelin administered the church of Narbonne almost entirely through a vicar, yet no one criticized him for his absenteeism or for his involvement with the secular government. In 1295, when confirming Aycelin's special privileges in the archdiocese, Boniface VIII actually approved this conflict of interest on the ground that Aycelin could do more good for his church by his influence with the king than by his presence in the diocese.[23]

To ensure his freedom to staff the province, the bulls of 1291 gave him full control of appointments to benefices not already in the gift of the pope or the king; in addition he could accept resignations from the cathedral chapter and create new canons. He was given power to provide dispensations for the appointees of his choice in cases of plurality and in cases where men had not taken the orders required by their offices. Finally, he could absolve his benefice-holders from any canonical sentence they might incur without reference to the pope.[24] In sum, his control over his subordinates in Narbonne was complete.

This freedom of action was further confirmed during his stay in Rome in 1297, when he was given the right to confer specific benefices outside his own diocese. In addition, the pope permitted him to neglect his duties of visitation if he believed it necessary, or to send deputies to carry them out.[25] On 25 February 1301 Aycelin's control over appointments to benefices was again con-

23. *Reg. Bon. VIII,* 297: "Sicut nobis significare curasti, dilectus filius frater Petrus de Morrone, olim Celestinus papa quintus, antecessor noster, intellecto quod ad sedandum dissensiones et scandala que in illis partibus nonnunquam pacis Emulus suscitabat, te de loco ad locum transferre sepius oportebat, necnon ad curiam carissimi in Christo filii nostri regis Francie illustris, cujus existis consiliarius, frequenter accedere pro executione obsequiorum dicti regis et etiam pro negotiis ecclesie ac provincie Narbonensis in eadem curia utiliter promovendis et defendis, et sic per te ipsum non posses provinciam tuam comode visitare, tibi per litteras suas sub certa forma concessit ut usque ad triennium quotiens dictam provinciam visitando aliquam ipsius provincie diocesim, quam visitare inceperis contingeret te exire, visitatione hujusmodi non completa, libere posses redire ad illam vel ad aliam, prout tibi necessarium videretur, et visitationem perficere sic inceptam, constitutione a felicis recordationis Innocentio papa quarto, predecessore nostro super hoc edita et qualibet alia contraria non obstante."
24. *Reg. Nich. IV,* 5183–97.
25. *Reg. Bon. VIII,* 2006–17.

firmed when Boniface ordered the Bishop of Béziers to revoke any statutes of the chapter of Narbonne interfering with the archbishop's rights.[26] This bull was strengthened by the granting of permission to the archbishop to collate two new prebends in the diocese and receive the first fruits from five to fifteen clerical benefices there.[27]

The success of Aycelin's administration shows that he must have used his privileges wisely, although in at least two cases he bestowed benefices on members of his own family.[28] Even these beneficiaries, however, can be classed as having been given to qualified persons: Jean Aycelin was capable enough to be appointed to the bishopric of Clermont a few years later. Arbert, Gilles' nephew, would later take over the same see; at the time of his appointment to minor benefices in Narbonne, Boniface recognized Arbert's need to absent himself to continue his legal studies.

While securing his ecclesiastical rights in Narbonne, Aycelin was also concerned to confirm, and, if possible, enlarge his temporal rights. One of his first acts in office was to seek the recovery of his rights in certain alum mines which had been illicitly exploited by the Count of Foix. Characteristically, when he failed to receive satisfaction from the count, he took the case to the Parlement of Paris where a judgment in his favor was passed in 1293.[29]

Aycelin's general policy is clear from the beginning of his tenure. He would always try to strengthen his own juridical position, within the framework of Philip the Fair's efforts to establish himself as the ultimate giver of justice in France, by asking the royal courts for arbitration in his favor against his rivals.

There were even occasions when he was willing to join with his archenemy, the viscount, to this end. Thus, in 1291, the rival

26. *Ibid.*, 3982. Boniface stated that he was acting on a complaint of the archbishop, probably made during his last trip to Rome in 1301, that the chapter had been claiming that legally they had the right to appoint to all vacancies in the church of Narbonne themselves without consulting the archbishop. From this, Aycelin claimed, benefices had been given to unworthy persons or not filled at all so that their duties were neglected, to the offence of God, the prejudice of the archbishop, and the scandal of the faithful.

27. *Ibid.*, 3966–67.

28. *Ibid.*, 2018–19.

29. De Vic and Vaissette, *Histoire de Languedoc*, X, 170.

lords appealed against the citizens of the bourg who were attempting to remove their consulate from the jurisdiction of both lords
in favor of the king. At their joint request, the seneschal of Carcassonne was asked to investigate the case.[30] Nothing more was ever
heard of this attempted revolt. Presumably, the legal claims of the
archbishop and the viscount were found to be justified and the
king made no effort to take illicit advantage of the offer of the
citizens. Thereafter, the question of the jurisdiction of Narbonne
is confined to the long struggle between the two lords.

Amaury, the son and heir of the Viscount of Narbonne, had
headed the military side of the mission to Rome of 1288 and presumably became acquainted with his future rival at that time. In
1292 he returned to Narbonne and began to act as his father's
procurator in the royal courts, taking over increasing powers before his succession to the title in 1298 brought the question of
homage to the archbishop to a head. He spent these earlier years
in a persistent effort to reach a position where he would not be
obliged to give the oath when it came due.

Having obtained the Parlement's recognition of his rights in
1291, Aycelin pressed for years to get the judgment executed.
Amaury's father, however, was never brought to do the desired
acts of homage. The case dragged on for years. As Aycelin sought
to prosecute it, the viscount tried to evade the issue by failing to
answer the court's summonses. On 7 September 1294 Aycelin excommunicated the viscount for the seizure of one of his ships,[31]
but the old lord made no response. Even as Aycelin's influence
grew in Paris and his position might seem to have improved,
Amaury added to the military duties he performed for the king,
thus keeping a balance in which he also was too valuable to be
alienated by an adverse decision.[32] It is unlikely that Amaury ever

30. *Ibid.*, X, 268, 7 January 1291.
31. Carbonel, *Histoire de Narbonne*, 180.
32. Philip maintained the correct legal position in that he formally upheld the
rights of the archbishop. However, his reluctance to take sides between two
valuable servants is typified by his order to the seneschal of Carcassonne in
January 1296, repeating his summons to the viscount. There he recounted at some
length the history of the case between "our beloved and faithful archbishop"
and "our beloved and faithful viscount." The seneschal was to call the viscount to
Paris, but he had no orders to enforce the invitation. De Vic and Vaissette,
Histoire de Languedoc, X, 296.

seriously expected a judgment in his favor in a case that had so little legal basis. He could gamble on the king's reluctance to take action against him, however.

As the price of his independence from the temporal authority of the archbishop, on several occasions he offered the king direct homage for his holdings in the city. As in the case of the consular offer, however, Philip refused. Though advantageous to himself, he eschewed a situation which would flout the legally established rights of the archbishop who, despite his own close attachment to the king, never wavered in pursuit of his rights.

The viscount and the archbishop were held in balance by the king's policy and their continued competition for his favor assured; but neither was reduced to servility. In general, their relations with one another and with Philip the Fair concluded in compromises not disadvantageous to any of the parties concerned.

After 1288 the principal fact of Aycelin's career was always his relationship with Philip the Fair. His advancement to Narbonne may have been inspired by the request of his brother, but through the rest of his life the evidence indicates that he considered himself primarily as the king's officer. Indeed, his effectiveness as a prelate can generally be traced to the strength of his connection with the royal court. On the other hand, much of his usefulness to the king was drawn from his impeccable position as a prelate.

His high ecclesiastical position, added to his legal training, fitted Aycelin for a great many roles. In partnership with Pierre Flote, he was one of France's leading diplomats—the builder, if not the architect, of royal policies in Rome, in Aquitaine, in Flanders, and in the Empire. Simultaneously, he labored at home in the great effort to untangle the complex of feudal and ecclesiastical jurisdictions and create a clear and effective machinery of government with the king, represented judicially by the Parlement of Paris, at its head. And, continually, he acted energetically in the affairs of the church entrusted to his governance.

The archbishopric of Narbonne was not a sinecure, and neither Aycelin nor the king treated it as one. Nor did the archbishop ever acquiesce in subordinating its rights to the interests of the crown. As a councillor, as a lawyer, as a feudal lord, and as a prelate, Gilles Aycelin was no tool of an aggressive monarchy. He was a conscientious and effective person in all these areas, capable perhaps even of enthusiasm for the great movements in which he was involved. It is the very complexity of his career and the talent with which he pursued each of its elements that gives it its special interest.

IV

The Complex Patterns of Policy

The long and fruitful partnership between Gilles Aycelin and Pierre Flote began in 1293. Flote had probably seen some royal service already as, of course, had Aycelin. According to one source, Flote, with other officials, acted as the king's representative at the Parlement of Toulouse in 1291, where he was instrumental in the arbitration of a settlement for the Abbot of Montauban.[1] Since the abbey was within the jurisdiction of the seneschal of Périgord, for whom he worked later on, it is probable that he was already a royal agent of some sort in that area. On the other hand, in October 1291 he acted as a witness to an agreement between the Dauphine Anne and the Archbishop of Vienne[2] which suggests that he was still working for the Dauphin. It is equally unclear on whose behalf he was acting on 28 September 1292 when he witnessed the ratification of an agreement between the citizens of Lyon and the King of France.[3] He may have been a royal agent helping to secure the citizens' recognition of the king's guardianship of that city. But his presence may have been the result of chance or some quite different business, since we have no record of his participation in the affair beyond his acting as a witness to the signing of the document. Whatever his status during these years, Flote's first assignment which could have brought him to the king's personal notice was that in which he joined Gilles Aycelin in 1293.

1. De Vic and Vaissette, *Histoire de Languedoc,* IX, 154, n.2, cite a document from the archives of the church of Montauban dated 3 April 1291. Père Anselme, *Histoire généalogique,* VI, 274, added that Flote appeared at the same Parlement in May to give information against the Lombards of Beaucaire, but does not give the source of the statement.
2. Digard, *Philippe le Bel,* I, 110, suggested that he appeared on the Dauphine's behalf in Vienne as a favor to his former employer because he happened to be in the vicinity.
3. Guigue, *Cartulaire municipal de la ville de Lyon,* 411.

Flote and the archbishop were assigned the complex task of settling the conflicting claims over the sovereignty of the County of Bigorre. The disputed lands were in Aquitaine and the conflict therefore represented only a single aspect of the greater problem of the duchy itself. The relationship between the King of France and his great vassal, the King of England, was never amicable; by 1293 it had reached a point of open hostility. Conflicts over assorted feudal rights in Edward's duchy were constant irritants. Loyalty to the two sovereigns was joined to inherent commercial rivalry in the competition between the Norman and Gascon sailors. With the beginning of reciprocal raids by these sailors on the French and English coasts, war seemed at hand.

Philip apparently was willing to meet the situation decisively. His outstanding difficulties with Aragon were no longer threatening to French security. The question of the lordship of Bigorre had been a problem since his reign had begun, and offered a good opportunity for a test of strength with Edward I. No less than six contestants claimed the homage of the county. Among them was Jeanne, Queen of France and heiress of Champagne and Navarre, which lands, she argued, included Bigorre. The conflict was made more deadly because the claimants might choose to give their own homage to the immediate overlord of the duchy, Edward I, or to bypass him in favor of direct homage to the King of France.[4] Initially, success favored Constance of Béarn, who governed the county with the support of Edward I to whom she had given her homage. In 1286 the question was brought before the Parlement of Paris by Edward himself among a series of disputed cases he wished to settle while he was in France to give homage to the new king.[5]

The immediate object of French policy appears to have been to oust Constance but not to press the matter of homage. Accordingly, the Parlement declared in favor of the claims of the bishop and chapter against Constance without discussing the position of the Duke of Aquitaine in the matter. For years thereafter the

---

4. A detailed history of the problem of Bigorre and the six claimants to its sovereignty is provided by Rochet, *Les rapports de l'église du Puy avec le ville de Girone en Espagne et le comté de Bigorre,* 133ff.

5. *Les Olim,* II, 40.

French made sporadic efforts to execute the decision. In 1291 the seneschal of Périgord was instructed to support the attempts of the bishop to oust Constance. Again in 1292 the seneschal of Toulouse was sent to seize the county from her, but she resisted successfully with the help of the Count of Foix, for many years the organizer of southern resistance to the extension of French authority.[6]

In 1293 the matter was turned over to the Archbishop of Narbonne, who was to go to the county to press the queen's claims. His task was to remove Constance and recognize the bishop and have him installed in the lordship of the county. Once in office, the bishop was not to give homage to Edward I but to the queen as countess of Champagne and Navarre. Aycelin was probably chosen for this task because the king was already familiar with his ability as a lawyer and as a negotiator. Flote may have joined the mission on Aycelin's recommendation since they were related to one another. It is, however, equally possible that he was sent as a military precaution by the seneschal of Périgord, who had had an interest in the area since 1291.

Though no record of any fighting was preserved, it is probable that some show of force assisted the archbishop in his successful completion of the mission. In any case, Constance was removed and the bishop upheld. Once in office, the bishop gave his homage to the Queen of France through Aycelin, who acted as her proxy because pregnancy prevented her from leaving Paris. The affair of Bigorre was settled. Or at least it was subsumed in the growing area of conflict between the French and English in Aquitaine.

Aycelin returned to Paris, where his services were given due appreciation. Later in the year he had the honor to stand godfather to the queen's third son. In 1294 he became involved in the highest levels of French diplomacy. Flote remained in the south. Under the direction of the seneschal of Périgord, he played an outstanding role in a series of French actions designed to undermine the entire English position in the duchy.

Southern resentment of the incursions of the French was encouraged by the rivalry of the two lords. Violence against royal

6. The relevant documents for the entire case are reprinted by Rochet, *Les rapports*, 223–35.

officials and French sailors had broken out in more than one of
the towns of Aquitaine. An outbreak in Bayonne shortly after the
French success in Bigorre was made the occasion for action by the
Parlement of Paris. In December 1293 the court issued a citation
ordering Edward, as Duke of Aquitaine, to appear before them to
answer charges of having encouraged his subjects to rebel against
their lord and his, the King of France. The seneschal of Périgord
was entrusted with the publication of the court's sentence. Prominent in his entourage, he included Pierre Flote, whom he praised
to the king for his devotion and energy.[7]

On December 10 the seneschal reported to Paris to describe
the difficulties of their progress. At Asterium, Edward's agent had
refused to receive a copy of the citation or acknowledge that he
had seen it. As an alternative, Flote ignored its lack of official
reception and read it aloud. At Agen, the city gates were closed
against them and the bells were calling the citizens to arms. Not
wishing to provoke violence, the seneschal had Flote read the
document to a crowd outside the walls. He explained its meaning
and denounced the townspeople as traitors. At Saint Émilion they
were again prevented from entering the town and their agents
reported that armed men held the gates from within. The seneschal
concluded that, in accord with Flote's advice, he felt he must
request military assistance to quell the rebellion and secure the
country against the English fleet which was patrolling the coasts.[8]

Though his policy was to pretend ignorance of the summons,
Edward was in fact anxious to avoid both the commanded public
appearance before the French court and the penalty he would
incur by refusing to attend. His brother, Edmund of Lancaster,
was in Paris seeking to arrange a compromise. He was ingeniously
led to believe that Philip was as anxious as he to reach a settlement but was under pressure from public outrage against events
in Gascony. Philip pretended the need of some device to save his
dignity before he could accept a compromise. An interim agreement was made that Edward would give formal recognition of

7. *Les Olim*, 21, ". . . qui procul dubio ferventi animo anhelat, et incessanter
intendit ac studet summopere ad custodiendum utilitatem et honorem regie
majestatis, et ad ea que circa utilitatem et honorem predictos possunt congruere
et attendi."
8. *Ibid.*, 19.

Philip's sovereignty by admitting a token force of one or two officials into the key towns of Aquitaine.[9]

On 7 February 1294, after Edmund had instructed the seneschal of Gascony to open the gates of the strong towns, Pierre Flote entered Bordeaux. From there he dispatched the token forces that had been agreed on. Once they were in possession, however, he and his agents were followed by Raoul de Nesles, the Constable of France, and an army of occupation which gave him effective control of the duchy. Naturally, once this condition was established, the French had no further interest in a swift settlement. For years Flote and Aycelin would be involved in spinning out the discussions of a treaty which would spell a return to normal. Meanwhile, the private assurances given to Edmund of Lancaster that the citation of the Parlement of Paris would be revoked were ignored. On 19 May 1294 Edward was formally declared contumacious for his failure to answer the charges.[10]

Of course, the result of these maneuvers was war in Gascony. On 13 June Flote was in Toulouse with Raoul de Nesles, assisting with the mobilization of the military strength of Languedoc for the continuing struggle.[11] It is not known whether he participated in the successful military campaigns there of Charles of Valois and Robert of Artois in 1295–1296 but it is not improbable that he did. At some time in his life he lost an eye, and it is likely to have occurred in battle. In any case, he remained in the south into 1295, appearing briefly in November of that year in the Auvergne.[12]

By that time Flote had earned the title which he would most commonly use for the rest of his life: *miles regis*, the king's knight. This was apparently an honorific designation used by Philip the

9. The full story of the assurances given the English and the beguiling of Edmund is given in the prince's report to Edward I: Rymer, *Foedera*, II, 620.

10. *Les Olim*, 19.

11. De Vic and Vaissette, *Histoire de Languedoc*, X, 296–97.

12. On 24 May 1294 the seneschal of Beaucaire was commanded to assist Flote in collecting 2,000 marks owed by Robert of Andusia to the Bishop of Valentinois, Bréquigny, *Tables chronologique des diplômes*, VII, 377. On 10 January 1295 he collected monies due from the Count of Rodez, De Vic and Vaissette, *Histoire de Languedoc*, IX, 173. In November 1295 he joined William Aycelin in implementing a judgment of the Parlement of Paris against the Bishop of Clermont, *Comptes royaux*, n.8698, and in directing the seizure of the lands of Dreux d'Auvergne in the king's name, *Les Olim*, II, 385–86.

Fair to confer distinction on certain of his friends and officers. There is no basis for translating it, as did Renan, as "knights of the law,"[13] and no connection can be shown between the king's knights and the later nobility of the robe. Indeed, among the handful of men known to have held the title was Reginald da Supino, a petty Italian lord whose only distinction is that he provided Nogaret with troops for the venture at Anagni. Nogaret, one of the most famous holders of the title, left a definition of it in one of his apologies.[14]

While Pierre Flote was thus successfully engaged against the English in the south, the Archbishop of Narbonne was employed in countering their diplomatic maneuvers elsewhere. Neither as independent sovereign nor as vassal was Edward I alone in suffering the aggressive actions of the French. In the summer of 1294 the King of the Romans, Adolph of Nassau, declared that he would no longer tolerate French incursions against imperial rights in Arles and Burgundy. At the same time, a more serious threat to French interests was posed when the Count of Flanders announced in August that his daughter would marry Edward's heir.

Guy de Dampierre, Count of Flanders, had formerly followed a policy of friendship with France. In fact, he was godfather to Philip the Fair. But since 1290, Flemish sailors had been engaged in sporadic skirmishes at sea with the English. The count had, however, become increasingly resentful at Philip's failure to supply more than moral support to his seamen. He undertook to reach an independent settlement with the King of England. In 1293 their differences were compromised and their mutual alarm at the tightening of the French hold on their fiefs brought them steadily closer. Guy complained that the King of France had allowed the patricians of Bruges to disregard the count's jurisdiction by appealing directly to the Parlement of Paris against his

13. Renan, *Etudes sur la politique religieuse du règne de Philippe le Bel*, 6.
14. Dupuy, *Histoire du différend d'entre le pape Boniface VIII et Philippe le Bel Roy de France*, 517–18: "Numquam in productis per nos, nos [sic] diximus esse domestices et familiares regis, sed milites regis, ex eo quod per regem sunt in suos milites recepti, habent inde nomen honoris et dignitatis, et se milites regis appelant, ne sunt propter hoc domestici dicti domini regis et familiares; et sunt quasi infiniti tam in regno Franciae quam in Italia et locis aliis qui sumunt honorem et nomen hujusmodi dignitatis, nec sunt domestice, quod est ubique notorium."

financial reforms. Philip had further shown a reckless disregard of Flemish economic interests in his actions against Edward. He had prohibited the circulation of any but the notoriously debased French monies in Flanders and then forbidden the import of English wool, upon which the Flemish textile industry depended.[15]

Rather than attempting to placate his godfather by recognizing and correcting the wrongs he had suffered, Philip retaliated violently against the English alliance. In November he ordered the seizure of the goods of Englishmen in the count's service and expelled the Flemish merchants from the fairs of Champagne. French agents took possession of the town of Valenciennes, and the Parlement of Paris summoned the Count of Flanders to answer charges of breaking his feudal oath. When the count and his daughter appeared in Paris, they were summarily taken into custody.

Early in 1295, after this action, Philip dispatched Gilles Aycelin to Flanders to supervise the securing of the county. After a brief attempt at resistance, the count's sons submitted to the French. On 5 February 1295 Aycelin and his companions secured their signatures to a document pledging themselves for their father's loyalty and agreeing to leave their sister in Paris as a hostage for their good faith.[16]

After this success in Flanders, Aycelin left for the east to counter the threats of the emperor-elect by strengthening French ties with the Duke of Burgundy. At Vincennes, with the Counts of Evreux, Blois, and St. Pol, he helped arrange a marriage agreement between the duke's daughter and Philip's second son, the future Philip V.[17] When this document was signed on 2 March 1295, the east was protected against any attempt by Adolph of Nassau to enforce his rights.

These two treaties effectively isolated England. Edward was further distracted from immediate action by a revolt in Wales and the growing threat of a Scottish war, assisted by a French alliance.

15. Guy's complaints are recorded at length in his defiance of 1297: Limburg-Stirum, *Codex Diplomaticus Flandriae*, I, 133–45.

16. Funck-Brentano (ed.), *Chronique artésienne*, 7–8.

17. Dumont, *Corps universel diplomatique*, 292–94. On 1 July 1295 Boniface VIII provided a dispensation for this marriage, *Reg. Bon. VIII*, 218.

It remained clear, however, that English action had only been postponed. With much of the diplomatic threat relieved, it was still necessary to mobilize France by raising men and, above all, money for the defense of the realm.

Perhaps the most difficult problem confronting any government is the question of taxation. Medieval man, moreover, was by no means as certain as we are that taxes rank with death as one of the few inescapable facts of life. In France, the traditional belief that the king should live of his own was still cherished by his subjects, though Philip the Fair sought every means of demonstrating that it had become untenable in the face of the growing responsibilities of the government at home and the constant expenses of his many wars.

As early as 1294 he had exhausted his normal sources of revenue and was forced to seek new methods of financing the approaching war with Edward of England. In that year he attempted to go completely beyond the traditional means of raising money by the introduction of the *maltôte*—a general tax on all subjects, including the normally exempt clergy. To soften the blow, he tried to raise the fervor of his subjects by an intensive propaganda campaign so violent that Edward I claimed that he aimed at the total annihilation of the English people.[18]

As lord of the bourg of Narbonne, Aycelin supported the king by compelling his subjects to send an accounting of the taxable hearths in the city, despite their objections to the extraordinary demand. But as a prelate, he placed clerical exemptions above the king's interests and excluded all clerks—even married and unbeneficed clerks—from the rolls.[19] The general resistance to the new tax was so strong that Philip was soon obliged to revoke it and look for other means of assistance. In particular, he hoped to compound with his clergy for grants from their considerable revenues.

Theoretically, the clergy was exempt from royal taxation but,

18. Rymer, *Foedera*, 689. In summoning the "model parliament" of 1295, Edward wrote to the Archbishop of Canterbury: ". . . ad expugnationem Regni nostri insurgens, classe maxima et bellatorum copiosa multitudine congregatis (cum quibus Regnum nostrum et Regni ejusdem Incolas hostiliter jam invasit) Linguam Anglicam. . . . omnino de terra delere proponit."
19. De Vic and Vaissette, *Histoire de Languedoc*, IX, 174.

under Philip the Fair, it was becoming common for the proceeds of the *decima*—originally a church tax controlled by the pope—to end up in the royal treasury. Aycelin had begun his career in the king's service by negotiating such a grant with Nicholas IV, and the favor had been repeated by Celestine V. Early in 1295 Philip bypassed the pope altogether by requesting his prelates to organize local synods to vote him further subsidies.

Among the six prelates known to have complied with this request was the Archbishop of Narbonne, who wrote from Paris instructing the Bishop of Uzès to hold the meeting. Accordingly, a synod at Béziers gathered and voted a two-year tenth.[20] This readiness to supply the king with money on request should not be construed as the act of sheep willing to agree to any demand without complaint. Aycelin's suffragans successfully demanded an investigation of the abuses of the royal seneschal of Beaucaire in exchange for their grant.[21]

In general, the attitude of the French clergy on these occasions was very businesslike. They used their power to grant money to the king as a means to pressure him into the correction of abuses by his agents or the extension of the existing liberties of the clergy. There is no reason, however, to interpret the complaints they made to the king as evidence of their intolerable oppression. Rather, it is evidence that they believed the king could and would grant them the improvements they requested in return for their financial assistance.

The following year a similar occasion arose. Once more the king asked his prelates for money and again they prepared to consider his request. Aycelin and his prelates had already gathered for this purpose when, quite without warning, they were confronted with the bull *Clericis Laicos*.

---

20. Ménard, *Histoire civile, écclésiastique et littéraire de la ville de Nismes*, I, *preuves*, 128.
21. *Ibid.*, 91.

V

Clericis Laicos

Boniface VIII had occupied the papal throne for a year and it was increasingly evident that Rome's policies were changing. His predecessor had been a man of ineffable sanctity and a pope of incomparable ineptitude. Boniface seemed fated to attract notoriety of a different sort, but he was an administrative genius capable of correcting the many disorders which impaired the operation of the hierarchy. He was Italian by birth and internationally minded in outlook. While not hostile to the French, he was not particularly partial to them either. He was anxious to recapture the church's independence of action politically, ultimately to revive the crusade. His immediate ambition was to act as arbiter of a general peace in Europe.[1] Fiery-tempered and determined, Boniface did not hesitate to begin his work of reconstruction in the Curia. Before his first year in office was out, deadly enmities had been rooted at the core of his administration, and among the cardinals who were to contribute to the pope's destruction were the two who were closest to Gilles Aycelin: his brother Hugh and Simon de Beaulieu, with whom he had worked in Clermont.

Hugh Aycelin had remained one of the closest confidantes of Celestine V through his brief pontificate. Favors and privileges were showered upon him as upon many others of the pope's friends, and only once was he apparently disappointed of his requests.[2] When the hermit pope abdicated in December 1294,

1. His efforts along these lines have recently been recapitulated by Renouard, "Les papes et le conflit franco-anglais," 915–16.
2. Stefaneschi, *Opus Metricum,* stated that Hugh was disappointed to find that one of his nominations had been excluded from the final list of Celestine's cardinals. Lelius Marini, *Acta Sanctorum,* 522, a later chronicler, claimed that the candidate was Hugh's nephew, but he had no nephew even remotely eligible for the appointment at that time. If the nominee were a member of his family,

Hugh had more than enough cause for future discontent. However, he was on good terms with the new pope at that time. It is almost certain that no breach had yet occurred between Aycelin and Benedict Gaetani, who was executor of Hugh's will.[3] Although the voting in the conclave was secret, there is very good reason to suppose that Hugh voted for Gaetani in the papal election.[4] But shortly after his election, Boniface quarreled violently with the Bishop of Ostia and there is reason to suppose that Aycelin never stopped nursing his resentment of his treatment at that time.[5] Related as he was to the Archbishop of Narbonne, Hugh was in a position to act as one of the vital links between the French court and the growing party of cardinals who resented the high-handed methods of the new pope.

The admirers of Celestine V had been disturbed from the first over the abdication of the hermit pope. When Boniface determined to place his predecessor in protective custody to prevent his friends from attempting his restoration, their misgivings turned to alarm. More worldly members of the College of Cardinals, most especially the Colonnas, were resentful of the new pope's attempts to build an independent temporal base through the aggrandizement of his family. Simon de Beaulieu, who had been appointed by Celestine V and arrived in Rome shortly after the election, was an old enemy. Their quarrel dated back to 1290 when Gaetani

therefore, it must have been one of his brothers: Jean, who was a priest by that time, or, more likely, Gilles.

3. This fact is known only from Hugh's statement in a later will that he was changing his executor because Benedict Gaetani was too overburdened with the cares of the papacy to maintain the responsibility. Duchesne, *Histoire des cardinaux*, 231.

4. In 1297 Hugh signed the statement made by the cardinals in opposition to the charges raised by the Colonnas that no serious protest had been made against Gaetani's candidacy: Denifle, "Die Denkschriften der Colonna," 515. Analyzing the probable division of votes in the conclave, both Finke, *Aus den Tagen Bonifaz VIII*, 45, and Seppelt, *Studien*, 19, argue that Gaetani could not have been elected without the votes of Aycelin and the other French cardinals.

5. Trivet, *Annales Sex Regum Angliae*, 334: "Hic Bonifacius octavus vocatus, statim post suam creationem episcopum Ostiensem super quibusdam in praesentia cardinalium arguens durissime, pallii usu privavit; et nihilominus ab eodem ante restitutionem pallii coronatur." Though Trivet is the only chronicler to mention this incident, there is no reason to doubt his statement. Like Hugh, Trivet was a Dominican and present at the time in Rome. The cause of the quarrel is unknown, but from this time on there is ample evidence of a change in Hugh's feelings toward his erstwhile friend.

had been papal legate in France. At the synod of Sainte Geneviève, he and Beaulieu quarreled bitterly and publicly over the question of mendicant privileges at the University of Paris.[6] Subsequent events seem to prove that Beaulieu had never forgiven the quarrel and, with his powerful friends on the royal council, he could be a deadly enemy. He may already have known Hugh Aycelin, as he knew his brother. If not, they must have been brought together very soon after Beaulieu's arrival in Rome.

Boniface made every effort to repair the breach with Hugh Aycelin. Soon after his coronation he appointed him to the important office of chamberlain, which gave him the congenial responsibility for the disbursement of papal funds and the direction of consistorial discussions of financial issues.[7] He bestowed special favors on his family in August,[8] over and above his earlier special exemption of the privileges granted by Celestine to the Bishop of Ostia from his general revocation of his predecessor's grants in April.[9] Despite these efforts, however, the rift was not healed. At this time Aycelin changed his will, removing the pope as his executor.[10] The following year he was specifically named[11] as one of the cardinals involved in Simon de Beaulieu's efforts to secure French aid for a move to depose Boniface.

The pope seems to have been serenely unaware of these undercurrents at his court. One of his first acts in office, on 18 February 1295, was to appoint Beaulieu legate to France with instructions to cooperate with the legatine mission of Berard de Goth in England for the establishment of a peace, or at least a truce, between the two countries. To further their mission, the legates were entrusted with a variety of bulls providing them with alternative powers to use at their discretion as conditions demanded them.[12] There is no indication that Beaulieu made any serious effort to

6. The text of their charges and countercharges appears in Finke, *Aus den Tagen Bonifaz VIII*, 3–7.

7. Kirsch, *Die Finanzverwaltung des Kardinalkollegiums*, outlines the history and responsibilities of this office. He includes documents from the period of Aycelin's tenure, 96–128.

8. *Reg. Bon. VIII*, 300–302.

9. *Ibid.*, 295–96.

10. Duchesne, *Histoire des cardinaux*, 231.

11. Höfler, "Rückblick auf P. Bonifacius VIII," 72.

12. *Reg. Bon. VIII*, 697–731.

pursue this mission. On the contrary, the evidence shows that during the two years he spent in France he consistently worked to undermine the pope's reputation there and to induce an open quarrel between the pope and the king.[13]

The time could not have been better for the legate's purposes. In January 1296 an English force landed in Aquitaine and laid siege to Bordeaux. It was a moment of national crisis and the French were quick to respond to any suggestion of further hostility from any quarter.

In cooperation with French plans to repel the invaders, Gilles Aycelin called a meeting of his suffragans to discuss a new grant of money.[14] Pierre de Latilly and another royal representative attended the meeting, which apparently took place in April or early May, to present the king's case. Luckily, we have an excellent, though often neglected, account of the subsequent events from the testimony of Berengar Frédol before a papal commission of 1309.[15]

Frédol, who was then Bishop of Carcassonne, participated in the deliberations of the province of Narbonne. They concluded that the king had not offered enough in the way of privileges for their money and accordingly sent Frédol and Etienne de Suizy to negotiate with Philip, offering him a tenth for two or three years in return for the desired liberties.

The two bishops had reached Limoges when they were overtaken by a messenger from the archbishop. He had a copy of *Clericis Laicos* and a letter from Aycelin describing the steps that

13. A full account of Simon de Beaulieu's successful efforts to provoke the first quarrel between Boniface and Philip the Fair has been provided in McNamara, "Simon de Beaulieu and *Clericis Laicos*."

14. It is probable that the letter of January 22, written soon after the English landing at Bordeaux, published by Martène and Durand, *Thesaurus*, IV, 217–18, convoked this council. The editors ascribed it to "Aegidius of Bourges" (Aegidius Romanus), but since it was found in the Archives of the Archbishop of Narbonne, its author was probably Aegidius (Gilles) of Narbonne. The letter urged the meeting and an agreement to support the king on the ground that the danger of the invading English was a threat not only to the kingdom but also to the entire Gallican Church.

15. Höfler, "Rückblick auf P. Bonifacius VIII," 75ff. While none of the testimony given to this commission can be trusted too far as regards its major purpose —to clear Philip of complicity in the later events at Anagni—Frédol is excellent for our purposes. He had no reason to distort the events he describes here, and his evidence is borne out by succeeding events.

had already been taken in Paris by the Archbishops of Rheims, Sens, and Rouen. Considering the content of the bull, the archbishop warned them not to make any promises to the king. The envoys decided to go with their report to Philip. Upon their arrival, they gave the king assurances of the good will of the province of Narbonne and recounted the results of their meeting. Then they asked him to excuse them from giving him immediate assistance since the pope's bull bound them not to take such an action.

The rest of Frédol's account is concerned with Philip's reaction and as such is most enlightening. The king of England flew into an outraged temper the following November when confronted with the same situation and drove the Archbishop of Canterbury into near-outlawry. Philip the Fair received the report from Narbonne in his council with a remarkable show of self-control (which makes one suspect that he had already been warned of what was to occur). With a display of tact rare among monarchs, he graciously sent his thanks to the province for their good will and asked the delegates if they thought they could give him the money he needed so badly. In return, he assured them he was ready to give them the privilege requested. He added that he would not have them transgress the papal bull, demonstrating his respect for the obligations of the prelates to their ecclesiastical superior. After giving the expected refusal, the bishops left court. Later Frédol said that many people suspected that the pope had acted specifically out of enmity to the King of France.[16]

It is likely that no one could have been more surprised at this development than Boniface VIII, if he had known of it. *Clericis Laicos* had been sent to the legates in both countries in April, but its release was to be delayed.[17] As Boase suggested,[18] it was most

16. *Ibid.*, 76.

17. *Reg. Bon. VIII*, 1584: "Verum quia non est fragilitatis humane prescire futura—intentionem nostram a vobis caute servandam presentibus aperimus, ut si dicti reges per treugas vel sufferentias voluntarias vel per viam alicujus concordie seu alias a bellicosis aparatibus et prosecutione cessabunt—et sic per consequens videritis quod non expediret ad treugarum hujusmodi publicationem procedi, discretioni vestre committimus ut in hoc casu treugarum presentatio differatur; ubi autem de congressu hujusmodi verisimiliter timeretur, presentatio et publicatio nullatenus omitatur." He proceeded to explain that the "other letters" he was sending were to be delayed for emergency use.

18. Boase, *Boniface VIII*, 136.

probably the pope's intention to use the bull to reinforce the peace negotiations. His only immediate move in the direction indicated by the bull was a mild request that both legates ask the kings to press less onerously upon their clergy.[19] His main object was the proposal itself, which the legates were to publish on 24 June.

There is no hint of any discussions of a truce proposed by the pope or anyone else in France during that spring. In May, with Bordeaux still under siege, when Aycelin's suffragans were meeting, the only word from Rome appeared to be the obstructive bull which reminded them that they could not finance the king without papal permission. Nor did Beaulieu mention the truce in his letter of 20 May to the French clergy, though he summoned them to meet in Paris on 22 June, two days before it should have been published. He spoke only in guarded terms of the great ruin that was threatening the Gallican Church—a calamity that could only be defined as possible repercussions from *Clericis Laicos*.[20] This letter of convocation was sent to the prelates of Narbonne, Auxerre, Bourges, Lyon, Tours, and Bordeaux with supporting letters from the bishops of Rheims, Sens, and Rouen whom Beaulieu had consulted in Paris. This is probably the letter Aycelin mentioned in his note to Frédol.

It is likely that Philip's careful reaction to Frédol's statements was part of a plan made by this group. The king had determined not to alienate his clergy, and in return they appear to have taken immediate steps to rescue him and themselves from the papal strictures. The royal tact had saved them from a painful situation and assured the king of their loyalty in the difficult days ahead. Completing his account of these events in 1309, Berengar Frédol burst out:

19. *Reg. Bon. VIII*, 1585: "Sollicite insuper vias decentes studeatis assumere in evitandis oneribus intolerabilibus ecclesiarum regnorum eorumdem quas intolerabilia prexerunt hactenus onera et pressure, in eis ecclesiastica libertate quasi totaliter enervata, ex quibus divinam non ambigimus potentiam fore graviter provocatam et nisi provocantes saniori ducti consilio ad ejus celeriter misericordiam revertantur, timeri potest et merito quod misericordiam ejus convertet in iram et ad vindictam vibrabit gladium contra eos."
20. Martène and Durand, *Thesaurus*, 219–20: ". . . pro salubrius remediis exquirendis quibus ipsa ecclesia cui grandem videmus, proh· dolor! imminere ruinam, auctore domino fulciatur."

> It is my experience that if the king had bad will toward Boniface, he had cause for it that I know of. At the time when there was war between him and England, Boniface worked for the destruction of the king.[21]

The clergy had already determined their position and dispatched a delegation to Rome to request the pope's release from the restrictions of the bull. The French government had already retaliated on 17 August by sequestering the funds collected for the crusade[22] when the pope ordered the publication of *Clericis Laicos* on 18 August 1296.[23]

The pope undoubtedly thought that the combination of the exhibition of his growing impatience to settle a peace and the release of *Clericis Laicos* would finally force some action in France. But he could not have anticipated the news of the organized French resistance that must have reached him in mid-September. At that time, threatened with new wars in Sicily and apprised of the unabated preparations in France and England for a continuation of their struggle, the pope apparently recognized that a new attempt to force a truce on the belligerents was hopeless, for he said no more about it. Instead he attempted only to repair the disastrous misunderstanding with France of which he had finally become aware.

The text of his bull of 20 September, *Ineffabilis Amoris*,[24] reflected Boniface's genuine bewilderment. He maintained that he had never acted against the best interests of France but rather had exhausted himself in unremitting labors on the king's behalf. To save the French alliance with the papacy, he was not above threatening Philip with the dangers of alienating so warm a friend at a moment when France was surrounded by enemies. But the repeated argument of the bull is that some misunderstanding must have occurred, for there could be no other explanation of the actions of the French. Although he admitted that the cause of the confusion might be *Clericis Laicos*, he claimed to view the possibility as irrational.

---

21. Höfler, "Rückblick auf P. Bonifacius," 75.
22. *Les Olim*, II, 397.
23. *Reg. Bon. VIII*, 1644.
24. *Ibid.*, 1653.

Boniface apparently still had faith in the integrity of his legate for he did not recall him. Searching for the source of the king's hostility, he could think of no possibility except the enmity of "evil councillors." For the first time he exhibited that conviction which was to haunt him for the rest of his life—that someone was playing the role of Achitophel in France, deliberately scheming to alienate the papacy from its eldest daughter, the Gallican Church. In the end, he would come to identify Pierre Flote as the man, but in 1296 Flote was only beginning his career of goading the unstable pope.

Flote's first major role in Philip's council was the preparation of an answer to *Ineffabilis* for presentation at the meeting of the Parlement of Paris on 1 November. The object was to present an argument which would justify the king's aggression. A simple recognition that a misunderstanding had occurred would not serve royal policies. To strengthen his position, Flote apparently received his appointment to the highest office in the council at this time.[25] The tact with which Philip received Aycelin's initial refusal to grant subsidies without papal permission demonstrated that the king had no desire to compromise his clergy in the coming quarrel. When it became necessary to concoct a defiant answer to *Ineffabilis Amoris,* it is understandable that he preferred to make use of a layman who was not vulnerable to reprisals from Rome.

Ineffabilis was probably received about mid-October, and may never have been seen by anyone outside the king's closest circle. It is very probable that the only version of its contents that most officials ever received is that given in Flote's speech of 1 November. The records of the meeting of the Parlement of Paris have not been preserved, but it seems likely that the substance of Flote's speech has been preserved in the document called *Antequam Essent Clericis.*[26]

25. No evidence has yet been discovered to pin down the exact date on which Flote came to office or the exact title which he held. Perrichet, *La grande chancellerie*, 154, discussed the problem at some length. He found no satisfactory official documents giving Flote's title, though in an unofficial document he signed himself "Petrus Flote, miles, domini regis cancellarius." The date at which he came into possession of the seals is equally obscure, but Perrichet argues convincingly that it occurred in the spring of 1296.

26. This tract was found in the royal chancery by Dupuy, *Histoire du différend,*

Flote's speech was made before the assembled lay and clerical dignitaries, including the Archbishop of Narbonne, who had come to Paris for various causes to be considered in the Parlement of Paris. It was strong, even violent in places, but there is no indication that it was meant to do more than justify the king's request for money and, perhaps, alarm the pope with a demonstration of French opposition. No further threat to the clergy was made and they were left undisturbed while further action from Rome was awaited. The main arguments were directed against the pope's putative claims—and opposition to a reigning pope cannot be considered synonymous with anticlericalism. No diminution of existing ecclesiastical liberties was suggested except for a general condemnation of the view, erroneously attributed to Boniface VIII, that the liberties of the clergy freed them from the responsibility of assisting the king in the defense of the realm.

Since the pope had suggested no such attitude, it can only be assumed that Flote's purpose was to alarm the pope and to stiffen the clergy in support of the king at a time when they would not yet have known of the release of *Clericis Laicos* in England. When Flote had finished with his attack on the pope's pretensions to unfounded authority, Pierre de Paredo, Abbot of Saint Médard, spoke, developing an attack on the person of the incumbent pope by repeating the charges of Beaulieu in 1295 that Boniface was a heretic and usurper. Paredo had been dispatched to Rome the previous summer, after the first appearance of *Clericis Laicos,* and by November the abbot was back with letters from various cardinals supporting Beaulieu's charges. In 1309 he stated that

---

21–23. The arguments of Scholz, *Die Publilizistik zur Zeit Philipps des Schönen,* 333, attributing its authorship to Flote or someone working under him in the chancery, have been generally accepted. Entitled "Responsiones nomine Philippi Regis, ad bullam Bonifacii PP. VIII datam Anagniae II Kalend Octor. Pontificatus anno secundo," the tract clearly purports to be an answer to *Ineffabilis Amoris.* As demonstrated by Langlois, *Saint-Louis,* 134, it could never have been sent to Rome or intended for the pope's eyes. Therefore, the most logical explanation for its composition is for use at this meeting of the Parlement. *Antequam* has generally been interpreted as the exposition of the new "secular" point of view growing up at the French court. In addition to Scholz, the argument has been advanced by Schleyer, *Die Anfänge der Gallikanismus,* 90ff., Rivière, *Le problème de l'église et de l'état,* 98ff., and most recently by de Lagarde, *La naissance de l'esprit laïque,* I, 204, who presents the tract as a full-scale attack on the whole system of clerical immunities.

these included corroborating letters from Hugh Aycelin, Pietro and Stefano Colonna, and other cardinals.[27] Having examined this testimony, the Parlement instructed Paredo to return to Rome where he could keep in contact with the dissident cardinals, though he was to take no concrete action against the pope beyond warning him that he was being accused of serious crimes.

The chief purpose of this meeting of the Parlement appears to have been propaganda. It was the first of those carefully staged dramas at which Flote—and after him, Nogaret—became adept in years to come. The theme is always the same: the traditional rights of the king were alleged to be under attack by an unjust and intemperate pope, ambitious to extend his power into the temporal sphere. Except for Paredo's assignment, no plans for action were formulated. Nothing at all, not even the promise of future subsidies, was asked from the clergy. Apparently, it was enough to have set the terms of the king's defense and show him as a righteous and innocent victim.

The subsequent actions of Pierre Flote should not be viewed as the expression of a new, anticlerical spirit in the French court, but as the response of a talented man to a specific political problem. Soon after these events, the long diplomatic partnership of Flote and the Archbishop of Narbonne was established. Their relationship in the years to come, until Flote's death in 1302, demonstrates concretely the general atmosphere of cooperation between those of the king's servants who had been rewarded with ecclesiastical office and those whose careers were entirely secular. Far from opposing one another, or representing different traditions, they complemented one another admirably in carrying out policies designed not so much to destroy the power of the Church as to maneuver the pope into support of French policies.

---

27. Höfler, "Rückblick auf P. Bonifacius," 72. Paredo's testimony was confirmed by Napoleone Orsini (p. 50) and Jean Lemoine (p. 52).

VI

Aycelin and Pierre Flote

Dramatic as it was, the quarrel with Boniface VIII by no means monopolized the attention of the king's councillors through 1296. During the summer, when French resistance to the pope was at its hottest, Aycelin was equally occupied with meetings of the Parlement of Paris. Among many lesser issues, the Parlement was absorbed in development of a policy against the Count of Flanders. Since his submission of 1295, Guy de Dampierre had been subjected to constant pressure from the French. In the summer of 1296 he sought alleviation by an appeal to the Parlement of Paris. There he found no mercy.

The Parlement's verdict was expressed in a series of acts issued in August.[1] He was denied the right to reclaim the town of Valenciennes, which was proclaimed a direct possession of the King of France. The count was further ordered to make amends for several acts of disobedience, whose nature was not clarified, and to refrain from any attempt at reprisals against towns which opened their gates to the French. As a guarantee of future good behavior, he was required to place possession of and jurisdiction over certain towns in the king's hands. In turn, the king agreed "graciously" to send only a single representative to occupy each town—with the exception of Gand, over which he claimed to have sole jurisdiction.

The French appeared to be determined to strip Guy of Flanders of all his authority in the towns of his county by the same means already used successfully by Flote in Gascony. With his fellow judges, Aycelin must have helped devise the Parlement's answer to the count's demand for a judgment by his peers. They maintained that the court, whose membership included some of the greatest men in France, constituted a court of peers and was

1. *Les Olim*, II, 394–96.

therefore the highest authority in the count's case. In 1298, when Dampierre turned with the same complaint to Boniface VIII, Aycelin was prepared to refute his charges of injustice with a copy of the records of the Parlement. The pope himself was at that time prepared to recognize the justice of the Parlement's claim.[2] By this device, Philip the Fair and his councillors had successfully defined the conditions under which they would conduct their future relations with Flanders. The county was not an independent power in their view. It therefore had no right to seek alliances and assistance from abroad. It was a fief of the King of France who had the final authority to regulate its affairs. If Guy de Dampierre desired to fight further for his rights, he must undertake the role of rebellious vassal. Recognizing that he had exhausted the possibilities of legal remedy, the count decided on this course. He sent representatives to Paris with a letter of defiance, renouncing his allegiance to Philip the Fair. Upon receipt of this letter, the king called together the great men of his court. The Archbishop of Narbonne was in attendance on 21 January 1297 to hear Flote's reading of the defiance into which he had helped to drive the count.[3]

The royal answer was a protest of outraged virtue. The King was a lord who had never failed to do justice as he should. God helping him, he never would! The count was a recreant vassal declared contumacious by the Parlement of Paris. The Parlement further deprived him formally of all his holdings in Flanders and restored the towns he held to their ancient liberty.[4]

Shortly after the Flemish defiance was received in France, Edward I announced a renewal of his alliance with the count, swearing to sustain him with both men and money. Philip's complicated maneuverings had brought him to a dangerous pass but they had also given him a legal, if not a moral, advantage. He could claim to be the injured party, not the aggressor in the war that was about to begin. He could act as a victim forced to defend

2. Kervyn de Lettenhove, "Etudes," 43.
3. The text of the letter was published by Kervyn de Lettenhove, *Histoire de Flandres*, II, 574. On p. 391, he dates the meeting February 1298, but the date I have used is confirmed by the documents printed by Limburg-Stirum, I, 133–49.
4. *Les Olim*, II, 28–33.

himself and his realm against rebellion within and invasion from without. The argument was important in view of the need to persuade his own subjects to support him with men and money. It was vital in regard to the greater necessity of completing the immobilization of Boniface VIII.

During the period immediately after the November Parlement, the question of *Clericis Laicos* was quietly abandoned. The pope's protestations in *Ineffabilis* were ignored, but an independent statement issued from the court stated that the prohibition on the export of gold—which had held up the crusading monies—was not intended to apply to any funds but those which might be used to support the enemies of the kingdom. By 28 November the crusade money had been released.[5] The pope answered this move with a letter explicitly stating that Philip could not be considered to have incurred the automatic excommunication threatened in *Ineffabilis* and specified in canon law for those who despoiled church property, since Philip had never intended that his edict be applied to the clergy.[6]

As a result of these moves, Philip had recovered much of his freedom of action as regarded subsidies in time to prepare for the threatened invasion of 1297. Accordingly, the clergy were convoked to a general meeting with the king on 1 February 1297 and asked for help in the coming emergency. With tranquil hearts, they could promise to exert themselves as far as possible. After the meeting, the pope was inundated with respectful letters from all the provinces of France requesting his permission that the French clergy be allowed to subsidize their king in his hour of need.[7]

Having destroyed the pope's design for peace, Philip still desired to ensure his support—or at least his neutrality—in the com-

---

5. Digard, *Philippe le Bel,* I, 272.
6. *Reg. Bon. VIII,* 2311.
7. Langlois, *Saint-Louis,* 135, established that the letter which Dupuy reprinted (p. 26) from the clergy of Reims was issued from this February conference. Kervyn de Lettenhove, "Etudes," 20, provided evidence that the letter was only one example of a form followed by twenty-two other French prelates, including Gilles Aycelin. This is corroborated by the pope's answer, *Reg. Bon. VIII,* 2333, addressed to him among other prelates. Strayer, *Studies in Early French Taxation,* 30, attributes this action to pressure applied on the clergy by Pierre Flote, but there is no reason to suppose that any prodding was needed.

ing war. To do so he had already entered into a series of complicated schemes, being directed in part by Paredo in Rome, and the
final reaping of their fruits was imminent. For this purpose he
dispatched Aycelin and Pierre Flote to Rome in the spring of
1297. Every first-class diplomatic assignment during this period
was entrusted to the archbishop and his one-eyed companion.

The daring, mocking Flote has long occupied the center of the
stage whenever the first half of the reign of Philip the Fair has
been discussed. His astute and inconspicuous superior on these
missions has, as a result, been almost overlooked—or, at best,
treated as a pompous cipher. Flote, endowed with a law degree
by later historians, invariably has been credited with all the results of the various missions in which he participated. By infer-
ence, the Archbishop of Narbonne (whose name so frequently
heads the list of representatives) could have been no more than a
figure-head, providing an imposing facade behind which Flote
could operate unhampered.

Such assumptions are totally unjustified. The scanty mention
of their specific deeds in the accomplishment of their missions
rather indicates that they functioned as a uniquely compatible
team. Aycelin's training in the law and his success in his independent missions argue that he was a real force in those he shared with
Flote. There are hints that they divided their responsibilities in
such a way as to take advantage of their individual talents. Flote,
free of the inhibitions imposed by ecclesiastical dignity, seems to
have played a special role in French dealings with Boniface VIII.
The pope, like others who reported on the missions, consistently
saw him in the role of provocateur. The business of goading the
papal temper, of expressing extreme ideological positions, and of
hinting that the King of France was prepared to be violent appear
to have been his specialties. Audacity was his stock in trade, and
it is most likely that his role was to shock and unnerve the oppo-
nent; to prepare him for a prudent and sympathetic archbishop
only too eager to pour oil on the troubled waters by cooperating
in a design to avert the imaginary dangers created by Flote—by
providing France with privileges and advantages.

Their mission of April 1297 was to ensure that the pope would
not interfere in the coming war and to secure what assistance they

could. His ability to act as arbiter to prevent a French invasion of Flanders had been neutralized by the acts of January which turned the war into a feudal rebellion, a domestic affair of no concern to the papacy. Though Guy of Flanders appealed to the pope to act as arbiter in his quarrel with the king of France, Boniface made no response.[8] His effort to make peace had come to nothing. He was alarmed and anxious over the apparent violent misunderstanding with which his bulls regarding taxation of the clergy had been received in France. He may already have been aware of the plots against him that were being brewed among his cardinals—especially by Pietro and Stefano Colonna—and of the activities of the French agent, Pierre de Paredo, who was keeping them in communication with the French court.[9]

All of these factors were known to Aycelin and Flote, and they were prepared to manipulate them to gain their object with the pope. They wanted a papal pronouncement which would effectively make *Clericis Laicos* a dead letter in respect to the coming war. Symbolic blessings were to be obtained for the French monarchy by the canonization of Louis IX. In addition, the ambassadors must have had general instructions to prevent any move to renew papal intervention in the war and, if possible, to persuade the pope to condemn the count of Flanders. To implement this general policy, they appear to have been given a free hand in dealing with the cardinals whose discontent was being kept alive by Paredo. No doubt, Aycelin in particular could be expected to confer with his brother on this question.

Just before their departure there was a public performance in France whose purpose is a mystery but which may well have been intended as some sort of prologue to their mission. On 20 April 1297 Beaulieu and Berard de Goth, who had left England and joined his fellow legate in France, presented the king with papal letters threatening him with the penalties included in the truce of 1296 should he continue his plan to invade Flanders.[10] Since

8. Kervyn de Lettenhove, "Etudes," 27–29. On 25 January the count wrote an account of his case to the pope, arguing that as a vassal he had acted blamelessly, issuing his defiance only after the king had repeatedly violated his own commitments.

9. Höfler, "Rückblick auf P. Bonifacius," 59.

10. The scene is described by the legates in their report to Boniface VIII,

the pope had written no letters regarding the truce since the previous summer, it can only be imagined that the legates were presenting the truce that Beaulieu should have published the year before. In any case, since the pope had already recognized that a state of emergency existed in France in his bulls modifying *Clericis Laicos*, the application of penalties for breaking a nonexistent truce was totally irrelevant. The scene can therefore only be explained as either a final trick of Beaulieu's or as a staged threat to the pope to warn him against resting too securely at a time when a French mission was leaving for Rome.

Philip had obviously been fully informed of the legates' intentions beforehand, for he refused to hear their message until he had delivered himself of a resounding statement of principle: that he and no one else controlled the temporalities of his realm and that he recognized no superior in matters concerning them.[11] It is probable that the whole scene was arranged for the sake of these remarks which, included in the legatine report, would reach the pope's eyes a few weeks before the appearance of the French representatives.

There is a second, though entirely conjectural, possibility that this move by Beaulieu was intended in some manner to be coordinated with the culmination of the plot being nurtured in the

---

Dupuy, *Histoire du différend*, 27–28. The date, 1297, is confirmed by the text, "anno tres of the pontificate" and by the presence of de Goth, who remained in England until the winter of 1296.

11. *Ibid.*, "Cumque dictas litteras praesentaremus [the legates speaking] dicto Regi Franciae legendas, idem Rex incontinenti, antequam eadem litterae legerentur, nomine suo, et se praesente, fecit exprimi et mandavit in nostri praesentia protestationes huiusmodi, et alia quae sequuntur: videlicet regimen temporalitatis regni sui ad ipsum Regem solum et neminem alium, pertinere, seque in eo neminem superiorem recognoscere, nec habere, nec se intendere supponere vel subiicere modo quocunque viventi alicui, super rebus pertinentibus ad temporale regimen regni: sed potius se intendere feoda sua iustitiare, regnum suum defendere continue, iusque regni per omnia proseque cum subditis suis, amicis, et valitoribus, prout haec Dominus ministrabit: maxime cum dictarum treugarum indictionis virtus, vel indicentis intentio, ipsum Regem aliquatenus non impediat in praemissis, vel aliquo eorumdem, ut dicebat, nec aliquem obicem contrarietatis opponat; sed dicti Regis regnique sui turbatores et aemulos arctius deprimat, illorum compescat audaciam, ausus frenet, ac excommunicationis sententias, si contra tenorem treugarum ipsarum venire praesumpserint, ipso Rege, dictoque regno suo, remanentibus non ligatis, iuxta declarationem per dictum dominum Papam factam litteris suis patentibus, ipsi Regi directis; a quibus declaratione et protestationibus, verbe vel facto, nunc, vel in futurum, idem rex non intendit recedere, ut dicebat."

Curia by Paredo. Only six days after this scene the Colonnas rebelled openly against the authority of Boniface VIII, and their manifestos—published in May, with one written especially for presentation to the King of France and the University of Paris—give some evidence that they expected French support.[12] Pietro Colonna's testimony of 1309 strongly suggests that Aycelin and Flote received specific instructions regarding the rebel cardinals before their departure from Paris.[13] One of the cardinals' messengers met the ambassadors on their way to Rome and spoke with Flote, who appeared to be fully informed of the Colonna situation. Pietro Colonna claimed that Flote was in possession of letters empowering the ambassadors to denounce Boniface as a heretic and usurper and begin proceedings against him. Flote gave the messenger assurances of the king's sympathy with their cause and promised to meet the Colonnas at Palestrina, presumably to coordinate their joint strategy.

Although the Archbishop of Narbonne was the formal head of the mission, his name never appeared in connection with the Colonna affair—and was probably never intended to appear. After their arrival in Rome in July, it was Flote who continued to meet with the representatives of the Colonnas, promising to come to Palestrina and providing them with other encouragement. Throughout this time negotiations with the pope were proceeding smoothly and it seems likely that this was Aycelin's responsibility because of his greater legal knowledge and his imposing ecclesiastical title.

The ambassadors were with Boniface from 3 to 9 July, and probably helped secure his argument to the king's various requests by spicing their conversations with allusions to the Colonnas. While Flote kept the rebellious family on the strong, possibly by dispensing to them and their supporters at least a portion of the 1,200 pounds he spent "on the king's secret business" during this mission,[14] Aycelin must have secured the promulgation of Louis

12. The Colonna manifestos and an introductory account of the events which provoked their rebellion are published in Denifle, "Die Denkschriften der Colonna," 493–529.

13. Höfler, "Rückblick auf P. Bonifacius," 59.

14. *Comptes royaux*, 20918.

IX's canonization on 9 July. On the same day, assured that the King of France would not interfere, the pope issued his bull deposing the Colonna cardinals with instructions to the inquisitors to take them into custody;[15] in September Boniface formally declared a crusade against them[16]—with all the trappings, including appeals to Christian soldiers and offers of indulgences.

Pietro Colonna was later to claim that the pope had tricked Flote and that he had followed a policy, which he had confided to others beforehand, of separating the French from the Colonnas and attempting to destroy them one at a time.[17] The historian of the Colonnas[18] believed that Flote betrayed the king on his own initiative, omitting the prosecution entrusted to him for the sake of the privileges Boniface offered to seduce him from his purpose. To Colonna, this version was confirmed by the fact that Boniface later suspended the same privileges. But it seems far more likely that the privileges Aycelin received were the real object of their mission, since even the pope could not have foreseen the events which would lead to their suspension in 1301. It was the Colonnas who were tricked and betrayed by Flote and the maneuver had probably been planned in advance and approved by the King of France.

While his companion was engaged in this complex diversion, Aycelin must have been applying his experience and understanding of the law to the amassing of the privileges secured in the bulls of 27–31 July sealing the rapprochement of Philip the Fair and Boniface VIII. New interpretations of *Clericis Laicos* were supplied, expressing the pope's anxiety that the bull would not be used to endanger the kingdom of France.

15. *Reg. Bon. VIII*, 2351.
16. *Ibid.*, 2352.
17. Höfler, "Rückblick auf P. Bonifacius," 59. At the same hearings (p. 72) Paredo claimed that he had delivered the warnings with which he had been charged at the November Parlement and that the pope's response had been angrily to rail against Gallic pride: "God confound me, if I do not confound the pride of the French! I see your king calls himself a friend of the Colonnas. Then I will make peace with the king, destroy the Colonnas, and then I will destroy the king and set up another king in France." On the face of it, this is a most improbable account. Paredo, at best an unappetizing character, most likely concocted it for his own purposes in 1309, which were to contribute to the contention that Philip was acting in good faith in attacking the pope at Anagni in 1303.
18. Möhler, *Die Kardinale Jacob und Peter Colonna*, 260.

Pope Boniface must have been only too anxious to escape from his false position. Even before he received the letters of the French prelates, he had written a series of further explanations of *Clericis Laicos. De Temporum Spatiis*[19] reiterated the claim that the bull had been issued only as a general statement in defense of the traditional liberties of the Church and had in no way been intended as a particular attack on the King of France. *Romana Mater*[20] was more extensive in stating that the clergy had never been prevented from giving free contributions to the king and that clerical privileges were not in any case intended to comprehend royal riefs or offices held by clerks or to cover married clerks or any others not living in strict conformity with clerical regulations. Upon receiving the letters of the French prelates he wrote *Coram Illo Fatemur*,[21] expressing his regret that the clergy of France should have experienced difficulties because of previous papal bulls and commending their request for his permission to aid the king in view of the new emergency. Claiming that he had never intended to endanger the kingdom of France, or any other realm, in time of danger or fear of invasion, he gave the prelates leave to act freely to assist in its defense.

This series of bulls has normally been interpreted as a surrender by the pope in the face of French resistance. But there is no real reason to suppose that the pope was not in fact making every effort to clarify a genuine misunderstanding. When Boniface wrote *Clericis Laicos* there was no national emergency and he fully expected a truce to be established, which the bull was designed to enforce. Conditions had changed by February 1297, and communications from France had shown the pope that his bull was being interpreted in ways he had never intended. Rothwell has contributed a persuasive argument on this problem in his discussion of the doctrine of "Necessitas" as the legal foundation for these bulls and for *Etsi de Statu* the following summer.[22] He argues that Boniface was acting as he said he was acting, in conformity with new political circumstances which had arisen in

19. *Reg. Bon. VIII*, 2308.
20. *Ibid.*, 2312.
21. *Ibid.*, 2333, 28 February 1297.
22. Rothwell, "The Confirmation of the Charters, 1297," 16–35.

January. Since a state of dangerous necessity had developed in France, the pope was acting logically and correctly in stating that his bull was not intended to operate against the urgent needs of defense. These conditions seriously weaken the arguments that Boniface surrendered or that the French clergy had, from servility, bowed to the aggressive will of Philip the Fair.

As soon as the pope's answer was received, the prelates met on 27 March to arrange for the concession of new subsidies. Before he had begun the journey to Rome, Aycelin had spent a week negotiating on the king's behalf with other prelates to arrange the terms of their grants.[23] The bull *Etsi de Statu*, arranged for by Aycelin in Rome—which repeated the proviso that the pope's earlier bulls had never affected the freedom of the clergy to make voluntary gifts and loans to the king[24]—placed the seal of papal approval on these arrangements and, indeed, seems to have given the French clergy almost complete liberty to negotiate grants at will. Among the further concessions, the king's power to imprison clerks suspected of treason during time of war was recognized, an important abrogation of clerical privilege which would later be used against the Bishop of Pamiers.[25] To ease his financial difficulties, Philip was given permission to appoint a single canon or prebendary in each of the French cathedrals, including those of Lyon and Viviers which were not normally under his jurisdiction.[26] A further concession of first fruits[27] on all ecclesiastical offices below the episcopal and abbatial levels for the duration of the war was added on 8 August.

These grants represented the successful completion of the French mission. Nevertheless, Flote and Aycelin remained in Rome at least until 28 October, at which time Flote was given the authority to settle certain outstanding problems in France concerning the money which the legates had collected for the prospective crusade.[28] It seems likely that the reason was simply a sense

23. Martène and Durand, *Thesaurus*, I, 1277–80. They date the documents "1296," but the text is dated third year of the pontificate, or 1297.
24. *Reg. Bon. VIII*, 2354–55.
25. *Ibid.*, 2357.
26. *Ibid.*, 2356.
27. *Ibid.*, 2367.
28. *Ibid.*, 2091. On 8 August Boniface had already granted Philip's request to make these monies available for the prosecution of the war, *Ibid.*, 2361–66.

of caution, an unwillingness to desert Rome and leave a Flemish representative near the pope while the outcome of the summer's campaign was still in doubt. They probably left Rome after they had been informed of the signing of a truce favoring the French on 10 October. Despite the continued presence of the Flemings in Rome, they must have felt the position of France required no additional vigilance on their part.

En route back to Paris, Aycelin and his companion stopped to fulfill a papal commission regarding the troubled affairs of the city of Lyon. Although the city was legally part of the Empire, Philip the Fair had long been attempting to bring it under his own jurisdiction. For this reason he interested himself in the constant disputes between the Archbishop of Lyon and the citizens, claiming that his father had once taken the city under his guardianship. On his side, Boniface VIII had been interested in protecting the city's liberties since he had studied the problem during his legatine mission in France in 1290. It is clear, however that he did not wish to make the case the cause of a quarrel with France.[29] It may well be that he thought that the appointment of a churchman in such high favor with the king would secure him a free hand as arbiter.

Before Aycelin arrived in Lyon the quarrel had grown so intense that the king had helped the citizens by taking captured church goods into royal custody. The archbishop had retaliated by placing the city under interdict and excommunicating several of the citizens. Boniface VIII gave Aycelin full power to act in imposing at least a temporary settlement by releasing the goods held by the king, lifting the interdict, and citing anyone—including the archbishop if necessary—to appear at Rome for a final arbitration. To avoid potential difficulties in securing the goods, Boniface provided Aycelin with a curious legal solution. A second bull appointed Philip the Fair, with the Bishop of Auxerre and the Duke of Burgundy, as official guardian of the goods of the

---

29. *Ibid.*, 2370. Among his letters of direction to Aycelin, giving him power to act in Lyon, he directed him: ". . . taliter providere curetis sicque studeatis sollicite regere terram sub vestro dominio constitutam, ut per eam et ipsius incolas prefatis regi et regno nullum dampnum nullaque injuria possest favente Domino irrogari, neque in ea inimici vel emuli dicti regis receptationem vel refugium aliquod invenire."

church of Lyon until the difficulties of the prelate could be resolved.[30]

Aycelin's negotiations with the archbishop and citizens of Lyons were reinforced by Flote, who accompanied him with a group of armed men detached from the service of the seneschal of Macon.[31] Neither party to the quarrel was willing to accept more than the temporary truce thus achieved. During the following year, French officials continued to hold the disputed property in custody. When Aycelin was again at Rome, in July 1298, he must have conferred with the pope on the question, for Boniface wrote to Auxerre and Burgundy complaining that they had not taken effective steps to safeguard the property placed in their hands.[32] Aycelin was given a letter to the king requesting him to release the property, at least until Christmas, by which time the pope hoped to reach a final settlement.[33]

The Archbishop of Lyon did not wait for further action from the pope. Before any other settlement could be reached he gave homage to Philip the Fair in 1298. The presence of Aycelin and Flote as witnesses to this act suggests that it occurred on their return from their second trip to Rome.[34] This outcome of his arbitration suggests that, at the very least, Aycelin was not so energetic as the pope hoped he would be in assuring the Archbishop of Lyon of papal support and in persuading the king to allow Boniface to proceed unimpeded to a settlement. Moreover, Flote's disbursement of royal monies to citizens of Lyon at this time was likely to be related to this affair.[35] The pope did not give in lightly. In July 1300 he wrote again to Aycelin, instructing him to see that the Archbishop of Lyon and representatives of the citizens appeared in Rome at the earliest possible moment.[36] Even then, though angry at their failure to answer his earlier summons, the pope displayed no suspicion that his chosen arbiter was failing in his duty.

30. *Ibid.*, 2374, 28 August 1297.
31. Guigue, *Cartulaire*, 168.
32. *Reg. Bon. VIII*, 2717.
33. *Ibid.*, 2718.
34. Menestrier, *Histoire civile ou consiliaire de la ville de Lyon, preuves*, 99–100.
35. Viard, *Journaux du trésor*, no. 1442.
36. Guigue, *Cartulaire*, 427.

The question remained unsettled until 1306, when Philip took advantage of his presence at the coronation of Clement V in Lyon to assert his lordship over the imperial enclave.[37] Since Aycelin was at that time conferring with the pope-elect on various topics of interest to the king, it is not improbable that he arranged this final outcome of the fate of Lyon.

Aycelin and Flote had at last returned to Paris to attend the royal council meeting on 17 December 1297. They had succeeded in keeping the pope inactive while the French took control of Flanders,[38] and Philip had been released from all meaningful restraint on his ability to negotiate freely with the clergy for grants of money. Moreover, papal concessions had greatly strengthened royal control over the Gallican Church and assisted its extension in Lyon and Viviers.[39]

For years to come the pope would be too preoccupied with the Colonna rebellion to pursue a strong policy elsewhere in Europe. On the eve of the war in 1297, he had certainly been rendered too vulnerable to interfere with French plans. Philip the Fair may not have been fully privy to the various plots that had been hatched against Boniface VIII; he may not have controlled their timing and development; but Aycelin and Flote had maneuvered brilliantly on his behalf, to ensure that the only benefits of the whole affair accrued to France.

---

37. Bonnassieux, *De la réunion de Lyon à la France*, 83ff.

38. That summer the French swept across nearly three-quarters of the county, capping their success by trapping both the count and Edward I in their siege of Gand. For details, see *Chronique artésienne*, 13, and Funck-Brentano, "Courtrai," 246.

39. The accomplishments of the embassy were reported to the French clergy by the king in a meeting of 17 December 1297, recorded by Guillaume de Nangis, *Chronique latine*, 580.

VII

The Peace of Montreuil

The campaign in Flanders had progressed very satisfactorily for the French while Aycelin and Flote had been in Rome. After their return, the pair were sent to Flanders in January 1298 to undertake further negotiations with the English and Flemings. The primary aim of the diplomats at this point was to remove the English from the struggle, leaving the Count of Flanders isolated to be treated as a recreant vassal. It was not, however, desirable to accomplish this end at the price of any tangible concessions regarding Aquitaine, where the status quo was very favorable to the French.[1]

In pursuit of these aims, the French avoided the establishment of a permanent peace. Instead, they dealt with Edward alone, excluding the Flemings, to secure a truce. The Truce of Tournai was signed on 28 January and ratified three days later by Philip the Fair. Fighting between the French and English, without reference to the Flemings, was suspended for a year. Edward promised to make no future alliances against the King of France and guaranteed that the Count of Flanders—whom he had formerly promised to include in all his negotiations—would honor the truce even though he had not been asked to sign it.[2]

The French had bound themselves to nothing, either in Flanders or in Aquitaine, and had secured an end to the fighting at a moment when they occupied a position of maximum strength in both areas. Their only concession was a tentative agreement that representatives from both sides would meet later in the year at

1. The credentials of the representatives on both sides are printed in Rymer, *Foedera*, II, 804. The Archbishop of Narbonne headed the French mission with the bishops of Amiens and Auxerre, the dukes of Burgundy and Brittany, the Count of St. Pol, the Constable of France, and Pierre Flote, who is listed as Lord of Revel.
2. *Ibid.*, 804.

Rome, where they would ask the assistance of the pope in forging a permanent peace. After the rapproachment of 1297, the French had little reason to fear Boniface VIII. Nevertheless, they were anxious to prevent a revival of his claims to arbitrate the quarrels of independent sovereigns. Before going on to Rome, Aycelin and Flote spent some time with the king in Paris, where a policy regarding papal arbitration was worked out conforming to Philip's earlier rejection of papal authority over temporals.

The papal legates present at Tournai had been excluded from the truce negotiations. Their signatures, even as witnesses, had not been appended to the final agreement.[3] Following the new arrangement, Philip agreed to send his representatives to Rome on the condition that the pope would agree to undertake the arbitration as Benedict Gaetani, a private person, and not by reason of his papal office.[4]

A month or so before the arrival of the French mission in Rome, an envoy from Flanders arrived at the Curia to appeal to the pope to take over the arbitration of the quarrel between the count and the king. He based his request on the ground that Philip's mistreatment of his vassal constituted a matter of conscience. His initial reaction had been optimistic and he wrote the count that he had received assurances of good will from the pope and many of the cardinals.[5] With the English alliance perceptibly weakening, the Flemings were rightly convinced that their last hope of salvation lay at Rome. Count Guy, however, was not sanguine about the probable result of the effort. He was all too keenly aware of the power of French influence in Rome—so much so that he unjustly accused Boniface of actually favoring the war:

3. The presence of the legates is attested by Nicholas Trivet, *Annales*, 369. Noting the absence of their signatures, Digard, *Philippe le Bel*, I, 352, suggested that Flote had excluded them to deprive the pope of any juridical claim to the arbitration.

4. Rymer, *Foedera*, II, 812. Philip wrote to the pope on 4 March announcing the truce and his plan to send Aycelin, Flote, and others to Rome. On 7 March he persuaded the papal legates to act for him in his efforts to include John of Balliol, his Scottish ally in the truce: Dumont, *Corps universal diplomatique*, I, 305. Digard, *Philippe le Bel*, 352, n.8, suggested that the designation of "Benedict Gaetani" was intended to encourage the Colonnas and to remind the pope that the charge of usurpation still hung over him and had not been forgotten by the French.

5. Kervyn de Lettenhove, "Etudes," 412.

All the tribulations which we suffer today come from the court of Rome. In truth, the pope, who should hold the place of God on earth and preserve the peace, is not what he should be; he encourages perpetual war which will never end. We believe that neither we nor our predecessors nor the house of Flanders have deserved this treatment on the part of the pontifical court. Whenever you have a favorable opportunity, we wish you to explain our complaints to the cardinals. For you should know, that if the pope fails us we can no longer resist.[6]

Aycelin and Flote arrived in Rome some time prior to 11 June, well supplied with funds to aid them in persuading the Curia of the justice of their cause.[7] Aycelin lost no time in attacking the legal basis of the Flemish appeal. The count's representatives had asked for papal support on the grounds that Philip had provoked the count's defiance by denying him his rightful privilege of presenting his case to a court of peers after he had been unjustifiably deprived of the rights which his father had always enjoyed. On 11 June the Flemings were invited to an audience with the pope at which the French emissaries were present. Boniface angrily informed them that the Archbishop of Narbonne had given him a copy of Philip's letter in answer to the count's defiance of 1297. There it was clearly stated that the count had incurred his condemnation by refusing to appear when summoned to a court of his peers. Philip was acting on the principle that the Parlement of Paris, which had condemned the count, was, by reason of the presence of some of the great nobles among its members, a properly constituted court of peers. Convinced that the Flemings had been deceiving him, the pope furiously informed them that their only hope was to submit their affairs unconditionally to his judgment.[8]

In despair, the Flemings answered that they could make no answer to the pope's demand until they had consulted their English allies. But someone, probably Pierre Flote, had already visited

6. Kervyn de Lettenhove, *Histoire de Flandres*, II, 414.
7. *Comptes royaux*, n.3161–68, records a partial account of the allotments from the royal treasury to members of this embassy.
8. The full account of this meeting and those that followed appears in the reports of the count's son, Robert of Bethune, in Kervyn de Lettenhove, "Etudes," 41–44.

those unsteady allies. The head of the English mission, Amadeus
of Savoy (who had known Flote in their years in Dauphiné), met
Robert of Bethune with cold comfort. He told the Flemings that,
as the English viewed the developing situation, they could see no
course of action open to Flanders that was free of deadly danger.
So true was this that the Count of Savoy said he feared to advise
them at all. He confined himself to restating their position with
terrible clarity:

> The King of France is powerful and he hates you. He holds much
> of your country. You cannot be sure of the assistance of your
> neighbors. The King of England is occupied in Scotland, Gascony,
> and England itself and will not always be able to help you. If
> you don't do the pope's will, you will lose his favor and he could
> do you much mischief.[9]

Thus brutally informed that they could no longer depend on
their ally, the Flemings decided to submit to the pope—although
they probably had few hopes in such a course. Bethune thought
he might achieve something by appealing to Boniface's vanity,
and on 12 June informed him that Flanders would trust utterly in
the pope, who stood in the place of God on earth, and was "Sou-
verains dou roy de France en espirituel et en temporel." This, of
course, was a direct contradiction of Philip's frequently stated
contention that the pope had no authority in temporals. Boniface
knew it as well as anyone, and, far from being pleased at this expression of his unreserved power, he showed himself alarmed and
angry. He informed Bethune that he had been ill advised to speak
so, and that the pope would hear no statements designed to alienate him from the King of France.

Bethune gave up. He put his father's interests wholly into the
pope's hands with the wistful proviso, "saving the English alliance
and my father's honor." In his report he admitted that he expected
little help from Boniface, but felt that the Count of Savoy had
been right in warning him that it would be too dangerous to
alienate the pope entirely. Having been given a free hand, Boniface proceeded on 26 June to suspend all judgment on the appeals
of the count of Flanders, though he appended a reservation that

9. *Ibid.*, 43.

the bull was not to be considered prejudicial to the count's status.[10] On 30 June[11] he nullified all conventions between the King of England and the Count of Flanders. Specifically, the bethrothal between Philippa of Flanders and the Prince of Wales was dissolved.

Flanders was left alone with only a few insubstantial promises from a preoccupied pope to sustain it. French armies occupied much of the country and the French diplomats had set them free to act without impediment. This was the goal Aycelin and Flote had been pursuing. The ostensible purpose of their mission, a settlement with England over Aquitaine, no longer depended on the threat of an attack on France in the north.

More than one writer has imagined that Philip entertained hopes of driving Edward completely off the Continent, emulating the successes of Philip II in Normandy. Realistically, he probably reposed little hope in so definite an outcome of his designs on the duchy. The most that could have been achieved by a settlement arranged in the circumstances prevailing in 1298 would have been a confirmation of his position as Edward's overlord and a justification of his confiscatory actions. Possibly, he could have demanded some territorial concessions as surety. In exchange, however, the French would certainly have been obliged to withdraw their armies from occupation of the Gascon strongholds they had held since 1294. Under these conditions, it was preferable to avoid both a new war and a final settlement—in short, to preserve the status quo which left the French in effective control of the duchy. Accordingly, Aycelin and Flote negotiated a tentative agreement with the English on 29–30 June, which presented the appearance of a settlement while changing nothing concrete. As evidence of the good will of both parties, the future Edward II, now freed from his engagement to Philippa of Flanders, was betrothed to Isabella of France.[12] A territorial settlement was reserved pending further discussions between the kings. Meanwhile, the disputed lands were to be placed under the guardianship of the Bishop of

10. *Reg. Bon. VIII*, 2854.
11. *Ibid.*, 2809.
12. *Ibid.*, 2826.

Toulouse—in whose name the French officials would continue to occupy them.[13]

Some further light can be thrown on the course of these negotiations by the report of an English ambassador in 1300. In an interview during that year, Boniface VIII described his earlier attempt to create a settlement in Aquitaine. The pope's account suggests that Pierre Flote played his accustomed role as a gadfly during their discussions. It is thus possible to imagine that he softened the pope sufficiently to make him amenable to an apparently well-meaning suggestion by the tactful Aycelin that he settle for an agreement which saved appearances, even though it changed nothing in reality.

When in 1300 the English renewed their complaints that the French were still holding their position in Gascony, the pope advised them to seek their aim indirectly by trying to persuade Philip to put the duchy in the pope's hands, since he did not believe the French king would ever willingly restore it to the English. He reflected that in 1298 he had warned the French to let the Gascons go because they were a restless people who would never willingly submit to a single lord, preferring to have two to play off against one another. But he felt that he had failed because of the French king's greed: "What he takes once, he never lets go. They who have dealings with the French must take care, for an affair with the French is an affair with the devil."[14]

In fact, the pope continued, he had protested at that time to Pierre Flote against the insatiability of the French demands, saying that it was enough that they had taken Normandy from the English king. He demanded to know if it was their further intention to take all his overseas possessions. Smiling, Flote suggested that indeed the pope had hit upon the truth. Boniface remonstrated with him in vain, pointing out that such a course would not be to the king's profit or to his honor but would only bring perpetual war with the King of England. With pride and mockery, Flote responded: "Hoo, le Rois de Fraunce, ne lerra pur rien son honur."

13. *Ibid.*, 2627.
14. The text of the report describing this interview is in Black, "Edward I and Gascony in 1300," 518–27.

It is clear, then, that Boniface VIII was ruthlessly balked in his efforts to obtain some clear concessions from the French. Aycelin may have stepped in at this juncture soothing him with a suggestion for a spurious compromise. Boniface's pride could be salvaged by an interim agreement that would place the disputed lands ostensibly in the hands of the Church. Thus, further quarreling was averted at the time. But the incident stuck in the pope's mind and still galled him two years later when he told the story. No doubt the memory contributed much to his conviction that Flote—bold, one-eyed, eternally mocking—was behind the puzzling shifts in his relationship with Philip the Fair. It is equally clear that the onus for the mission's failure was never laid on Aycelin. His name is never mentioned in any of Boniface's invectives against the evil councillors of the King of France, and, until the final breach in 1303, the pope gave every sign of continuing to trust the archbishop.

Despite the apparent failure of negotiations over Aquitaine, the French mission of 1298 was a brilliant success. Aycelin and his partner had achieved everything they could have hoped for. They returned with copies of papal bulls confirming the isolation of Flanders and the meaningless agreement with the English. In addition, Flote placed another mysterious document in the royal archives. He later claimed that Boniface had entrusted a special letter to him in which he promised to make no final pronouncement in the future regarding Aquitaine without first securing the approval of Philip the Fair. The bull does not appear in the papal registers, and was found by Dupuy in the French archives only in a highly suspicious form.[15] Since Flote never made any use of the letter, his ultimate design is unknown. He might have believed that a final settlement could be delayed until Boniface was replaced by a new pope who might accept the promise as an authentic commitment.

Negotiations between Edward and Philip continued after both groups of ambassadors had reported to their respective

---

15. *Histoire du différend,* 41. The document was listed as a copy of the original letter. The notary who wrote it stated that its authenticity was confirmed by Pierre de Belleperche, Bishop of Auxerre, and Pierre Flote, who saw the original. He does not offer any explanation as to the fate of the original bull.

masters and received additional instructions. The French, secure in their advantageous position, approached the problem in a dilatory manner, persistently introducing additional complications into the course of the negotiations. On 15 January 1299 Aycelin and Flote, together with other luminaries of the French court, participated in a meeting with the English representatives at the Louvre. The English knights requested an exchange of prisoners during the truce. In addition, they were charged with presenting Edward's complaints against the French failures to observe the terms of the truce. Speaking in the king's name, Flote disposed of the English objections with a flat denial that his master would ever countenance fraud or truce-breaking, but would take the precaution of making an investigation of Edward's complaints.[16]

After this conciliating answer to their complaints, Flote had a surprise for them. No further negotiations would be undertaken and no exchange of prisoners arranged without the inclusion of the King of Scotland and other Scots held captive by the King of England. For, he stated firmly, they are the allies of the King of France. Once in possession of their persons, Philip would be willing to ask the pope's advice about their future disposition. In fact, he would even be willing to have them placed in the hands of certain French prelates who would hold them in the pope's name until a decision could be reached. If the pope ruled that they should be restored to England, they would be sent back in the end, but they must have their freedom immediately.[17]

Edward needed a settlement in Aquitaine. Philip would be happy to continue to occupy the land indefinitely—in fact he did occupy it until 1304 despite all the agreements he made for its ultimate restoration. Edward had been forced to abandon his

16. Dumont, *Corps universel*, 305, and Bréquigny, *Tables chronologiques*, VII, 470, date this meeting in 1298. However, that date conflicts with the presence of Flote and Aycelin at Tournai. I am therefore following the date used by Limburg-Stirum, *Codex Diplomaticus*, 269–71, in his edition of the report of the apostolic notary describing the meeting. Flote's speech is given on p. 270.

17. *Ibid.*, 271. Flote concluded this ultimatum by piously proclaiming: "Hec vobis offero pro conservatione honoris mei, et alius non possum facere sine nota parjurii et infidelitatis, cum istud debeamus facere equaliter et fideliter; unde se redderem vobis captos de parte regis Anglie et vos non liberatis captos de parte regis Francie, scio equaliter nec fideliter ageremus."

allies in Flanders despite his solemn promise never to do so. Now Philip confronted him with his own loyalty to the Scots, whose inclusion in a final settlement had never previously been mentioned, and his audacious spokesman boasted that the King of France kept *all* his agreements with friends and enemies alike. Edward balked, but in the end he had to give way. John of Balliol was released.

The Flemish ambassador in Rome, still attempting to save something for his master, wrote bitterly:

> Sire, certain news has come to the pope that the kings of France and England have made peace together and that all things are agreed according to what the pope pronounced at Rome. As to you and the peace that you desire, no word has been breathed. The King of Scotland and his sons, thanks to the King of France, have been remitted into the pope's hands. And it seems to us, to our small sense, as well as to others, that the king of France has better helped the King of Scotland, of whom no word was ever spoken in the war or in the treaties, than the King of England has helped you, you who have been in the war and in the truce and through whom the King of England has been enabled to gain peace.[18]

And so it was. Philippa of Flanders was left forgotten in prison and her father stood alone at the mercy of the French. For the sake of the long-sought peace, Boniface, too, abandoned the Flemings, though he promised them publicly that he would seek other means of helping them despite their exclusion from the ultimate peace.[19] The French had exacted a gratuitous concession from the English and still returned nothing in Aquitaine.

At last, when all these concessions had been secured, Aycelin and Flote were dispatched to meet once more with the English. On 19 June 1299 they met in the presence of the papal nuncio, the Bishop of Vincenzo, who formally repeated the pope's agreement to act as a private person because of his great desire to see peace among Christians.[20] By 14 July the two parties had concluded the Peace of Montreuil, establishing a general peace in

18. Funck-Brentano, *Phillippe le Bel*, 302.
19. *Ibid.*, 302.
20. Rymer. *Foedera*, II, 840.

Flanders and a tentative agreement on the future disposition of
the disputed lands in Aquitaine—they were to go as a dowry to
Philip's sister, Marguerite, who was to marry the widowed Edward
I. Eventually, they were to revert as an independent duchy to the
eldest son of this marriage. Their betrothal, with that of the
Prince of Wales and Isabella of France, was announced to seal the
agreement.[21] Once again the French mission had been headed by
the Archbishop of Narbonne, who signed the final treaty. Pierre
Flote was included among the emissaries and apparently occupied
some special position in the formalities. His name does not appear
among the signatories, but in the appended document of ratification Philip solemnly swore to keep the promises made by Flote in
his name.[22]

The formal signatures were placed on the treaty on 3 August,
but Aycelin did not leave the meeting without a parting shot. On
the same day the truce was signed he went to the papal nuncio
and persuaded him to publish a testimonial letter stating that the
Archbishop of Narbonne had presented a formal protest in the
name of the King of France that, if the King of England should
attribute to himself the title of Duke of Aquitaine, or if others
should attribute it to him, it could not be considered detrimental
to the claims of the King of France.[23]

In those years, not only skill but luck served Philip the Fair at
every turn. The final member of Edward I's anti-French coalition,
Adolph of Nassau, King of the Romans, was deposed on 23 June
1298 by the German princes and died shortly thereafter. The
newly elected King of the Romans, who had not yet received any
response from Boniface VIII to his request for papal recognition,
was Albert of Hapsburg, long a friend of the French. As early as
1295 he had sought the hand of a French princess for his son
Rudolph.[24] The request was renewed immediately upon his election in 1298.

Philip promised the new emperor-elect an early meeting to

21. *Ibid.*, 847–52.
22. *Ibid.*, 852.
23. Dumont, *Corps universel diplomatique*, I, 319.
24. Boutaric, *La France sous Philippe le Bel*, 398.

discuss this question. No ambassadors were sent, however, until the spring of 1299. On 10 April Aycelin and Flote met the imperial representatives at Neufchâtel in Lorraine to begin a series of discussions which proceeded slowly through July. During this period they were constantly shuttling back and forth from Lorraine to Montreuil to resume talks with the English. They undoubtedly were able to extract the best advantage from both projects by using progress on one front to put pressure on the other.[25]

The negotiations were brought to a happy conclusion on 21 July and confirmed by the principals in August at about the same time as the ratification of the Peace of Montreuil. A board of arbiters was to be set up to settle all outstanding differences concerning the frontiers between France and the Empire with the exception of those involving Burgundy—to whose protection Philip the Fair was deeply committed. Princess Blanche was to have the counties of Alsace and Fribourg for her dowry. Finally, the two sovereigns agreed to meet on 8 December at Vaucouleurs to issue a statement of mutual friendship. At this meeting, a final treaty of alliance was issued whose exact terms have been a matter of disagreement among historians for centuries.[26] The marriage itself was solemnized at Paris in February.

The great international problems which had troubled France during the early years of Philip the Fair's reign seemed to have been triumphantly brought to an end by 1299. Indeed, with the single exception of the continuing struggle in Flanders, the king's satisfaction would have been more than justified. And no one had worked harder or with better effect to this end than the Archbishop of Narbonne. He had by this time established himself

25. This is the view of Leroux, *Recherches critiques sur les relations politiques de la France avec l'Allemagne, 1292–1378,* who published the documents for these negotiations, p. 99ff. He opposes earlier commentators who thought the discussions at Neufchâtel were aimed at an antipapal coalition on the grounds that the French were at the moment friendly with Boniface VIII and the pope had not yet refused to recognize Albert's election.

26. On the basis of references to the treaty in an anonymous memoir of 1300 edited by de Wailly, *Mémoires de l'Academie des Inscriptions et Belles-Lettres,* XVIII, 435–94, Leroux, (p. 107) believes that Albert may have offered France the lands between the Meuse and the Rhine. There is no further reference to such an agreement except in the claims of sixteenth- and seventeenth-century jurists.

securely among the most influential members of the royal council—a position he would continue to occupy for the rest of his life.

After the conclusion of the treaties of 1299, the principal ob-
jects of French policy were to retain the gains they had made,
complete the subjection of Flanders, and restrain the pope from
interfering with the status quo. By 1300 Boniface VIII had brought
the war with the Colonnas to a successful conclusion. In addition,
he had set in train a series of administrative reforms in the Church
and published his own additions to canon law. In 1300, displaying
his renewed confidence, he presided over the great Jubilee in
Rome. But his cherished project for the renewal of the crusades
seemed further away than ever. His years of compromise with the
French had brought him no nearer to that goal. By 1300 he was
apparently ready to attempt a somewhat more aggressive policy
by opening tentative conversations with the discontented enemies
of Philip the Fair.

He expressed his resentment of the Treaty of Vaucouleurs in
an interview with the Flemish ambassadors in January of 1300,
confiding to them that he believed the King of France to be the
victim of bad counsel.[27] Accordingly, he refused to ratify the treaty
and charged Albert of Hapsburg with the responsibility for the
murder of Adolph of Nassau. He refused to recognize the deposition of Adolph or the election of Albert. A few months later, in an
interview with the English ambassadors, who were seeking a
firmer foothold in Aquitaine than that provided at Montreuil, he
criticized the French in the sharpest terms.[28]

On 6 January 1300 Cardinal Matthew of Aquasparta preached
in the presence of the pope and the other cardinals. His sermon,
followed by the proclamation of the great Jubilee, served notice
to the world of a change in the papal position. As reported by the
Flemish ambassador,

> Matthew of Aquasparta preached that the pope is the only lord
> in temporals and spirituals over all who are, by the gift God
> gave to Saint Peter and the apostles after him, and whoever
> wishes to claim exemption to this cannot without opposing him

27. Kervyn de Lettenhove, "Etudes," 76.
28. Black, "Edward I and Gascony in 1300."

and the church and being condemned as miscreant by the authority of the temporal and spiritual swords and the power of God.

The ambassador believed that there was at last reason for his countrymen to hope that the pope would come to their aid.[29]

Encouraged by the pope's anger, the Flemings again appealed for his assistance, renewing their flattering resolution to depend on him alone as supreme judge of spirituals and temporals. "Cannot the pope depose the emperor, the first of all secular princes?" they asked him. "Has he not also the right then to depose the King of France who recognizes no prince above himself?" This time, they were obliged to record no angry rebuff.[30]

The Count of Flanders was desperately in need of this gleam of hope. Philip the Fair had not been wasting his opportunities to take a strong hold on the county during the truce period. Since his victories of 1297, he had been establishing his own officials in the Flemish towns. Throughout 1298 complaints were constantly presented to the papal nuncio of their infractions of the truce. In alliance with the town patriciate in the wealthy city of Bruges, the Constable of France had begun to erect a series of new fortifications. Taking the part of the commoners, Count Guy complained repeatedly of the constable's oppressions, describing him as a bird of prey feeding on the country, whose every deed was aimed at destroying all authority in Flanders but that of the king.[31]

Strong papal action in favor of Guy de Dampierre at this point could have proved embarrassing and inconvenient for the French, who were preparing to launch a new offensive against the county in the spring when the truce expired. Naturally, it would have meant little in terms of armed forces, but it might have placed new impediments in the way of the king's collection of subsidies and would certainly have created a distasteful situation in view of Philip's constant care to give his aggressions the appearance of

29. Kervyn de Lettenhove, *Histoire de Flandres,* II, 585.
30. *Ibid.,* 421.
31. Funck-Brentano, *Philippe le Bel,* 320ff. gives these complaints in detail. He adds that in fact the constable was so moderate and conciliatory in his government of the town that pro-French chroniclers accuse him of approaching treason in his neglect of the kings' interests.

irreproachable legality. Moreover, the French wanted the pope to recognize the Treaty of Vaucouleurs and to cooperate in the implementation of a plan, broached in December 1298, for a new approach to the Italian situation.[32]

Despite the assistance of James of Aragon, the pope was still unable to gain a definitive victory over Frederick of Sicily and his supporters in northern Italy. By the beginning of 1300 he was again seeking French help, and with it a new disposition for the heiress to the Latin Empire in Byzantium, Catherine de Courtenay. In December 1299 the wife of Charles de Valois had died, and Boniface now proposed that he marry Catherine. In exchange for future assistance in the crusade, the French prince would become the pope's new protector in Sicily and Tuscany.

These projects had been brought to a point where a mission to Rome to undertake preliminary negotiations was required. Apparently not feeling that he had reached a point in the negotiations requiring that such distinguished councillors as Flote and Aycelin disengage themselves from their activities at home, Philip the Fair entrusted the mission to a relative newcomer in his service, Guillaume de Nogaret. He had been for some years a professor of law at Montpellier, where it is very likely he instructed several of the men who had come to sit on the king's council. There are therefore several possible candidates for the dubious honor of having introduced Nogaret to the royal court. The most likely, however, was Aycelin. Though it is not known where he studied, Montpellier was the most convenient school and therefore the most likely. More important, however, Nogaret's first documented appearances in Paris associate him with the Archbishop of Narbonne.[33]

Very little came of Nogaret's mission, and possibly little was intended to come of it but a distraction for the pope. Boniface continued to oppose the election of Albert of Hapsburg and there is no indication that the French were really prepared to insist on

32. Boutaric, *Notices et extraits*, XX, 130.

33. In 1298 he is listed as a witness at the Parlement of Paris in the company of Aycelin and others from Languedoc, *Les Olim*, II, 408. In the following year, he and Aycelin joined to sponsor an appeal of Arnald of Villanova to the pope, Denifle, *Chartularium Universitatis Parisiensis*, II, 86–87.

his approval. They may well have perceived that they had little reason to complain of a situation which left the King of the Romans with no friend but Philip the Fair. The Flemish truce ended while Nogaret was still in Rome, and French armies, led by Charles de Valois, moved to complete their conquest of the county. By 8 May 1300 they were victorious, and Guy de Dampierre was once more in a French prison. Nogaret's presence at the Curia, in the company of the German ambassadors, may have been intended only as a demonstration to the pope that he could not afford to move to the aid of Flanders.

By autumn, with the Flemings helpless, Philip was ready to turn to the question of Charles de Valois' expedition to Italy. In addition, there were several other affairs that required negotiation with the pope. To complete these discussions, Aycelin and Flote traveled once more to Rome. The date of the mission can be established as early November 1300 by a letter from Aycelin to his suffragans on the Sunday after All Saints, excusing himself from attending the consecration of the new Bishop of Carcassonne.[34]

The pair had reached Genoa by 1 December. While there, they made an unsuccessful effort to prevent the citizens from supplying arms to the Sicilian insurgents. They had also been given power to settle the discords between the commune and the pope. Although he did not know the result of these efforts, the King of Aragon's informant warned his master that they could put his brother Frederick in grave danger.[35] For his part, Pope Boniface awaited the French in a cooperative mood. With Florence in re-

---

34. Baluze, *Miscellanea*, III, 105: ". . . tam pro Domini Regis Franciae illustris et regni quam ecclesiae nostrae negotiis habeamus ad Romanam curiam in praesenti necessario profisci." Digard, *Philippe le Bel*, II, 45, computes their presence in Rome for January–March 1301 on the basis of expense payments for 179 days recorded in the *Journal du trésor*.

35. *Acta Aragonensia*, I, 88–90: "Unde nos de novo intelleximus per plura paria literarum, quod dominus rex Francie mitit magnam ambasatam comuni nostro et domino papa et intendimus, quod vult concordare discordia, que sunt inter nostrum comune et domino papa et rege Karullo. Nomina de ambasatoribus sunt ista: Comes de Sampolo, Archiepiscopus Nerbone, Dominus Petrus Floto. Super predicta nesimus, que finem capiant. Quare vos suplicamus, quod super predita provideat vestra magestas, quia si comune nostro perveniret ad finem de dito discordio, facta domini regis F. fratris excellencie vestre essent in maxima aventura."

volt, he was in no position to reject any of their demands. Rather, he must do everything in his power to bring the negotiations concerning Charles de Valois to a swift conclusion. Even the French failure to pay certain sums of money promised by Flote at this time did not discourage Boniface from placing his hopes in Valois for the following summer. The French representatives assured the pope that the prince would shortly be dispatched.[36] On every other subject opened for discussion, however, they showed themselves to be as intractable as ever.

The pope was still seeking a concrete settlement of the disposition of the strongholds in Aquitaine, pending the marriages arranged at Montreuil. The French remained unwilling to move. The new discussions with the English in the pope's presence at this time resulted in nothing but an extension of the existing truce. That Boniface was growing restive and increasingly suspicious of French intentions is clear from his letter on the subject to Edward of England, 26 February 1302.[37] But on the surface, the French star seemed to be completely in the ascendant in Rome. On 14 September 1301 the Aragonese ambassador described the pope's welcome of the long-awaited Charles de Valois, ending: "And now the will of Philip the Fair is his command."[38] The ambassador was misled. Boniface needed Valois and the army he was bringing into Italy, and had sacrificed every other aim of his policy to get him there. But he had not forgotten his humiliations. As he confided to the English ambassadors, the course of the negotiations of 1301 were marked by angry outbursts. Later on the French would charge that he was a heretic because he did not believe in

36. Petit, *Charles de Valois*, 373, quotes a letter from the pope shortly after the departure of the French mission describing its accomplishments and begging the king to make the deposits with the Spini as Flote had promised.

37. Rymer, *Foedera*, II, 876–78: "Ne ille malignus Angelus Satanas, humani generis hostis antiquus . . . adeo in hac parte tibe et praefato Regi Franciae cupiditatis aestum adhibeat, adeo virus infundat invidiae, quod irremediabilia nocumenta producat, Ecce! adhuc te ad ea quae tuae saluti expediunt, honori et utilitatibus tuis et ipsius Regni conveniunt, salubribus exhortationibus invitamus. . . . Intuerberis insuper quod, circa recuperandam hujusmodi particulam dicti Regni, de qua contenditur, et ob quam videtur scintilla ignis obnoxii remansisse, non absque aviditate deduceris, et avaritiae vitio retorqueris, cum inter te ac praefatum Regem Franciae tot et tales sint, ut nostri, parentelae contractae, quod licet ispe fervore juventutis impulsus, pravis seductus consiliis et adulatorum malitia instigatus, se nimis in hac parte tenacem exhibeat atque duram."

38. *Acta Aragonensia*, I, 71.

the immortality of the soul. Their testimony was based on his outburst during this period that he would rather be a dog or an ass than a Frenchman, so beyond bearing was the pride of the French. Scarcely held in check, the pope's anger grew until it broke loose in a flood of bulls at the end of 1301.

The focal point of his attack at that time was a series of events in Aycelin's archdiocese of Narbonne.

VIII

The Liberties of Narbonne

During his frequent absences on the king's business, Aycelin had never entirely neglected the work of his diocese. He was a loyal servant of Philip the Fair without giving up any claims to independent privileges as a prelate. As long as he was able to deal with the king alone, there was never any indication that his two roles did not harmonize with one another. The entire question of the relationship of the Gallican clergy with the king has been distorted by the great quarrels with Boniface VIII and the subsequent subjection of Clement V to French demands. The traditional portrait of Philip, derived from this context, as an anticlerical king has as little validity as the picture of his prelates as servile cowards, unable to rise to the standards of a Becket or a Winchelsey:

> Par les prelatz qui veulent plaire
> Au roy, et tout son plaisir faire,
> Deschiet aujourd'hui sainte église . . .[1]

The Gallican clergy were not an isolated group of men whose interests and policies can realistically be treated as hostile to the secular world represented by the lawyers who served the royal government. On the contrary, many of them were those lawyers. The Archbishop of Narbonne is typical of the higher clergy in that he occupied seats in both supposedly antithetical camps. The dependence of the French prelates on the king's favor in securing advancement has been studied in some detail,[2] but, in treating the prelates by titles, the duality of their occupations was not made apparent. As members of the royal council, men like Aycelin were active in the formulation of the policies that were later applied in their dioceses.

1. Quoted by Langlois, *Saint-Louis*, 240, from the *Roman de Fauvel*.
2. Baumhauer, *Philipp der Schöne und Bonifaz VIII.*

Philip did not pursue a policy of reducing his clergy to subservience or depriving their churches of their liberties. The problem which always presented itself in the daily routine of his government was the need to clarify the boundaries between the temporal and spiritual spheres. The king naturally wished to maintain his own rights and expand them where feasible. Likewise, he aimed at defining the rights allotted to the clergy by law and custom and establishing their limits. The clergy for their part could cooperate with a clear conscience in this effort. Real difficulty only arose at that point where their relationship to the pope was involved. Philip could not make himself the chief lord of the clergy or even the principal defender of their liberties without a conflict with the Chief Priest of Christendom. Before that point was reached, however, there was a great deal of work to be done on a local level. There the competence of a prelate like Aycelin was allowed free play, to the advantage of both king and Church.

Aycelin rarely exhibited any sense of tension resulting from the fact that he operated in both the temporal and spiritual spheres. He brought to the administration of his diocese the skills of a lawyer, a businessman, and an administrator. In a period when many churches were complaining of financial ruin, he managed his finances so well that he was able to begin the construction of a new cathedral. He turned his frequent absences—especially his missions to Rome—to advantage by securing privileges for his church from the popes with whom he was negotiating and from the king as reward for his services. His legislation in the diocese, his applications of papal bulls and royal charters, did much to clarify and strengthen the position of his church.

It must not be forgotten that during five of the seven years of the pontificate of Boniface VIII the King of France was on reasonably good terms with Rome. During these periods Aycelin was able to claim papal support for his ecclesiastical programs, and the pope could count on the cooperation of the archbishop in applying the broad policies of his government to local conditions.

Through the bulls he had acquired from Nicholas IV, Aycelin had achieved control over the clerical personnel in his diocese at the beginning of his tenure. The main expression of his authority was control of the ecclesiastical court system, where he was con-

cerned with the practical application of the separation of Church
and State. Conflicts between the agents of the secular and spiritual
courts were frequent to the point of monotony everywhere in
France. Both Philip the Fair and Boniface VIII were anxious to
establish a legal system which would end these repeated struggles.

Before his election to the papacy, Benedict Gaetani had studied
this question during his legatine mission to France in 1290. He
had then directed a vast inquest into the complaints of the clergy
and the king. Many of his recommendations had been taken up by
Philip the Fair and made into laws in France.[3] Baillis were forbidden to interfere with the goods or jurisdiction of prelates without a special mandate from the king. They could constrain clerks
who worked as merchants or artisans to pay customary taxes, but
they must respect the fiscal immunities of clerks living clerically.
Royal jurisdiction was to control cases involving wills, questions
of real estate, dowries, inheritance and feudal rights, but clergymen would be allowed to act as procurators in the royal courts.

All of these questions would be brought up repeatedly throughout the reign, but these early pronouncements represented a basic
program to be applied by royal officials. Prelates like Aycelin, who
worked simultaneously on the royal council and in the ecclesiastical
hierarchy, had the primary responsibility for working out the
details of the relationship between the two systems of justice.

Philip the Fair's policy was to establish a clear-cut hierarchy
of courts in France, with the royal court as the highest appellate
tribunal. By clarifying his relations with secular lords and acting
aggressively against them when need arose, he was fairly successful in the temporal sphere, as we have seen from his adventures
with his vassals in England and Flanders. The system of ecclesiastical courts, however, provided a separate complication. The
king demonstrated no ambition to destroy their competence or
deprive the clergy of their immunities—except insofar as he preferred to substitute his own court for that of Rome as the court of
last appeal. On the lower levels, his object was to establish a clear
line between the lay and ecclesiastical worlds, defining the exact
qualifications for membership in the ecclesiastical class and limit-

3. *Ordonnances,* I, 318.

ing the extent of the church's jurisdiction to that which was established by custom. This policy conformed with the legislation of Boniface VIII, and was put into practice by Aycelin and other prelates at the local level.

No deliberate challenge was made to ecclesiastical jurisdiction in France until the middle of the fourteenth century.[4] The ordinances of Philip the Fair were designed only to clarify the relationships of ecclesiastical and lay courts and define the limits of each. His judicial practices did, however, continue a long-standing effort to make the royal court supreme arbiter in conflicts between the two, an effort which foreshadows—though unintentionally— the eventual submission of the entire court system to the king.

One of the most difficult problems that beset ecclesiastical and secular courts at the end of the thirteenth century was that of defining the "clerk." In principle, the ecclesiastical courts had sole jurisdiction in cases involving clerks and the Archbishop of Narbonne, according to a privilege granted by Boniface VIII in 1297, had the power to excommunicate anyone guilty of violence against the clerks in his diocese, including agents of the secular courts.[5] All men who had taken orders above the rank of subdeacon were indisputably protected by this power so long as they conformed to the rules of celibacy and practiced the clerical profession. Below this rank, however, there were large numbers of men who at one time or another had received minor orders. These men were not included under the rule of celibacy. Moreover, since Alexander III had deprived married clerks of their ecclesiastical functions, they could and indeed had to, practice secular professions to earn their living.[6] Throughout the thirteenth century the debate raged between the secular and ecclesiastical authorities on whether or not such men were eligible to receive benefit of clergy. The problem was somewhat relieved by Gregory IX, who instructed his legates to subject married clerks in secular professions to the fiscal responsibilities of laymen toward the State and to confirm the jurisdiction of lay courts over them in cases involving taxation.[7]

4. Lot and Fawtier, *Histoire des institutions*, II, 452ff.
5. *Reg. Bon. VIII*, 2010.
6. For the detailed history of this problem see Génestal, *Privilegium Fori*, 81ff., and Gaudemet in Lot and Fawtier, *Histoire des institutions*, III, 267.
7. Génestal, *Privilegium Fori*, 92.

The entire problem of their answerability to other types of cases remained open. In France, the question became acute after the reversion of Languedoc to the crown in 1271.

In Narbonne, as elsewhere in Languedoc, Aycelin found a situation in which the courts were constantly agitated by the extraordinary extension of clerical privileges. The rights of the suffragan church of Toulouse were so extensive that Baudouin[8] has ventured to state that if the county had not reverted to the crown when it did, it would probably have become at length a confederation of small theocratic states. Quasi-impunity for crime, and even exemptions from taxes, were extended to large numbers of men in all the dioceses under Aycelin's control by the simple device of giving them the tonsure and allowing them to wear ecclesiastical dress, although they lacked any qualification to be clerks. Artisans and tradesmen, who were free to marry and pursue their trades, were recognized as clerks in the eyes of the law. Secular officials complained that in some cases they were given the tonsure by a complacent clergyman *after* the commission of crimes for which they were being brought to trial.

In 1300 Philip the Fair appointed a series of commissions to undertake investigations into the practices of ecclesiastical courts in France. In Normandy, where royal authority was relatively strong, Pierre Dubois complained at length of the various tricks which both laymen and clergymen employed to circumvent adverse judgments in the royal courts.[9] The report from Languedoc revealed an aggressive policy in the ecclesiastical courts that bordered on violence, and transgressed even the papal order to subject certain clerks to normal taxation. Ecclesiastics were accused of habitually compelling laymen to plead in their courts, even in property cases, and of actually forcing royal notaries to make copies and instruments of their acts in such cases and obliging royal officers to execute their sentences. They used the threat of excommunication to force laymen to pay debts to ecclesiastics and to pay legacies made by others, and compelled royal baillis to execute sentences confiscating the goods of such laymen. They declared that anyone remaining excommunicate for

8. Baudouin, *Lettres inédites de Philippe le Bel,* Introduction, ii.
9. De Wailly (ed.), "Summaria Brevis."

a year or more was to be suspected of heresy. They defended married men in secular professions as though they were clerks, even where they refused to contribute to the common tax burden on goods which had always been subject to the *taille,* and they protected common criminals by providing them with the tonsure.[10]

Numerous attempts had previously been made to rectify these conditions. In 1274 Philip III had passed an ordinance prohibiting the extension of clerical immunities to married clerks, merchant clerks, or clerks carrying arms. In addition, he declared that criminal clerks must be tried according to custom and, where the custom was not clear, written law—with its tendency to favor the secular courts—was to be applied.[11] But at the Council of Lyon in the same year, Gregory X confirmed the full privileges of married clerks except in cases where the clerks in question had been degraded by the ecclesiastical court for the commission of a serious crime.[12] Independently, the prelates of Languedoc tried to clarify the confusion by urging the king not to appoint clerks as his officials, and in some cases they forbade clerks to exercise military or artisan professions on penalty of automatic degradation. In cooperation with this effort, the king instructed his agents not to apply corporal punishment to an accused clerk until he had been degraded in the ecclesiastical courts.[13]

Obviously, these were but makeshift solutions. The problem remained and created difficulties in Aycelin's province during the early years of his tenure. Between 1292 and 1297 a stream of royal letters supported actions of the seneschal of Toulouse in his efforts to prevent laymen from obtaining the tonsure on easy terms and thus escaping the penalties of secular law.[14] A final solution was provided only in 1298 with the publication of the *Sext,* Boniface VIII's compilation of additions to canon law. One of the lawyers commissioned by the pope to undertake this work was Aycelin's suffragan bishop, Berengar Frédol, who undoubtedly worked with the problems of his own province clearly in mind.

The *Sext* delineated a compromise that was welcomed in

10. Boutaric, *Notices et extraits,* 132–35.
11. Gaudemet, in *Histoire des institutions,* III, 327.
12. Génestal, *Privilegium Fori,* 93.
13. *Ibid.,* 98.
14. Baudouin, *Lettres inédites, passim.*

France and applied there as law for centuries: by virtue of having married, the clerk was to forfeit his immunities in civil cases, but he would retain it in criminal matters. Since this provided a satisfactory means of dealing with those problems in which he was involved by reason of his secular way of life, there was little opposition among royal lawyers to the continuation of his immunity in criminal questions.[15]

This legislation was expressed in the most general terms, since it was intended for use by the entire Church. As was usual in the thirteenth century, its specific applications were left to the decisions of the bishops, usually taken in consultation with provincial councils.[16] In most parts of France, apparently, little need was felt to take extensive action of this nature following the publication of the *Sext*. Most of the French bishops were content to register the laws of Boniface VIII in their own churches.[17] Aycelin, however, was anxious to use the legislation to solve the problems of his own province. Accordingly, in 1299, he held a council of his suffragans in Béziers to recognize the new laws and regulate their application in Narbonne. Boniface had imposed the wearing of the tonsure and habit of a clerk as the test of a man's clerical status. Aycelin added provisions regulating the conditions for conferring the tonsure and habit: to avoid a situation where a man might obtain them for purposes of defrauding the secular courts, they were to be given only where the candidate's clercial way of life gave full warrant to his claims.[18]

In addition, Aycelin tightened the requirements for the reception of candidates to ecclesiastical orders from the minor orders through the priesthood, including a requirement that each applicant be examined by his bishop to ensure his fitness. Secret marriages, false testimony, and the extortion of extraordinary fees

15. Génestal, *Privilegium Fori*, 100ff.

16. This process of adapting and applying papal legislation in the diocese is fully described by Lefebvre, in Lebras, *L'age classique*, 188–93.

17. Hefele and Leclercq, *Histoire des Conciles*, VI, pt. I, remark on the general "indifference" of the French toward the publication of the *Sext*, describing Boniface as a general abandoned by his lieutenants. They dismiss the Council of Béziers as a relatively meaningless gesture of courtesy toward Berengar Frédol.

18. The canons of this council are reprinted in Martène and Durand, *Veterum Scriptorum*, IV, 225–27.

for burials and other services were also strictly prohibited by the council, and priests and monks were forbidden to practice as surgeons or doctors.

With these laws Aycelin had achieved a legal, if not a moral, reform among the clerks of his diocese, and had provided an answer to the most pressing complaints against them. By tightening the definition of "clerk" and stiffening requirements for entrance to that order, Aycelin had taken steps to correct most of the outstanding abuses of the courts in his province some months in advance of the submission of the report of the king's investigators. Strengthened by this evidence of cooperation with royal efforts at reform, the archbishop and his suffragans could then address themselves to the more congenial task of defending and extending their own liberties.

Having corrected the conditions leading to the worst abuses charged against their courts, the bishops at the Council of Béziers passed a series of laws restating their own privileges. Anyone who persisted for more than a year under sentence of excommunication was to be restored to the Church by force if necessary. The bailli charged with assisting the Church in such cases was to provide the archbishop with a written explanation if he failed to bring in the culprit. In particular, the penalty of excommunication was to be applied to anyone who failed to pay pious legacies made by deceased members of his family. As a final act, to predispose the king to respect their decisions, the bishops voted to grant him a new *decima*.[19]

This synod of 1299 was designed as part of a larger effort which would engage Aycelin's attention sporadically until his translation to the see of Rouen in 1311. While he had corrected some of the abuses included in the report of the royal commission, he had defended others of these practices and had enforced them with the new laws. Certainly he must have been one of the men against whom Pierre Dubois was complaining when he wrote that the efforts of individual royal officials to attack the abuses of the ecclesiastical courts were rendered useless by the efforts of some

19. Strayer, "Consent to taxation under Philip the Fair," *Studies in Early French Taxation*, 32.

of the most influential of the king's councillors, prelates who labored to crush their opposition.[20]

Aycelin's program was to reform and clarify his jurisdictional rights and then to guarantee the structure with royal privileges. Accordingly, he approached the king early in 1300 with a request for redress against the abuses of the royal agents, to which the king tendered a gracious replay on 3 March.[21] After instructing his agents generally to observe the customs of Saint Louis in their assizes and to do no injury to the servants of the archbishop, Philip provided a specific series of privileges for the church of Narbonne. Notaries were not to be taxed on any benefices they might hold but only on their salaries. Vacant benefices in which the king had the right to collect annates and first fruits in the province were to be committed to good and honest persons who would take from the goods only what they required for their own sustenance. In their administration they would respect the customs of the Church, and under no circumstances were they to tamper with the movable property entrusted to them, particularly books and chalices.[22] No vacancy was to be created fraudulently in order to get control of its revenues and no vacancy would be extended beyond a year, nor be permitted to occur twice in a single year. No one in peaceful possession of any church was to be compelled to produce titles for its property. The goods set aside for charity and church administration would not be included in the assessment of annates.

On the same day, Philip addressed an ordinance regarding the privileges of the cathedral establishment in Narbonne to the archbishop personally.[23] He promised that the archiepiscopal goods would not be placed under royal guardianship for any reason ex-

20. De Wailly (ed.), "Summaria Brevis," 452.

21. *Ordonnances*, XII. 338: Philip promised redress of the archbishop's grievances, with a flattering reference to his many services to the crown: "Eorum, igitur, in quibus sincerae devotionis, et proptae nostris desideriis affectionis gratitudinem invenimus, supplicationibus inclinati, super praemisses graveminibus, molestiis, oppressionibus, et injuriis sic duximus providendum."

22. The necessity for such strictures is graphically demonstrated by the complaints of the Bishop of Angers regarding the behavior of royal officials in his diocese during vacancies: "Le livre de Guillaume le Maire," *Coll. doc. inéd.,* XI, pt. 2, pp. 187–537.

23. *Ordonnances*, XII, 339.

cept contumacy or failure to pay a debt, in which case royal exactions would be limited to the extent of the legal fine or debt. No secular judge in Narbonne would compel ecclesiastical persons to his court and his officials would not attempt to tax any clerk living clerically without fraud, married or unmarried. In addition, royal judges would observe the customs of the city in giving the archbishop complete control of cases involving wills, despite royal practice elsewhere.

Thus, by early 1300 Aycelin had achieved all his major goals in his diocesan administration. His position at the royal court had paid handsome dividends for the Archbishop of Narbonne in his church. Less successful were his dealings with Amaury of Narbonne, who was still dragging out the case of his homage to the archbishop by his failure to appear for judgment before the Parlement of Paris. Far from penalizing him, in September 1298 the king instructed the seneschal of Carcassonne to assess the subjects of viscount and archbishop equally in raising subsidies for the defense of the realm.[24] A year later Aycelin had become so anxious over the case that he mobilized the clergy of the province to join him in his protest to the king. The prelates assembled at Béziers in 1299 wrote to Philip in support of the legal claim of the archbishop; at the same time they demonstrated their value to the king by voting a new subsidy. In this remonstrance they went so far as to remind the king that support of Count Amaury's unjust pretensions would justify the disolution of the traditional bonds of loyalty joining the church of Narbonne to the throne of France:

> When the head languishes, the members are compelled to sorrow and thus we mourn with the Church of Narbonne and share in her infirmities. Long did the viscount hold the bourg and half the city from the archbishop: the father of the present viscount did homage accordingly. . . . He who is now viscount, led by no good spirit, has offered, as we hear, to recognize the said fief from your majesty, against the fidelity and oaths of his predecessors registered in your court. . . . Moreover, he got letters from the king . . . and this is to your own prejudice because it would dissolve the conventions contracted by your predecessors with

24. Regné, *Amaury* II, 95.

the archbishops dividing the said fief between the kings of France and the archbishops of Narbonne.[25]

Thus, in a purely domestic question of the rights of his own church, Aycelin displayed courage and determination to the point of threatening the king himself, although his attitude changed abruptly whenever any intervention from outside France was suggested.

The archbishop had helped to formulate and execute Philip's initial policies toward the Colonnas in 1297. After their first deceptive encouragements, the French had given the rebel cardinals no assistance against the pope, but in 1299, when they were fleeing in defeat, they found asylum and financial support in France. Stefano Colonna, whose attack on the papal gold shipment had been the immediate cause of the quarrel, took refuge with his brother-in-law, Amaury of Narbonne, and the archbishop tacitly cooperated in protecting him from the pope's vengeance.[26]

Having received word of Colonna's presence in Languedoc, Boniface wrote to Edward of England (as Duke of Aquitaine), Philip of France, and the Archbishop of Narbonne, requesting Stefano's apprehension and restoration to Rome. By virtue of his vows of obedience to the apostolic see, Aycelin was specifically commanded to get what help he needed from the secular arm to secure the fugitive.[27] The prelate took no action, however. It is not even recorded that he answered the papal letter. Although he might gladly have taken this opportunity to attack his rival, Amaury, he was probably checked by the king's protection of other members of the Colonna family. The friction between Aycelin and the king and between Aycelin and the viscount did nothing to lessen their mutual loyalty in the face of papal interference.

The delicate balance of their relationship in the case of Narbonne seemed to have frozen. By 1300 Aycelin must have realized that he could no longer expect a concrete decision from the king.

25. Mansi, *Sacrorum Conciliorum*, XXIV, 1213–14.
26. The relationship between the Colonnas and the house of Narbonne through their marriages with Jeanne and Gaucerande de l'Isle-Jourdain, is detailed by Martin-Chabot, "Contribution à l'histoire de la famille Colonna," 137–90.
27. Möhler, *Die Kardinäle Jakob und Peter Colonna*, 213–14.

Rather than refer directly to the pope as arbiter, he worked out a tentative agreement with Amaury to share in the jurisdiction of the city as equals without making a formal territorial settlement or deciding the question of homage. He then wrote to the pope requesting formal approval of the treaty. Boniface answered with a heated defense of the liberties of the church of Narbonne, followed by an expression of papal confidence that the archbishop would never diminish the goods of his church, nor subject it to "miserable servitude." He concluded with a reminder of the prelate's vow of obedience, threatening him with excommunication and loss of his ecclesiastical dignities if he should make any agreement without apostolic sanction.[28] In a second bull of the same day he expressed his determination to settle the affair himself, citing the archbishop and the viscount to appear at Rome within three months.[29]

Boniface apparently was trying to withdraw the affair completely from royal jurisdiction. But for all his determination to secure his rights in Narbonne, the archbishop was not prepared to cooperate with the pope. Neither he nor the viscount responded to the summons, despite the fact that Aycelin had once more (in June) failed to force Amaury's appearance at the Parlement of Paris and was claiming that by his absence he had defaulted his case.[30] As to the problem of the pope's threats, Aycelin could have claimed a technical obedience to his command by his appearance in Rome early in 1301 on the king's business, although there is no indication that the question of Narbonne was discussed at that time.

Aycelin had pinned all his hopes for a settlement on the royal courts, with a temporary agreement with the viscount as an interim arrangement. Philip continued to withhold a decision for years as the final quarrel with the pope developed. By holding this balance, he encouraged both claimants to continue to seek his favor by energy in his service. In 1302, for example, while Aycelin was organizing the French clergy in support of the royal demand

28. *Reg. Bon. VIII*, 3666, 18 July 1300.
29. *Ibid.*, 3667–68.
30. Regné, *Amaury II*, p. 100.

for a council against Boniface VIII, Amaury of Narbonne was touring the south with Guillaume de Plasians, securing the adherence of the Languedocian lords.[31]

Their mutual loyalty to the king and their temporary agreement did little to correct the troubled state of the city. In the summer of 1302, with both lords absent, rioting broke out in the streets. The viscount's agents accused the personnel of the archiepiscopal court of having set a murderer free rather than ask the help of the secular arm in punishing him. The archbishop in turn complained at length of the viscount's violence in interfering with his courts.[32] The viscount's men were charged with an armed attack on the cathedral itself and with the murder of both clerks and laymen within its precinct. The viscount retorted that they had been attacked because they had used the sanctuary as a base from which to assault the viscount's tower, throwing stones into the very room where the viscountess lay in labor. Clearly, Amaury contended, they would assassinate his entire family if they could.

By delaying a decision through the years of crisis that followed, the king prevented either claimant from taking advantage of his quarrel with the pope. The case was drawn out until 1305. On 11 October of that year, at the king's order, Amaury finally asked the archbishop's pardon for the attack on the cathedral. Aycelin, for his part, absolved him from blame on the ground that he had been absent during the violence.[33] In this new spirit of amity, they undertook to cooperate in support of the royal currency reform by issuing a new minting of the money of Narbonne. With the king's support they were able to ignore the claims of the consuls of the city to participate in the venture.[34]

It is perhaps worthwhile to note here an incident of the same year to illustrate that, despite their commitments to the king neither lord was prepared to surrender any of his own

31. Amaury's travels can be traced from the documents in Dupuy, *Historie du différend,* 123ff.

32. A detailed account of these complaints is supplied by Regné, *Amaury II,* 153ff.

33. De Vic and Vaissette, *Historie de Languedoc,* IX, 275.

34. *Ibid.,* 276.

privileges to the royal favor. In 1306 the Jews were expelled from France and the king attempted to add the property of the Jews of Narbonne to the store of confiscated wealth he had accumulated elsewhere. Though the Parlement of Paris supported the king's right to this claim, both Amaury and Aycelin stood together against it. The city, they claimed, had but two *Juiveries* —one in the archbishop's and one in the viscount's territory. They, not the king, had the sole right to confiscate goods there, and they demanded that the royal agents restore what they had taken. The case was argued for three years until, in 1309, the two lords were reimbursed.[35]

The viscount and the archbishop had perforce learned to cooperate with one another against a power that now threatened to overwhelm them both. They had recognized the right of the king to arbitrate the quarrel between them. The archbishop had even refused the pope's help. For years the king had delayed a decision, and thereby avoided losing their loyalty in time of crisis. The case of the Jewish goods, however, amply illustrated that they must in future present a solid front to the encroaching royal power if the liberties of Narbonne were to be preserved. Accordingly, on 17 April 1309 the viscount finally gave homage to the archbishop and the pair celebrated their accord with another joint issue of new money in the city.[36]

The case of Narbonne shows Philip the Fair in an "antifeudal" light insofar as it strengthened his courts' appellate claims. Both claimants recognized his right to adjudicate their quarrels to the exclusion of all others, including the pope. On the other hand, Philip's success was secured essentially by his tact in failing to exploit his opportunities. He desired a stronger foothold in the city, but he refused offers from both the viscount and the consuls to give it to him without a proper legal basis. Similarly, he recognized the justice of the resistance of both lords to his attempt to secure the confiscated Jewish goods. He gained and held his position as sovereign overlord by delay, evasions, and favor to

---

35. Regné, *Amaury II*, 116–17.
36. De Vic and Vaissette, *Histoire de Languedoc*, IX, 276.

both sides. Finally, the case throws a new light on the "legist spirit" by illustrating that one of the foremost lawyers of the royal court was as strong in the defense of his own feudal privileges as ever he was in defense of the king's claim.[37]

37. The dualities of interests among the lawyers of the royal council has recently been noted by Favier, "Les légistes et le gouvernement de Philippe le Bel."

IX

Heresy and Treason

The disputes and violent confrontations of the two lords were not the only manifestations of unrest in the archdiocese of Narbonne. For all his undoubted capacity as a church administrator, Aycelin was seriously limited as an ecclesiastic. His interests and abilities appear to have been entirely secular. There is no evidence of any kind that he was ever touched by those mystical impulses that made possible the strange career of his contemporary, the hermit pope Celestine V. He showed no sensitivity to the deep spiritual problems that troubled many souls in his own diocese of Narbonne.

The most revered leader of the "spiritual" wing of the Franciscan order, Peter John Olivi, was in residence at the order's convent in Narbonne while Aycelin was archbishop there. After his death in 1297, Olivi became something of a cult figure in the province.[1] Only a few years after Aycelin's translation to Rouen in 1315, Narbonne emerged as one of the major centers of spiritual Franciscanism; in 1317 forty-three Narbonnese were cited to answer heresy charges by John XXII and ultimately five of them were burned at the stake.

During Aycelin's episcopate, however, Narbonne presented a deceptive air of tranquility. The archiepiscopal court actually condemned only one heretic who, suspiciously perhaps, was formerly a subvicar of the viscount's court.[2] R. W. Emery suggests that the reason for the lack of condemnations was not the absence of heresy but the absence of an inquisitorial court. He shows that no serious effort was made to uncover heretics in the city throughout the thirteenth century.

Aycelin displayed an awareness of their presence on several occasions, though he undertook no determined step to prosecute

1. Douie, *The Nature and Effect of the Heresy of the Fraticelli*, 81–119.
2. Emery, *Heresy and Inquisition in Narbonne*, 105.

them. His single official display of concern with the problem was included in the records of the synod of Béziers in 1299. There the bishops were urged to undertake more frequent investigations of suspected heretics and to enforce the laws recently published by the pope to the full extent of their authority. But Aycelin himself made no noticeable effort to establish a court in his own see or to pursue the problem in any fashion, despite the fact that in the same year twenty-five citizens of Albi were arrested on charges of Catharism.[3] More alarming were the Spiritual Franciscans and their followers, whose influence was growing in the diocese. The text of the synodal statement condemned them strongly, noting that pretended piety was only too common an evil among the religious orders, seducing the laity with their devotions.[4]

But Aycelin's decree was not the starting point for any program of action—a program which he would have known well enough how to formulate and execute had he been seriously moved to root out heresy in his diocese. He was not, however, the sort of man to be seized with a desire for purely religious reform. He contented himself with a formal statement in condemnation of the unorthodox which was in no way designed to create a stir in his diocese. This might in the long run have proved embarrassing to himself and to the king, considering that Stefano Colonna had already taken refuge in or near Narbonne and that Philip the Fair was still inclined to flirt with the Spiritual Franciscans of Italy, who had never forgiven Boniface VIII for replacing their adored Celestine V.

Aycelin involved himself seriously in the question of heresy

---

3. Davis, *The Inquisition at Albi.*

4. Martène and Durand, *Veterum Scriptorum,* IV, 226, n.4: ". . . praedicantium multis finem mundi instare, et jam adesse vel quasi tempora antichristi, novosque poenitentiae modos et abstinentias vestiumque colores utriusque sexus personis suggerentium, et nihilominis virginitatis ac castitatis vota recipientium a pluribus ex eisdem, ad hoc suis exhortationibus prius tractis, quae vota a pluribus violata fuisse noscuntur: quam plures utriusque sexus ad novae superstitionis cultum pertracti fuerunt, Beguini seu Beguinae vulgariter appellati, qui conventualia prohibita facientes, et frequentes de nocte officium praedicationis verbi Dei temere usurparunt, in suam excusationem fictitio praetendentes, quod non praedicant, sed loquuntur de Deo se invicem consolantes, et quasdam novas observantias custodire conantur, a communi ritu ceterumque fidelium discrepantes, e quibus nonnulla scandala sunt suborta, et non modica pericula huic provinciae, quam haereticos olim publice frequentasse est certum, nec dubium est, licet clam adhuc ab aliquibus frequentari immineri noscuntur."

only when the actual authority and practice of the Church, as represented by the Inquisition was challenged by the Franciscans. Popular resentment of the extraordinary powers of these tribunals had long smoldered, occasionally erupting into violence throughout Languedoc. Between 1295 and 1299 the strength of this opposition was steadily increasing.[5] At the same time, the over-frequent applications of the traditional penalties of excommunication and interdict had made the population callous and scornful of their effects.[6]

At intervals throughout his reign, Philip the Fair had issued ordinances to his officers to investigate complaints against the inquisitors. After the entire city of Carcassonne had submitted to an interdict in 1298 rather than obey the demands of the Inquisition, Boniface VIII asked the king to strengthen the royal machinery against heretics. Philip responded by ordering the nobility and royal officials to assist the bishops and inquisitors in the capture and detention of heretics and their defenders.[7] On 27 April 1299, just prior to the synod of Béziers, the Bishops of Béziers and Albi held an assembly of the clergy and nobility of Carcassonne to reach a settlement with the rebellious citizens. Their summons was ignored, though a second assembly of 8 October was somewhat more successful. All but twelve of the most obdurate heretics received absolution at that time.[8]

While anxious to maintain his reputation for piety and orthodoxy, Philip was also prepared to use his authority to protect his subjects from false accusations of heresy. Thus, when a new revolt against the Inquisition broke out at Carcassonne in the sum-

5. The inquisitor Bernard Gui, *Historia*, in Martène and Durand, *Veterum Scriptorum*, I, 437–39, described the riots but dismissed them as the work of men previously convicted of heresy. But the widespread support gathered around Bernard Délicieux in 1300 suggests a far broader base of discontent.

6. De Vic and Vaissette, *Histoire de Languedoc*, X, 199: 13 October 1297, the pope instructed the inquisitor of Carcassonne to investigate complaints from Béziers that heretics in that city sought to have ecclesiastics subjected to taxes and other common imposts. They were saying that they did not approve of interdict and excommunication and spoke evil of the pope and his authority, asking the help of the secular judges in escaping censures against them. *Reg. Bon. VIII*, 2140, in 1298 the pope claimed that even though under the interdict, the citizens of Carcassonne boasted that they slept well and enjoyed their food as much as ever.

7. *Les Olim*, II, 413.

8. Davis, *Inquisition at Albi*, 58–59.

mer of 1300, he did not dismiss the leaders without a sympathetic hearing.

Bernard Délicieux, a Franciscan, took the lead in the movement addressing the complaints of the citizen to the Archbishop of Narbonne and his suffragans on 4 July 1300.[9] Receiving no satisfaction locally, he sought out the king at Senlis in December. According to his own report of the meeting, Délicieux received some encouragement, for the king stated that he believed their testimony to be honest and thought the Dominicans (representing the Inquisition), who besieged him daily, were lying. Philip turned the testimony of both parties over to Aycelin for investigation and two days later, following the archbishop's recommendation, a fine was pronounced against the Bishop of Carcassonne. The Dominicans were requested to appoint a new inquisitor. When they refused, Philip appointed the Vidâme of Amiens and Richard Leneveu to investigate the complaints locally and reform the disorders in the country.[10]

Aycelin could have had little to do with the course of the subsequent investigation. To have arrived in Genoa in the same month (December 1300), he must have departed almost immediately upon giving the king his recommendations. It is therefore impossible to guess how much he knew or approved of the turn taken by the activities of the royal agent. Considering his position at court, however, it seems impossible that he had not been informed that, among their other duties, the investigators were instructed to examine the evidence of sedition in the province which deeply implicated one of Aycelin's suffragan bishops.

Aycelin continued to be busy in Philip's diplomatic affairs. He was preoccupied again with matters in Flanders when, on the night of 12 July 1301, two commissioners broke into the bedchamber of Bernard Saisset, Bishop of Pamiers, and summoned him to appear at the next session of the Parlement of Paris to answer charges of treason.

Bernard Saisset was almost unique among the prelates of France—he was the pope's man and the pope's man only. His dio-

9. Hauréau, *Bernard Délicieux et l'inquisition albigeoise, 1300–1320,* "Pièces Justificatifs," 172.
10. *Ibid.,* 33.

cese had been especially carved out of the overlarge diocese of Toulouse and he had been named its first bishop without prior consultation with the king. On 23 June 1295 Aycelin was informed of the partition for the first time and instructed by the pope to ordain his new suffragan to the episcopal dignity.[11]

The appointment was unwelcome to the king on several counts. Not only did he dislike Saisset personally and resent the partition of a diocese held by one of his own relatives, but Saisset was the first prelate appointed in France during Philip's reign without prior approval from the court. Possibly under instructions from the king, Aycelin delayed the installation of the new bishop as long as he could. On 5 February 1296 the pope wrote him a sharp note ordering him to proceed without delay with Saisset's investiture.[12]

Aycelin had his own reasons for disliking the appointment. In running his diocese, he consistently kept himself in the position of intermediary between king and pope and his bishops. The latter played a subordinate, consultative role in forming the goals of the province through their synods, but Aycelin alone acted as their spokesman before the higher authorities. Bernard Saisset, however, was a personal friend of Boniface VIII and a personal enemy of the king. Moreover, he would not be easily controlled by his archbishop: his reputation as a firebrand and troublemaker was already old. He was connected by birth and friendship with the most dangerous dissident elements among the southern nobility. In the past, as an abbot, he had relied on appeal to the pope rather than to the king in his many quarrels over the temporal rights of his monastery. His violent defence of his claims had seriously compromised the king himself at one point. Philip had just sealed a crucial and hard-bought agreement with the Count of Foix by transferring to him the rights he held in Pamiers by virtue of an earlier pariage (a profit- or revenue-sharing contract) with the abbot. Saisset, however, refused to recognize the agreement on the grounds that he had made the pariage with the king only and with no understanding that the king's rights could be transferred.

11. *Reg. Bon. VIII*, 411–412.
12. *Ibid.*, 891–892.

In 1290 even Benedict Gaetani, the future pope, had tried to persuade Saisset to yield on this point without success.[13]

Saisset's quarrel with the Count of Foix was similar to that between Aycelin and the Viscount of Narbonne, but Saisset had none of the archbishop's tact. Nor was he willing to take the king's problems into consideration. At the time of his appointment to the new bishopric he was in Rome, having taken refuge with the pope after the Count of Foix had occupied and burned sections of Pamiers. He had persuaded Boniface to write the king, admonishing him for his transfer of the disputed pariage.[14] After his return as bishop, he continued the quarrel from 1296 to 1299. He brought it to Rome again. He brought it to Paris. But there is no suggestion that he ever looked to his archbishop for help or advice. In turn, Aycelin at no time showed any inclination to involve himself in the quarrels of his troublesome suffragan.

According to the testimony collected against him in 1301, the bishop's complaints during these years passed all the bounds of tact and diplomacy. In 1298, while Aycelin was in Paris for the ceremonies celebrating the translation of the relics of Saint Louis, his suffragan came to court to renew his demands against the Count of Foix. Infuriated by his failure to receive satisfaction, he began to voice his criticisms of the king and his government. Various members of the court who talked with him at that time later described his insulting remarks: he told one man that the king was surrounded by corrupt and lying courtiers and indeed was as bad as any of his men.[15] To another he said that Philip the Fair was neither man nor beast—only a statue incapable of any action—able only to stare and stare. He even questioned the king's legitimacy, saying that if he had been of the true line of Charlemagne, he could never have wreaked such havoc in the world.[16]

Not content with these grumblings, he then entered into open defiance. In the presence of Aycelin, Flote, and others, he told the king that the crown had no authority over Pamiers other than that represented by the pariage. If Philip did not renew it, he

13. The details of Saisset's background and his conflict of jurisdiction with the Count of Foix are provided by Vidal, *Bernard Saisset*.

14. *Reg. Bon. VIII*, 161–62.

15. Dupuy, *Histoire du différend*, 648, testimony of William Montaneri.

16. *Ibid.*, 649, testimony of Roger de Alariaco.

must recognize the perpetual alienation of Pamiers from his authority. Two witnesses recalled this event and testified that he added that Saint Louis, in his last sickness had warned the king's father that their dynasty would end in his generation unless he and his sons clung to their customary devotion to the Church.[17]

After this attempt to reach an agreement on the jurisdiction of Pamiers through the king's court, Saisset began a series of independent negotiations with the count, and on 17 February 1299 finally secured the pope's agreement to a compromise which would enable them to share in the jurisdiction of the city.[18] On 18 May Boniface wrote Aycelin, giving him the authority to arbitrate the details and seal the agreement—with a threat of excommunication against any member of the count's family who might dare to break it.[19] Perhaps this impending settlement inspired Aycelin's own attempt at this time to reach a similar contract with Amaury of Narbonne. If so, the pope's curt rejection of his request for confirmation must have been doubly galling in the light of his complacence toward Saisset.

Meanwhile, Aycelin was in possession of an appeal from the citizens of Pamiers, asking for redress of certain grievances of their own against Saisset. They had written to him and to the pope as the bishop's spiritual superiors, and to the king as his temporal lord. These new difficulties in Pamiers coincided with the more general difficulties of the province and were included in the problems to be taken up by Leneveu and the Vidâme of Amiens in their investigation. Before further action could be taken, however, Boniface VIII acted in support of his friend, striking the town with an interdict and the citizens with excommunication.[20]

The royal commissioners had a great deal more ammunition against the quarrelsome bishop than a single complaint of abuses from the citizens of his town. An immense dossier of various charges had been compiled against him in the summer of 1301.

17. *Ibid.*, 637–38.
18. *Reg. Bon. VIII*, 2907.
19. *Ibid.*, 3092.
20. *Ibid.*, 3340, 28 November 1299. The revolt in Pamiers and the appeals to Paris are discussed in detail by *Vidal*, 47.

One of the king's chief informants was Saisset's supposedly
reconciled enemy, the Count of Foix. The Count claimed that
Saisset began to formulate a series of confused treason plots
aimed at destroying the authority of the crown in Languedoc,
which were disclosed to the count when they met on 27 June
1300 to complete the terms of their reconciliation.[21] On that
occasion, the count said, the bishop promised him the lordship of
Toulouse, a base from which the French could be driven from the
entire country. According to the Count of Comminges, Saisset
at the same time was offering *him* the lordship of Toulouse.[22]

Foix also testified that Saisset called Philip a counterfeiter—
in fact, he claimed that the pope himself had made this charge
against the king to Pierre Flote. This remark was clarified by
another witness at the same meeting who stated that while he
was giving the count money to repay a debt, Saisset said that the
money was of no value to him in any case because it had been
coined by the king and was thus unlawfully debased.[23]

No one has ever succeeded in extracting any indisputable
truth from the masses of testimony against the Bishop of Pamiers
beyond the self-evident fact that he had a loose and malicious
tongue. His charges and complaints, however, have added interest
in that they appear to reflect the growing bad temper of Boniface
VIII, especially toward Pierre Flote. Flote had frequently loosed
verbal barbs at Boniface at their various meetings, and as French
success in war spread, Flote's aggressiveness also grew. In 1300
he laughed at Boniface's objections to French plans in Aquitaine.
A more serious quarrel, described by William Rishanger,[24] could
only have occurred in the spring of 1301. According to that chronicler, Flote so exasperated the pope as to provoke him to threaten
the chancellor with the penalties of both the spiritual and temporal powers at his command. To this Flote rejoined: "Yes, lord,
you have both powers; but your power is made of words and
ours is real." Saisset, like Boniface, believed that Flote was the

21. Dupuy, *Histoire du différend,* 633.
22. *Ibid.,* 641.
23. *Ibid.,* 647.
24. *Chronica et Annales,* 197. Rishanger believed that this embassy occurred
after the imprisonment of Bernard Saisset, but the spring of 1301 is the last
occasion on which Flote and the pope can have met.

source of all the evil loose in France. On one occasion he told Peter de Bocenaco that, while the king's court should be a source of justice and good counsel, it was so corrupt that there could be no justice done since Flote would not act unless he were bribed.[25] On another occasion, criticizing the incapacity of the king, he added that France was the kingdom of the blind in which the one-eyed man was king, a probable reference to the disfigured Flote.[26]

When the royal commissioners arrived to investigate the treason charges made by the Counts of Foix and Comminges and the complaints of the people of Pamiers, Saisset had already seriously compromised himself with the royal representatives by such remarks. He compounded his error by refusing any cooperation with the commission, accusing them of exceeding the conditions of their appointment in making an investigation of his activities. When he refused to answer their citations they arrested his clerks, put his goods under the royal seal, and finally broke into his bedchamber to deliver their summons.[27]

In this dilemma, Saisset turned for the first time to his archbishop for assistance. He sent the Abbot of Mas-Azil to Aycelin, asking him to support his demand that the case be referred to the pope. The ensuing events were recounted by Aycelin in a lengthy letter to Boniface VIII, written in October shortly after he had taken Saisset into his own custody. Since Aycelin's purpose in writing is to justify his own failure to protect Saisset more effectively, the reader must necessarily be judiciously critical of the archbishop's account of what he had been doing and why. As a narrative of the superficial events, however, there is no reason to question the report since Saisset was free to confirm or deny it himself and the papal legate was a witness to most of the meetings with the king which Aycelin described.[28]

According to Aycelin's exposition, he was in Orléans when the abbot reached him with Saisset's message, on his way to Clermont to settle the affairs of the lately deceased bishop, his brother Jean.

25. Dupuy, 639.
26. *Ibid.*, 640.
27. *Ibid.*, 651, Saisset's letter of complaint.
28. Martène and Durand, *Thesaurus*, I, 1320.

Since he felt unable to delay his business to take up Saisset's appeal, he had entrusted the abbot with letters to the king asking him to give the Bishop of Pamiers license to carry his appeal to Rome, though he stressed that he did not consider the king legally obliged to fulfill the request. In a second letter, he asked the king to remedy the aggressions of his commissioners against the bishop's person and property.

As soon as he could, Aycelin assured the pope, he had hurried personally to the king and in the presence of the entire council supported the abbot in presenting Saisset's complaints against the royal representatives. At this point, however, Philip had explained the nature of the grave and terrible crimes with which Saisset had been charged—the archbishop presumably not having yet enlightened himself on that point. Graciously, Aycelin added, the king stated that he found the charges difficult to credit and assured the archbishop that he would be greatly pleased if the bishop were able to prove his innocence. To this end, he had summoned him to appear at the royal court in his own defense. Meanwhile, with assurances of his desire to please the archbishop, he had promised to release the person and goods of the bishop and referred the abbot to Chancellor Pierre Flote for the necessary letters.

Aycelin claimed that this royal answer had satisfied him that all was well, and he felt free to return to Auvergne and settle his brother's estate. He then had joined Flote and Pierre de Mornay with the intention of proceeding to Flanders on the king's business. On the road, the Abbot of Mas-Azil had contacted him again, complaining that the Vidâme of Amiens had refused to release the bishop, denying the validity of the letters the abbot carried instructing him to do so. Moreover, the vidâme had impounded the letters, refusing to return them until the king himself had verified them. His only concession was to provide the abbot with copies under the vidâme's own seal. When the copy was relayed to Leneveu in Toulouse, that gentleman answered that he would have to consider what he wanted to do next. Meanwhile, fresh letters had come, ordering the bishop to leave immediately for court in Paris. The abbot complained to Aycelin that the bishop was being conducted on the road like a common criminal, strictly guarded by soldiers who refused even to leave his room while he slept.

Aycelin stated that he could not leave his business in Flanders and therefore decided to delegate Berengar Frédol to handle the problem. Frédol was instructed to see the king at Tours and exhort him, for the good of his soul and to avert the danger of drawing canonical censures upon himself, to provide new letters. But Frédol wrote that fever and flux prevented him from leaving his bed. Aycelin then had sent a servant with letters to the king, his confessor, and each of the clerks and councillors believed to be with him, urging the relief of the Bishop of Pamiers. But, he said, the king did not answer these letters.

This report of Aycelin's exertions on behalf of his suffragan, to whom he owed protection, is touching and seemingly ingenuous. It cannot, however, be read as an impartial report of the exact course of events. For years the Archbishop of Narbonne had carefully preserved his credit with Boniface VIII and dissociated himself from the activities of his partner, Flote. Obviously, in making this report to the pope, he made every effort to put himself in as favorable a light as possible. Even so, it is apparent that he made no more than a few token gestures on behalf of Saisset. It is even possible that the original letters were supplied him for the sake of appearances and that he knew what would happen when they were presented. Likewise, it is not beyond the bounds of probability that he knew that Frédol would have a convenient attack of illness, delaying the whole process for weeks. In Paris, and again in Flanders, he was with Pierre Flote throughout this period and the two probably consulted on the best tactics to take in response to the bishop's complaints. Aycelin's feeble resistance to the aggressions of the vidâme and Leneveu was strictly in conformity with the king's gracious and reasonable responses to Aycelin's complaints. Master and man, they were distressed. They deplored any breach of delicacy in the bishop's treatment. They sincerely hoped that he would be found innocent. But they insisted on keeping him at Paris.

On his return to the court in late September or early October, Aycelin made contact with the papal nuncio, the Bishop of Spoleto, with whom he claimed to have made frequent and urgent appeals to the king for Saisset's release from his guards. With his accustomed air of sweet reason, the king replied that the bishop was not a prisoner and, in any case, the king had specifically forbidden any violence to his person.[29] Philip then sent the Count of Dreux and the Constable of France (both of whom had been in Flanders with Flote and Aycelin), to inform the archbishop that the king was ready to hold a public hearing at Senlis of all his complaints.

On Thursday, 18 October, the king presented Aycelin with the accusations against Saisset. In the King's name, Flote read the lengthy list of charges, running from an account of his malicious remarks to an exposure of a whole series of revolutionary plots involving the Counts of Foix and Comminges and the King of Aragon. In conclusion, Flote swore to the truth of the charges and requested the archbishop, as Saisset's lord, to take him into custody and judge and punish him for the crime of *lèse majesté*, "lest from your negligence or defect the king must look for another remedy in the absence of this justice."[30] Since Aycelin had taken such good care to bring the papal nuncio as a witness, there can be no doubt this scene took place just as he described it. It has caused more than one later commentator to express sympathy for the harried archbishop and admiration for his integrity, since he did not immediately collapse under the weight of such a threat.[31] But there is no reason to take his word for it that he knew nothing more of the case than what Saisset, and now Flote, saw fit to communicate in public. He was as high in the royal councils as any man. If he was out of the way in Flanders when the case came to a crisis, so also was Flote, whose intimate acquaintance with every turn of the case has long been beyond question. It is altogether unlikely that Flote plotted this scene without his colleague's knowledge. In fact, the whole sequence of events witnessed by the Bishop of Spoleto was probably a well-planned drama for which the archbishop had had ample time to consider his role.

29. *Ibid.*, 1323.
30. *Ibid.*, 1334.
31. Aycelin's most recent champion is Pegues (p. 93): "Aicelin took a vigorous part in Saisset's process, pleading not for his innocence or against the charges, but for order and regularity in the trial and treatment of the bishop."

Again, it is by his own account that we are told that the archbishop did his best to protect Saisset. He did protest the king's
demand that he take over the custody of the bishop on the slender
grounds that his archiepiscopal jurisdiction did not extend to the
north, where the bishop had been transported, and that he would
do nothing so illegal without the consent of his fellow prelates, his
suffragans, and particularly the pope. According to Aycelin, this
courageous exhibition of clerical solidarity so enraged the "great
ones" in the court that they began to threaten Saisset with immediate physical violence. The prelates at the court, the papal
nuncio, and even Saisset himself, panicked and begged Aycelin
to give the bishop his protection. The king and the Bishop of
Auxerre added their voices to the clamor, begging Aycelin to step
in and prevent the threatened violence. Seeing no other recourse,
Aycelin wrote regretfully to Boniface, he gave way. He took Saisset into custody to keep him from harm, to ensure that he would
remain under ecclesiastical jurisdiction, and for the sake of piety,
mercy, justice, and to prevent tyranny (obviously, the potential
tyrant was not the king.)[32]

This fortuitous scene enabled the archbishop to solve the
king's legal embarrassment. It could now be admitted that Saisset was, if not a prisoner (and Aycelin stood firm in his claim that
he could not be considered anything but a free man under armed
protection), then at least confined. Now it could be claimed that it
was the Church, not the king, who was doing the confining. The
king's good will had been demonstrated: he had shown his respect
for the rights of ecclesiastical jurisdiction and his well-founded
anxiety for the bishop's safety had been displayed. Aycelin could
report to the pope that he had done everything in his power.

The situation of the Bishop of Pamiers was unaffected by all
this rhetoric. The archbishop protested to the pope that he repeatedly stipulated that Saisset's correspondence and movements
should be uninhibited. But, against his will, the royal guards continued to occupy his chamber, censor his letters, and even listen to
his conversations with his servants. How it must have moved the
pope to read Aycelin's pitiful description of himself—always in

32. *Ibid.*, 1324.

company with the papal nuncio—haunting the king's presence to protest the indignities visited upon Saisset and begging Philip to release the bishop to the pope's custody or at least to send him to some strong place in Narbonne! The king, on his side, was always patient, repeating that he had written to the pope himself and was waiting for an answer. At last, however, the fabulous patience of the king was worn out under the incessant importunities of the petitioners. Carefully losing his temper, he told the Bishop of Spoleto, "Lord Bishop, if you like, I will take my guards away and you can guard him yourself."[33]

Even after thus threatening to leave Saisset to the violence he deserved, the king was not free of Aycelin. The archbishop told the pope that his exertions were so undiminished that many people around the court began to whisper that he must be a traitor himself, or at least a supporter of the conspiracy. At last the king himself publicly questioned his zeal for the welfare of the kingdom. He demanded that the archbishop admit that he had the Bishop of Pamiers in his custody, despite his lack of jurisdiction, and discard the pretense of simple protection. Humbly Aycelin assured the pope he had answered that he was only acting through fear of God and fear lest he offend the pope and his brother bishops. But, he admitted, he owed justice to all and especially to the king and was not prepared to fail in that duty as far as he could act according to the law.

Happily for the archbishop, this fearful moral dilemma was solved by a meeting of all the prelates he could collect at Senlis (that is, those then attached to the king's service). They urged him to comply with the royal demands and even suggested that it would be a sin not to take the step to ensure Saisset's safety until the pope's answer could be received. Together they arranged a highly elaborate set of terms under which the imprisonment could be undertaken and obtained the king's approval of them. Finally, they covered their tracks by writing the letter to the pope.

The letters of Aycelin, confirmed by separate and less detailed accounts by other bishops, were designed to protect them from the

33. *Ibid.*, 1326.

pope's anger and to offer Boniface a graceful way of settling the problem by leaving the fate of Saisset in their devoted hands. At the same time, the king wrote his own letter of explanation to the pope, promising to send nuncios to Rome to negotiate a final settlement.[34] He recounted his complaints against the bishop with an interesting variation of the original list of charges. Some of Saisset's more scurrilous remarks about the king were omitted and additional charges were made that he was a simoniac, a heretic who had spoken against the sacrament of penance, and a blasphemer who had not stopped short of calumniating the pope himself.[35]

Taking the king's conciliatory tone together with the picture presented by Aycelin, it appears that the French believed that Boniface could be won around to countenance the aggression against Saisset. Philip went out of his way to demonstrate his respect for the pope and his willingness to go far beyond the strict limits of the law in order to act in conformity with his love for the Apostolic See.[36] However, he concluded, if the pope did not see

34. Dupuy, 627.

35. *Ibid.*, 628. ". . . quod dictus episcopus in blasphemiam Dei et hominum pluries dixit sanctissimum Patrem dom. Bonifacium summum pontificem esse diabolum incarnatum. . . . quae contra regiam maiestatem commisit dictus episcopus nec mirum cum gravius aeternam quam temporalem laedere maiestatem: quod insuper in Deum, vel fidem vel Rom. Ecclesiam committitur contra se commissum recipit dom. Rex praedictus, qui in sui progenitores defensores speciales fidei et honoris Romanae Ecclesiae semper fuerunt.

36. *Ibid.*, 630. "Licet insuper contra dictum Episcopum dictus dominus Rex aliis viis potuisset procedere ad finem privationis temporalitatis quam idem Episcopus tam ex se quam ratione Ecclesiae Appam. noscitur possidere; ipse tamen dom. Rex progenitorum suorum sequens vestigia qui privilegia et libertates Ecclesiae suae voluerunt servare, honoremque Romanae Ecclesiae matri, de cuius uberibus sunt lactati, usquequaque servare, praemissa significat ipsi summo Pontifici patri suo, qui nedum Dei iniuriam, cuius locum tenet in terris, sed etiam dicti dom. Regis filii sui et totius regni sui vindicare tenetur, requirit quod dictus dom. Rex ipsum summum pontificem, ut super praemissis sic celere remedium adhibeat, sic debitum officii sui exerceat, ut dictus vir mortis, ex cuius vita locus etiam quem inhabitat per ipsius enormitatem horribilem corrupitur, omni ordine suo privet, omni privilegio suo exuat clericali, quod suum est tollat, ita quod dom. Rex de illo proditore Dei et hominum in profundo malorum posito, de quo aliqua correctio vel vitae emendatio sperari, non potest, cum a iuventute sua semper male vixerit, et ad inveteratam consuetudinem, turpitudinem et perditionem suam deduxisse noscatur, possit Deo facere per viam iustitiae sacrificium optimum; tantum enim nequam est, quod omnia debent sibi elementa deficere in morte qui Deum omnemque creaturam offendit."

fit to condemn such a villain, the king would have to do so himself
with the assistance of his own prelates.

It does not seem that the embassy which the king said he
would send to Rome ever left. Probably Philip waited for an answer to his pacifying letter before pursuing the question further.
Digard even questions whether the letter was ever dispatched,
since the pope showed no sign of ever having received it.[37] But
Aycelin testified that the king did write to Boniface, though no
answer was forthcoming save the bulls of 5 December. Clearly,
the French were overly sanguine about the pope's state of mind.
Like the Aragonese ambassador earlier in the year, they must have
believed that the will of the King of France was the pope's command.

But the temper of Boniface VIII, never very cool, had boiled
over. A flood of bulls was suddenly poured into France. Philip
was ordered to set the Bishop of Pamiers at liberty immediately,
restore his goods, and place no impediment in the way of his appeal to Rome.[38] The Archbishop of Narbonne was ordered to secure his suffragan's freedom and to use his influence with the king
to help him get out of France.[39] Moreover, Aycelin was ordered to
investigate the case and send the bishop to Rome within three
months with a complete dossier. As soon as he received the letters,
on 21 February, Philip the Fair ordered the papal legate who had
brought them to get out of France and take Bernard Saisset with
him.

It is possible that in the meantime Boniface had received
Philip's conciliatory letter, for he wrote to the Archbishop of Narbonne and the Bishops of Béziers and Maguelonne in a softer tone
on 13 January,[40] admitting that he had long viewed most gravely

37. *Philippe le Bel*, II, 81. Rishanger (see above) believed that Flote headed
an embassy to Rome at that time and said that the quarrel with Boniface was
caused by the Saisset case. Baillet, *Histoire des démeslez*, 116–17, and Boutaric,
La France, 104, based their accounts on that single report, and it had thereby
passed into most subsequent histories. But if Flote went to Rome after 24 October,
he must either have been there or on his way by 5 December, when *Ausculta
Fili* and its accompanying bulls were issued. Yet he gave no sign of believing that
a crisis was building up. He did not hurry to the court but went to Scotland for
the final negotiations with Edward I at Linlithgow.

38. *Reg. Bon. VIII*, 4432.

39. *Ibid.*, 4433.

40. *Ibid.*, 4269.

the bitterness with which the bishop of Pamiers exceeded the limits of discretion and, with the appearance of insanity, neglected the episcopal decenies by bursting out against the King of France. The pope added that if he had been correctly informed, the bishop had not feared to give that prince great offence and requested fuller enlightenment on the matter, repeating his request that the archbishop send the bishop to Rome. The charges mentioned by Boniface do not include the slanders against himself recounted by Philip the Fair.

The tone of the letter of 13 January suggests that some change in the pope's attitude had occurred. Apparently he was no longer disposed to take his stand against the King of France on the questionable ground of Saisset's innocence. There was, however, no suggestion that Boniface intended to retract his earlier bulls of December, which included the famous *Ausculta Fili*. Either he foolishly underestimated the probable effect of their reception in France, or he had decided that they provided a more favorable position from which to fight. The latter case is probably the correct one. Boniface VIII was always more comfortable with large-scale pronouncements than with piecemeal corrections of individual abuses.

In any case, by the time that Saisset left France, his own case had fallen into the background since a more serious quarrel between France and the papacy developed around the letters of 5 December, in which the pope had turned his attention to the accumulated complaints of the French Church. Perhaps he believed that the attack on their fellow bishops would incline the Gallican clergy to support him, lest they should be similarly attacked. Perhaps, even, he was misled as to their state of mind by the account Aycelin had given him of the king's threats and his own reaction.

X

"That one-eyed Belial"

With a series of bulls issued on 5 December 1301, Boniface VIII moved from the specific problem of the Bishop of Pamiers to an attack on the crown's abuses of the privileges he had granted it during his pontificate. The pope at that point was determined to assume the role of the sole protector of the Gallican Church. Accordingly, he began a broad offensive to regain its ancient liberties and immunities by a blanket revocation of the privileges granted by himself and his predecessors to the King of France. Presumably he wished to remind the king as forcibly as possible that what he had granted he could take away. His excuse was that great damage had been done to the churches of France and to ecclesiastical persons by the king's misuse of his powers.[1]

With the case of Bernard Saisset before him, and having seen Aycelin's pitiful letter as well as numerous other reports concerning the attacks on clerical privileges by royal baillis, the pope apparently expected to gain the full support of the French clergy in this effort. The bull *Ante Promotionem* was an order to all the prelates of France to attend a council in Rome the following November to discuss means for correcting the multiple abuses of their privileges by the King of France and his baillis.[2] In a later letter of 13 December,[3] the Archbishops of Rheims, Narbonne, and others were convoked personally.

Accompanying these short bulls outlining the initials steps in the papal program was the famous bull *Ausculta Fili*, in which Boniface elaborated his complaints to Philip the Fair. He specified complaints against the activities of the royal baillis in attacking ecclesiastical jurisdiction, encroaching against clerical immunities,

1. *Reg. Bon. VIII*, 4422–23.
2. *Ibid.*, 4426.
3. *Ibid.*, 4438.

and abusing the regalian rights. Therefore, the pope explained, he felt obliged to make full use of the power of the keys vested in him to undertake a full-scale reform of the Church in France with the assistance of the French clergy. The bull therefore was a manifesto in the cause of the liberties of the Gallican church.

The papal nuncio arrived in Paris with the bulls on 11 February 1302. Immediately the royal council began to formulate a program to counteract the papal offensive. Although it is unlikely that the deed was announced by public criers and fanfares of trumpets,[4] *Ausculta Fili* was suppressed. In the excitement of the months that followed, there is abundant evidence that the French public was ignorant of the true text of the bull. All the polemics issued from France in this period, and even the brief descriptions of the quarrel which appear in French chronicles, suggest that the only version of the pope's bull to be released in France was the grossly misleading simplification of the papal arguments called *Deum Time*, which was issued from the royal chancery under the direction of Pierre Flote.[5]

Deum Time appears to have been an outline of *Ausculta Fili*, presenting the ideological content of the bull in a few sentences whose brevity and boldness entirely distorted the statements made by the pope. Omitting all of the pope's specific examples of abuses by the king or his agents, the false bull only retained his claim to judge them by virtue of the power of the keys. Furthermore, as summarized by Flote, this claim was converted into an unprecedented claim of sovereignty in both spirituals and temporals. Where the pope had simply revoked the special privileges which he had formerly granted to the king, *Deum Time* implied that he meant to dispossess all the clergy who had received their benefices by royal approval.

---

4. This story was long accepted, based on an "old manuscript" printed by Dupuy (p. 59). The editor gave no other description of the origin of the notice, and modern historians have been unable to verify its existence. The same story is repeated in the *Chronica Rotomagensis*, 346, and by Bernard Gui, *Rec. Hist.*, XXI, 712. In Rome, Matteo Rosso Orsini made the same charge in consistory, Dupuy, p. 79. On the other hand, Rocquin, "Philippe le Bel et la bulle 'Ausculta Fili,'" cites the failure of the Parisian chroniclers to mention the event and supports Philip's claim that he had not burned *Ausculta Fili* but an outdated bull concerning the privileges of Lâon.

5. Dupuy, *Histoire du différend*, 45.

Until well into the seventeenth century, *Deum Time* was still accepted as a genuine bull by French historians despite the fact that the only copy was to be found in the French archives, lacking all the formal apparatus of the Roman notaries. More recent historians, however, universally regard it as a forgery. Its very baldness has further convinced them that it was a concoction of Flote's chancery which could never have been seriously intended for public circulation. Beyond that, its true purpose is unknown. Noticing that it appears to be a distorted outline of the true bull, Digard suggested that it was intended for presentation as an abstract to the University of Paris.[6] Even more plausibly, as events will show, it may represent the "text" of the bull Flote claimed to be reading at the public meeting in Paris in April.

Whatever specific use was made of *Deum Time,* it represents the case the French planned to prosecute against the pope. Henceforward their entire argument was to be that Boniface had laid claim to absolute sovereignty in temporals—a claim that no law or custom had ever supported.

The next indispensable act for the king was to secure the cooperation of the clergy. Boniface VIII clearly intended to capitalize on whatever fears they might have that the Saisset case would prove a precedent. Nor was the pope mistaken in assuming that the aggressive behavior of the royal agents had created great dissatisfaction in France. However, he vastly underestimated the capacity of Philip the Fair to retrieve his position.

Even assuming that *Ausculta Fili* was suppressed immediately upon its arrival in France, its true contents must have been known to most of the members of the council. It is extremely unlikely that the Archbishop of Narbonne, who knew Flote so well, was not privy to his activities that spring. With the Flemish question beginning to boil up again and the quarrel with the pope reaching a peak, the king's need of Aycelin's assistance was too great to allow him to ignore or patronize the archbishop.[7] The king relied on him for further financial assistance in the forthcoming difficulty

6. *Philippe le Bel,* II, 97–98.
7. Aycelin's position at this time was too crucial to enable the king to treat him according to the formula advanced by Favier: ". . . on respecte l'archevêque de Narbonne, mais on ne suit pas toujours ses avis." "Les légistes," 99.

in Flanders, and in addition, he would play a crucial role in the mobilization of the Gallican clergy against the pope. Accordingly, at this moment—when he must be dissuaded from obeying the pope's summons and persuaded to assist the king—Aycelin procured an ordinance dated 3 May 1302 in favor of the churches of Languedoc,[8] which was lengthened and reissued after the death of Boniface VIII when the king was with Aycelin at Nîmes in February 1304.[9]

These ordinances repeated the privileges of 1300 regarding the protection of church property; the privileges previously confined to the archbishop were extended to all the churches he governed. Ecclesiastical jurisdiction was completely protected from the incursions of royal officials, who were forbidden to function or even to reside in lands under the jurisdiction of the prelate. The customs of Narbonne were reaffirmed in detail and the prelates were restored to their right to maintain their own armed forces. This grant may be construed as the first of the many charters of liberties which would later be won from Philip the Fair and his sons by armed leagues of nobles, prelates and commons.

The extended version of this ordinance, published in 1304, provided the church of Narbonne with the most valuable of all its privileges. The clergy of Narbonne were confirmed in their exemption from the *taille*, and the king promised never to exercise regalian rights over the benefices of the diocese.[10] The importance of this concession cannot be overestimated. In theory, the king's claim to regalian rights was modest and reasonable enough. As part of his duty of guarding the property of churches, he customarily administered their revenues during an episcopal vacancy, in return for which he claimed to enjoy the proceeds as compensation for his efforts.[11] Further, royal courts had developed a practice of basing their claims for the king's general feudal sovereignty over various churches on the existence of this right. Thus, Saint Louis defended his habit of referring cases involving

8. *Ordonnances*, I, 340.
9. *Ibid.*, 402.
10. These privileges were confirmed by a letter of 2 March 1307 to the seneschal of Toulouse, Baudouin, *Lettres inédites*, 22.
11. For a history of the extension of these claims, see Gaudemet, *La Collation*, and the section by the same author in *Histoire des institutions*, III, 243ff.

the regalian rights to the Parlement of Paris rather than to the pope for settlement.

That the agents of the king abused their rights during the periods of vacancies has been amply attested by the records of appeals brought before the royal courts as well as by references in the papal registers. Their activities were graphically described by Guillaume Lemaire, Bishop of Angers, in his complaints to Philip the Fair that royal officers took the precious vessels of the church, stripped the bishopric even of its stores of food, and inflicted permanent damage on the forests, fishponds, and rabbit warrens.[12] It is significant, however, in view of the common charges that Philip the Fair pursued an anticlerical policy, to note that Lemaire, like Aycelin, looked for redress at the king's court rather than through appeal to the pope. And he received it. On receipt of his appeal, Philip instructed the bailli of Tours to correct any injustices and repair any injuries against law and custom that his men had inflicted on ecclesiastics in the province.[13]

But, despite his anxiety to act as a responsible protector of his churches, Philip's grant of exemption from the royal exercise of the regalia to the church of Narbonne was unique. Although in earlier times the Kings of France had frequently been unable to exercise their rights over particular churches, they never surrendered their claims. Philip Augustus had made a few concessions of this sort in sensitive areas, but since his time only Aycelin received such a grant, which suggests the extremes to which Philip the Fair was prepared to go to retain his support. In 1310 Nogaret and Plasians, in their articles against Boniface VIII, tried to affirm the exercise of the regalia as a general right,[14] but as late as 1655 the clergy of Narbonne could state that it had never been exercised over their church.

Thus, in a limited sense, *Ausculta Fili* had achieved its end: the king ceased his abuses and restored his churches to their ancient liberties. But Philip was careful to represent his concessions as arising from his own concern for his people. In the years after the quarrel with the pope was launched, Philip's spokesman

12. Port (ed.), *Le livre de Guillaume Lemaire*, 358.
13. *Ibid.*, 331, repeated p. 341 (1294) and pp. 370–73 (1299).
14. Gaudemet, *La collation*, 40.

frequently stated that in fact the king had long planned to reform conditions in the French Church, and the pope's intervention had no effect but to delay their institution because Philip was unwilling to appear to have acted from subservience to papal command.

The publication of the reform ordinances changed the entire nature of the quarrel. Boniface had intended to act as the defender of the liberties of the Gallican Church. Philip now took this position for his own, and depicted the pope as a man driven only by his unbridled ambition for absolute spiritual and temporal authority. If the French could make this accusation plausible, the clergy would be relieved of much of the pressure to obey the papal summons while their inclination to do so had been weakened by various promised reforms.

As early as 15 February, the king and his council had determined that the best response to the papal offensive was to anticipate his projected synod of November with a great public meeting of representatives of the entire French nation. Accordingly, letters of convocation were sent out to prelates, barons, and townsmen throughout the country.[15]

In response, on 10 April 1302, the French clergy joined representatives of the other two estates of the nation to hear Pierre Flote address them on the subject of the papal bulls. Using the ideas expressed in *Deum Time*, the chancellor stated that Boniface was claiming that the King and kingdom of France were subject to him in temporals as well as spirituals, and that France should recognize this lordship though all the world had formerly believed that the king and his forefathers held their kingdom from God alone. Therefore, the pope's action in calling the prelates and theologians of France to a council in Rome was intended as a first move to convert this claim into reality. It meant that the pope intended to rob France of its most precious treasure and its shield—the wisdom of its clergy.[16]

Speaking in the name of the king, Flote responded to this

15. These letters of convocation were published by Picot, *Documents relatifs aux Etats Généraux*, 1ff., who compares them with those issued by Edward I in calling the Parliament of 1295.

16. The contents of this speech have survived in a report to the pope from the assembled clergy: Dupuy, *Histoire du différend*, 66.

papal "aggression" that the king would no longer allow such ravishing of his proper rights. Neither he nor his predecessors had ever recognized any temporal superior, and in this crisis he appealed to the assembly to help him in the noble resolve he had undertaken to protect the ancient liberties of the realm. Specifically, he needed assistance in carrying out the reforms he had long prepared to correct the exactions of his own agents which had damaged the property of the churches under his protection.

In retailing this speech to Rome, the clergy betrayed no awareness that Flote had in any way distorted the content of the papal bulls. Implying that they accepted his interpretation, they claimed that they attempted to delay a general resolution by the assembly but that the nobility and commons were so incensed by the pope's pretensions that they were forced to pledge their support to the king immediately. Accordingly, they requested the pope to protect them from further difficulties by canceling his letters of convocation. They could not in any case, they added, induce the king to give his permission for the trip. This request was reinforced by the immediate publication of a new royal edict prohibiting the export of monies from the kingdom and expressly forbidding the clergy to travel to Rome, threatening them with the confiscation of all their temporals if they complied with the papal order.

This exchange appears to have been a variation on Aycelin's tactics in the Saisset affair. As interpreted by Flote, King Philip was completely innocent of everything except an honorable desire to protect the liberties of his kingdom. Unhappily, his laudable desire to undertake reforms intended to improve the condition of the Church in his realm was being thwarted by the intervention of a greedy pope. Although it is beyond belief that none of the clergy knew the true contents of *Ausculta Fili*, Flote's presentation was the one they accepted. Their spurious narrative is piteous indeed. Perhaps they hoped the pope would be softened by their picture of themselves, harried by the most extreme threats from both their temporal and spiritual lords. Perhaps they hoped that, persuaded that Philip did indeed act from innocent intentions, the pope would dissipate his energies in a new effort to explain the apparent misunderstanding between himself and the French.

Indeed, that was Boniface's first impulse. He wrote to the University of Paris asking for support, complaining that they and the prelates of France had been grossly deceived by Pierre Flote on 10 April.[17] On 24 June, Matthew of Aquasparta spoke in consistory on the pope's behalf, blaming Flote for a serious and deliberate corruption of the papal letters—whose contents he outlined once more to refresh the cardinals' memories. Reading the letters received from France, he demonstrated that they could not refer to the same bull. Tactfully exonerating the French clergy, he laid the blame for the mispresentation on the king's evil councillors. Nevertheless, he added sarcastically, the complaints against the pope's convocation were hardly justified—the clergy had been summoned only to Rome, not to another universe.[18]

Pope Boniface, as might be expected, was even stronger in his condemnation. He was no longer content to refer to "evil councillors," but at last lifted the mask of Achitophel and displayed to the world the face of Pierre Flote, the man who desired to separate the Church of France and the Pope of Rome.[19] The consistory ended with the composition of letters to be sent by the French cardinals to their colleagues. They asserted that the letters read by Flote were not the ones the pope had sent, in whose composition the entire Curia had collaborated. Thus the chancellor's accusations were no better founded than a house built on sand.[20]

The letters from Rome might conceivably have opened the way to a settlement or to a change of heart on the part of the French clergy, but the atmosphere in France had changed greatly since April. No sooner had the meeting in Paris ended than Flote had departed once more to Flanders. While Boniface VIII was crying out in Rome against the "one-eyed Belial," Flote lay dead on the battlefield at Courtrai.

Interwoven with the events of the Saisset case and the quarrel with Boniface were the events leading up to the great French de-

17. *Chartularium Universitatis Parisiensis*, II, 96.
18. Dupuy, *Histoire du différend*, 75: ". . . et videatur in quo gravatur Rex Franciae, si Praelati sui regni vocantur ad tractandum super aliquibus, non vocantur alieni, non vocantur aemuli, non vocantur contrarii, sed vocantur familiares domestici, qui tantum diligunt honorem Regis et regni sicut pupillam oculi sui, vocantur etiam Romam non ultra fines mundi, non ultra universum, non perpetuo moraturi, sed expedito negotio revertentur."
19. *Ibid.*, 77.
20. *Ibid.*, 63.

feat in Flanders. The widespread social conflicts that harrassed that country had assisted Philip the Fair in his defeat of Guy de Dampierre, but as soon as the king effectively occupied the count's place he became heir to his difficulties. In May 1301 Philip and his queen made a great progress through the county and saw for themselves the evidence of the tensions there. In Gand, the commoners demonstrated their sense of conflict with the patricians by adopting a different form of dress when they appeared for the processions to greet the royal pair. At Bruges, fearing a repetition of the demonstration, the patricians barred the commons from the festivities. The latter retaliated by lining the streets in silence when the king entered,[21] and riots broke out shortly after his departure.

On his return to France in June, Philip began to take steps to reform the administration of the county. In addition, he again dispatched Flote and Aycelin to Flanders on a mission whose purposes have not been recorded. According to Aycelin's letter to Boniface VIII, they were in Flanders in August.[22] By September 5 they had returned and were reimbursed for their expenses from the royal treasury.[23] Probably they undertook preliminary consultations with the constable, Châtillon, on the general state of the country, in preparation for the general board of investigation which Philip opened in September to take up Flemish problems in detail. The most important achievement of this meeting was the promulgation of a new constitution for the city of Gand which broke the power of the local patriciate and confirmed the privileges and customs of the city.[24]

The position of Gand, however, was exceptional. The city had resisted the incursions of the French armies and none of the citizens had formed a French party. Thus, the French could alter its constitution without alienating any allies. But in Bruges, where the situation was even more desperate, the patriciate was still

---

21. Funck-Brentano, *Philippe le Bel*, 357ff.

22. Martène and Durand, *Thesaurus*, I, Col. 1320ff.

23. Digard, *Philippe le Bel*, II, 72, quotes the note from the *Journal du trésor*, which remarks only that they went to Flanders on the king's business.

24. Funck-Brentano, *Philippe le Bel*, 364–70, pointed out that this constitution was so soundly conceived that it remained unaltered for two centuries, being confirmed by Marie of Burgundy in 1476.

firmly allied to the French, inevitably throwing the commons into support of the count's grandson, William of Juliers, who was attempting to recover his family's position.

While the chief persons of the French government were absorbed by the quarrel with the pope, Châtillon faced a growing revolt in Flanders, which erupted into riots and resulted in his expulsion from Bruges. On 10 April, in addition to his attack on the pope, Flote found time to take up the crisis in Flanders, declaring that the pride of the Flemings must be broken and vowing that the king would make every effort to end a quarrel so shameful to France.[25]

By 29 April Flote had joined Châtillon and the French army before Bruges. The citizens held out until 17 May, but then were forced to give entry to the French. The mood of the city was noticeably hostile and suspicious, but this did not shake the self-confidence of the French.[26] It was dealt a severe blow by the events of that night. The people of Bruges, perhaps panicked by rumors which were flying about the city, massacred most of the French troops billeted in the town. Among the few who escaped the "Matins of Bruges" were Flote and Châtillon. As the news spread, so did the rebellion, and a new campaign in Flanders was about to begin.

Furious and humiliated, Flote threw himself into the mobilization of a new army to avenge the dead at Bruges and crush the rebellion. On 11 July 1302 he was in the vanguard of the cavalry drawn up to face the Flemings on the field at Courtrai. Michelet, mesmerized by his own characterization of Flote as a bourgeois lawyer devoted to the destruction of nobility and clergy, decided that there was some mystery regarding his presence on that perilous field.[27] He solved the problem by stating erroneously that Philip the Fair was at Courtrai, and that Flote was with him in order not to be separated from the king at a critical juncture in

25. Boulainvilliers, *Histoire de l'ancien gouvernement de la France,* II, 70.
26. The author of the *Chronique artésienne,* Funck-Brentano, ed., p. 41, stated that the representatives of the city had warned Châtillon privately that there would be trouble if he entered the city, but that "Messire Jacques (Châtillon) and Messire Flote"—trusting the Brugeois more than they should have—ignored the warning.
27. *Histoire de France,* III, 62–63.

the quarrel with Rome. Thus, said Michelet, "chancellor as he was, man of the long robe, he mounted a horse with the men of arms." The historian says at another point that Flote had the honor to be killed "just like a knight."[28] Accepting the same set of premises, Martin[29] suggested that Flote had been sent to Courtrai to preside over the trials expected to follow the victory.

Today no one disputes that Flote was a knight or that he would not behave as did his fellow knights in the face of impending battle. But beyond that, it is clear that Flote spent more time in this type of activity than he did in presiding over trials. Indeed, there is no evidence that he ever presided over a trial in his life, but earlier he had certainly been with the armies in Aquitaine, and in Flanders the month before. His appearance on this field is nevertheless still regarded as a mystery:

> No adequate reason has ever been given for Pierre Flote's presence on the battlefield of Courtrai. Despite the fact that he was a noble and owed military service, he could well have avoided the engagement. At his death, Philip was confronted with the need for a new chancellor and a new "first lawyer of the realm."[30]

However, if he is regarded—as he seems to have regarded himself most of the time—as a knight or a "king's knight," it seems reasonably clear that it would be unusual behavior if he failed to be at Courtrai after his humiliation at Bruges. Indeed the single account of his death that exists, fanciful though it surely is, depicts a very different man from the sober lawyer of modern fancy. According to Geoffroi de Paris,[31] Flote's natural common sense was uppermost at first. When the commander of the cavalry began to chafe against their position behind the foot soldiers, fearing that they would lose the chance of glory, Flote observed that the soldiers seemed to be doing very well and should be left alone. But when the Count of Artois taunted him for this lack of zeal, Flote flung himself ahead of the whole army and actually provoked the fatal cavalry charge—which brought about the death of

28. *Ibid.*, 33.
29. Martin, *Histoire de France*, V, 124.
30. Pegues, *The Lawyers of the Last Capetians*, 46.
31. *Chronique rimée*, 1186.

so many French knights that the Flemings named it the "Battle of the Golden Spurs" for the trophies brought to Courtrai church.[32]

Even if we discount Geoffroi's account as too highly colored, it is certain that Flote was in the battle and died there on the Flemish field. It was said that when the news reached Rome, Pope Boniface called the Flemish ambassador to his chamber in the middle of the night to join in his rejoicing.[33] Everywhere men said that the outspoken pope considered Flote's death an answer to his prayers.

There has been much speculation regarding the effect of Flote's death on French policy in the years that followed. Flote has been credited with a cool head and a steady hand which might have averted the outrage at Anagni and brought the quarrel with the pope to a more satisfactory conclusion. Certainly, Flote may have believed that he could get the pope sufficiently under control to repeat his performance of 1297, but he may also have been wrong in that belief. He was not yet aware of how deeply Boniface had determined to commit himself, as expressed by the letters of 24 June which Flote never saw. It is useless, however, to imagine what he might have done. Courtrai changed too many things. Abruptly, the seemingly unassailable position of the French everywhere was threatened. Whatever Flote's plans before he rode into that battle, they could not have included contingencies based on the pope's newly aggressive stance, the terrible defeat in Flanders, and his own death. But from what we can perceive of his character, Flote was as capable as Nogaret of conceiving the attack at Anagni. Surely Boniface VIII thought so as he sat in Rome, rejoicing that that "one-eyed Belial" had gone to join his true master.

32. All the known accounts of the battle have been examined and compared by Funck-Brentano, "Mémoire sur la bataille de Courtrai."
33. Giles li Muissis, in Funck-Brentano, *ibid.*, 305.

XI

"Deferentes homini plusquam deo"

At least one writer testified that Philip the Fair was often heard to bewail the noble men he had lost in Flanders, accusing the pope of having dealt him that wound.[1] As we have seen, the pope was certainly behaving as though he had done so. Several years later Nogaret charged that he declared a public celebration of the Flemish victory, gloating all the while: "Now the business goes well!"[2] Moreover, Boniface turned the knife in the wound by his unabated pursuit of vengeance against Flote, culminating in the bull *Ad malefactorum vindictam* of 3 November condemning Flote's memory and instructing that his sons be removed from all ecclesiastical offices of every rank.[3] These expressions of a hatred that reached beyond the grave could not fail to have their effect on Flote's friends, among them certainly the archbishop of Narbonne. Moreover, the persecuted sons of his dead companion in so many ventures were probably related to Aycelin in some fashion. For a brief hour he abandoned his customary discretion and stood forth among the pope's opponents.

Formerly, Aycelin had scrupulously avoided any public commitment between his spiritual and temporal lords. Flote had provoked the pope and borne the burden of his anger on their missions together. Even when most severely tested by the Saisset affair, Aycelin had dexterously extricated himself. His prudence was rivaled only by that of Philip himself, and it was this very sense of tact and care which made him so valuable. There were laymen enough to undertake more dubious assignments. The worth of Aycelin was measured by his respectability.

But during 1302–1303, as the differences between Rome and

1. *Chronique attribué à Jean Desnouelles, Rec. Hist. des Gaules et France,* XXI, 195.
2. Dupuy, *Histoire du différend,* 341.
3. *Reg. Bon. VIII,* 4847.

Paris hardened, Aycelin was drawn inexorably with the rest of the French clergy toward a harder commitment. The pope had summoned all of them, and Aycelin specifically, to attend him in Rome by November. Philip the Fair forbade them to leave the country. The pope turned a deaf ear to their pleas to be excused. Philip the Fair took a new interest in the cause of Amaury of Narbonne, who was industriously accompanying Guillaume de Plasians about the Languedoc securing the signatures of the local nobility to the promises of support against the pope formulated in April. Boniface was still refusing to countenance the agreement between the viscount and the archbishop regarding the jurisdiction of Narbonne and demanding the right to arbitrate the conflict himself. In July 1302 the king gave further force to his threat to confiscate the goods of clergymen trying to go to Rome. On the excuse that he did not want the effects of the unsettled dispute between Amaury and Aycelin to inhibit his efforts to raise a new army for Flanders, he took the jurisdiction of the city temporarily into his own hands.[4] Aycelin's ground for maneuver between the two powers was rapidly disappearing.

Neither pope nor king would give way, despite the efforts of Matteo Cardinal Orsini and the Duke of Burgundy to mediate their differences. Boniface refused to cancel the November council without assurances that the king's policies would really change. His initial demand was a formal admission from Philip that he had been misled by evil counsel. In an attempt to temporize, Aycelin and the other prelates asked permission to obey the papal summons and were refused. A select group including Aycelin held a conference at Paris and decided to send a delegation to Rome with their apologies to the pope.[5] In addition, Aycelin decided to hold a meeting of the clergy of Narbonne. On 11 August 1302 he summoned them for a conference at Nîmes on 15 September, stating that that city was close enough to the border to enable the clergy who wished to go to reach Rome in time for the pope's council.[6]

On 22 August he wrote again to his suffragans informing them

---

4. De Vic and Vaissette, *Histoire de Languedoc*, X, 236.
5. Baumhauer, *Philipp der Schöne und Bonifaz VIII*, 86.
6. Ménard, *Histoire civile*, I, 425.

of the king's threat to confiscate their temporals if they left the
country, explaining that the action had been taken because of the
need of the realm to defend itself in the military emergency.[7] No
doubt he repeated those remarks at Nîmes in September. Nevertheless, a few of his suffragans apparently chose to take their
chances and go on to Rome. One of them, Berengar Frédol, went
as an official delegate to convey the apologies of his fellow bishops.
The archbishop and most of his suffragans remained in France,
hoping for the best from a papal reception of their letters of
apology.

The French seemed to be faced with pressing emergencies on
every field. The perils posed by the defeat at Courtrai were
multiplied by a new threat from Gascony. The people of Bordeaux,
seeking to emulate those of Bruges, announced their rejection of
French sovereignty and declared themselves subject to no one but
the King of England. That situation was not improved by the news
that the Archbishop of Bordeaux had succeeded in getting out of
France to attend the pope's council in Rome. Moreover, the
angry pope began discussions with the Aragonese, suggesting
that the Sicilian question might be open to reexamination.

To forestall this move, French Ambassador Denis de Sens
spoke to the King of Aragon in the summer of 1302. He informed
him that the pope was attempting to subject all spirituals and
temporals to himself, implying that Aragon's turn would come if
France failed to defend the rights of kings everywhere. A summit
meeting of the two monarchs was decided upon, and Aragonese
ambassadors were dispatched immediately to Narbonne where
they were to discuss arrangements with the French.[8] By this
means, the Aragonese were kept immobile through the summer
and fall, past the date of the pope's council in Rome. On 27 November they wrote to Paris that, though they had been waiting in
Narbonne for several months, they had never seen the French
ambassadors.[9] The archbishop of that city, who would normally
have been one of the most eligible councillors for that task, was
in the neighborhood during that time and could have conveniently

7. De Vic and Vaissette, *Histoire de Languedoc*, X, 396.
8. *Acta Aragonensia*, I, 83.
9. *Ibid.*, I, 123.

met with them. But he kept out of their way, returning directly to Paris from the meeting of Nîmes.

Negotiations with the English were also continuing throughout the summer. Before Courtrai, on 12 June, a commission had been set up to settle the problems still outstanding in regard to Aquitaine. The difficulties in which they were involved may have served to convince the French that they would at last have to take concrete steps in that direction. The names of the negotiators were not included in the tentative set of agreements reached in September,[10] but Aycelin was in Paris throughout the summer and, since he had played so important a part in previous negotiations on this subject, it seems very doubtful that he would have been excluded from the commission of 1302. Certainly, on 25 November, when he should have been at Rome, he was in Amiens with the Dukes of Burgundy and Brittany and others, negotiating yet another extension of the prevailing truce with England.[11] He continued to play an active role in this affair until its conclusion on 30 May 1303. On that day the Archbishop of Narbonne presided over the formal betrothal of Isabella of France and the future Edward II.[12]

After completing the negotiations of November, Aycelin joined the king as he again took up the question of the Inquisition in Languedoc. By the end of 1302 Philip was himself threatened with excommunication, and may have considered it politic to listen more sympathetically to complaints against the papally controlled court. On Christmas Day he was in Toulouse with the queen, Nogaret, Plasians, Aycelin, and Frédol, who had just returned from the papal council. They heard a delegation headed by Bernard Délicieux complain that the Inquisition was needlessly persecuting the king's faithful and orthodox subjects. But when the rebel ended his peroration with the declaration that there had not been a single heretic in the Albi area for many years, Aycelin and Frédol vociferously denied it. They said there were certainly cases of avowed and proven heresy. Délicieux answered heatedly that no one could trust those false confessions. Saint Peter and

10. Rymer, *Foedera*, II, 901–902.
11. *Ibid.*, 913.
12. *Ibid.*, 928.

Saint Paul would be unable to justify themselves if they had to face an inquisitorial tribunal. The prelates replied that the king himself had already corrected these abuses and replaced the inquisitors against whom Délicieux had formerly complained. "Listen," Délicieux challenged them, "hear these complaints, and you will learn if the king's council, which should be his wisdom, has found the right remedy to cure this sickness!"[13]

Philip heard out these accusations with his customary impassive silence. He probably felt that decisive action would serve no useful end for him at that moment for he ordered none. Later, in 1304, he renewed the limitations formerly imposed on the Inquisition subjecting it to episcopal control—a solution obviously welcome to his friend the archbishop, to whom he made the mild recommendation that prisoners be treated more considerately. He continued, however, to deny that he, the king, had further competence to intervene in matters of church jurisdiction—an excuse that was probably no more impressive to contemporaries than it is to us.

By that time, Aycelin had made his decisions. As an archbishop, he had been efficient and courageous in defending the liberties of his church against the encroachments of the secular powers. But the affair of the Inquisition shows that, while he was always prepared to do the correct legal thing to suppress heresy or control the enemies of the church, he had little understanding of the deep currents of discontent that troubled his diocese under the prosperous facade he built for it. Nor, in the moment when his conscience was tested, did he show any real loyalty to the universal institution of which he was an officer. The conscience of Gilles Aycelin undoubtedly existed, but it was blind to the need for spiritual reform and the call for church unity. When he faced the moment of truth, he responded to the pull of those obligations which meant the most to him—his duties as a councillor of the king of France.

The papal council proceeded without him. In the presense of fewer than half of the prelates he had called, the pope opened the meeting with the condemnation of Pierre Flote. He responded to

13. Hauréau, *Bernard Délicieux*, 89ff.

the testimony of the empty seats with a restatement of the sacred principle of ecclesiastical unity, the bull *Unam Sanctam*. But the absent clergymen were already drawing closer to their king. On 1 December Philip felt strong enough to call a new meeting of the prelates and barons to be held on 9 February 1303. Thus he would be able to face the papal representatives bringing official letters of condemnation with a counterdemonstration of his own strength.[14] The Roman council had commissioned the French cardinal, Jean Lemoine, with a detailed list of the complaints they had formulated against the king of France and an ultimatum that, unless reforms were undertaken immediately, Philip would suffer the most extreme spiritual penalties. In the presence of the assembled barons and prelates, the king answered the charges in detail, and declared his firm intention to defend his kingdom and the French church against the pope himself if necessary.[15] Philip's answers were deceptively modest. His intention was apparently to clear himself of the imputation that he had deliberately precipitated the quarrel. With all the blame for the difficulties of the French Church transferred to the pope, he could direct a shift to a more aggressive policy to be revealed at the public meeting of 12 March.

The old rumors that Boniface was flagrantly immoral, a usurper, and a heretic, gathered new strength in the spring of 1303. The cardinals and councillors who testified in 1309 that Philip the Fair acted against Boniface in good faith are unanimous in their assertion that the pope's lapses constituted a public scandal at that time. The testimony of the Bishop of Bayeux that he had heard the charges from Pierre Flote, among others, suggests that a whispering campaign had been launched at some time before Courtrai, either after the reception of *Ausculta Fili* or even

14. Hervieu, *Recherches sur les premiers Etats Généraux*, 76ff., published the documents convoking this meeting. But, though he could find no supporting evidence, he believed that the meeting was postponed until 12 March. Digard, *Philippe le Bel*, II, 141, took the more probable position that the meeting was held as a formal reception for Cardinal Lemoine. He argued that it would have been such a gathering that would have approved of the king's answers. He further suggested that the demands were presented to this meeting upon which the March 1303 Ordinance of the Reform of the Church was based.

15. Both the papal charges and the king's answers are in Dupuy, *Histoire du différend*, 91–92.

earlier—possibly when Flote returned from his last trip to Rome.[16]

At least one of the favorite French charges cannot have been presented in good faith: that Boniface had high-handedly set aside the condemnation of the books of Arnald of Villanova by the University of Paris because he wished to take advantage of the services of the Aragonese doctor. Imprisoned as a result of the original condemnation in Paris in the summer of 1299, Arnald had appealed to the court of France for protection as a member of the Aragonese embassy. In 1300 Aycelin and Nogaret had procured his release and advised him to go to Rome, promising to support him in an appeal to the pope, which was ultimately successful.[17]

No satisfactory conclusion has ever been reached as to whether the more serious charges against Pope Boniface were either wholly or partially fabricated.[18] It is equally impossible to determine whether or not all the members of Philip's council were entirely privy to the full plan that was being unfolded, particularly regarding Nogaret's mission to Italy. However, it is easy to see that no prelate could hope to continue temporizing by the spring of 1303, and Aycelin in particular had already passed the point of no return. Moreover, the publication of the reform ordinances at that time simplified his problem. The rights and privileges of the Church in France were safeguarded, and the clergy were asked only to choose between a king who was proving himself energetically devoted to their welfare and a pope whose name was blackened by repeated scandals.

As the king's supporters were being bound to him by carefully constructed patterns of pressure and concession, the pope was

16. Höfler, "Rückblick auf P. Bonifacius," 78.

17. Arnald himself described their intervention in his favor in his letter of appeal to Boniface, *Chartularium Universitatis Parisiensis*, II, 88.

18. Individual testimonials describing his misdeeds range from the utterly outlandish to the entirely probable, and are indiscriminately included in the records printed by Dupuy, *Histoire du différend*, 346ff. The question had been tirelessly debated without any satisfactory result ever since. Most recently the putative heresies of the pope have been argued by Sommer, *Die Anklage der Idolatrie*, Scholz, "Zür Beurteilung Bonifaz VIII," Wenck, "War Bonifaz VIII ein Ketzer?" and Holtzmann, "War Bonifaz VIII ein Ketzer?" The debate between Wenck and Holtzmann, in particular, serves only to expose the impossibility of a decision at this late date.

again becoming the victim of his disastrous inability to judge his own men. In sending the French cardinal, Jean Lemoine, as his representative, he had made a choice comparable to his incredible designation of Simon de Beaulieu in 1296. Lemoine was one of the Celestinian cardinals who had long been known as a firm supporter of Philip the Fair. Boniface knew this, and apparently believed that such a choice would be a conciliatory move. He seems to have been totally unaware of how impossible conciliation had become, just as he was unaware that Lemoine had long nursed a grudge against him because he had once been the victim of Boniface's uncontrollable temper.[19]

Lemoine was supposed to present the papal letters to the king and then make contact with the French prelates who had failed to appear at Rome, probably to discover whether they had been prevented from coming by fear of the king and to test their willingness to cooperate in reaching a settlement between king and pope. Guillaume de Nangis[20] believed that he went so far as to call a secret meeting of prelates in Paris during Lent, at which time he obtained their promise to support the pope. This, on the face of things, is a most unlikely story. The men who feared to go to Rome would hardly have undertaken a defiance of Philip in his own kingdom.

It is probable, however, that a secret meeting—with the king's knowledge—did occur. He may even have been present while plans were formulated for further resistance to the pope. Lemoine was unquestionably plotting against his spiritual master during his sojourn in Paris. He was named specifically by several of the witnesses of 1309, who charged him with accusing Boniface of heresy in the king's presence—testimony which he personally corroborated.[21]

---

19. Lajard, "Jean Lemoine," *Histoire Littéraire*, XXVII, 201–204.
20. *Chronique latine*, 325.
21. Höfler, "Rückblick auf P. Bonifacius," 53. Lemoine gave no details but said that he had told the king that Boniface was a heretic. Frédol (*Ibid.*, 76) said that he was told by the king or by someone in his council that Lemoine made the accusation in the secret council. Napoleone Orsini (*Ibid.*, 51) said that Lemoine repeated the story to him, adding that he requested the king to take action against the pope, after his return to Italy.

Any doubts that Aycelin and his fellow prelates may have nourished about the propriety of their position would have been dispelled by the accusations of Cardinal Lemoine at this meeting of the secret council. Hugh Aycelin had been dead for several years, but his brother must have remembered the charges he had put in writing during the earlier crisis of 1296–1297. In any case, he cannot be exculpated from whatever guilt attaches to those who actively participated in the plans that were laid against the pope.

To a man, Philip the Fair's councillors kept faith with their master. The discussions that occurred during this time in council were never disclosed. It can never be known now to what extent any of the councillors believed the charges they formulated or whether or not they knew what was to occur when the quarrel had reached its peak. In justice, it must even be acknowledged that Nogaret himself may not have been completely certain about what he was going to do in Italy. But Aycelin was certainly a willing party to the attack which was being launched against the pope in France.

The charges against Boniface VIII were made public in a meeting of selected nobles and prelates on 12 March 1303. No one was present but dignitaries whom the king could trust completely. Only five prelates attended, and one of them was Gilles Aycelin.[22] The high point of the meeting was a speech by Nogaret, unveiling for the first time in public the full indictment against Boniface and inaugurating the idea of an appeal for a general council, one destined to have so long and exciting a history in the following century. Nogaret indulged in lengthy invective against the evil character of Boniface and charged that he had illegally usurped his office from the true pope, Celestine V. On the question of specific heresy charges, Nogaret was vague, simply claiming that he was a simoniac and guilty of criminal and heretical enormities that he had repeated in many times and places. The king, as defender of the faith, was requested to proclaim the text of the speech in a public instrument calling the pope to account for his crimes. After a show of hesitation and reluctance, Philip granted

22. Dupuy, *Histoire du différend,* 62ff.

the request and the Archbishops of Sens and Narbonne appended their seals at the head of the list of official witnesses.

The papal response was a new attempt to discipline the clergy of France. Although he made a relatively conciliatory reply to the king's official answer to his list of charges,[23] Boniface launched the full force of his anger against the rebellious prelates.[24] Recalling his convocation of the November synod, he praised those who had come in defiance of the king's prohibition. But those who had failed to present themselves, "tamquam inobedientie filii et rebelles, deferentes homini plusquam deo," were to come to Rome within three months to answer charges of disobedience and clear themselves with the pope under threat of deposition and deprivation of all ecclesiastical dignities and status. This command was laid specifically on the Archbishops of Sens and Narbonne, suggesting that the pope had already heard of their participation in the meeting of 12 March. He excluded by name a list of bishops whose fidelity he claimed to trust and whose excuses of age and illness he accepted as valid. The bull ended with a final rebuke to those prelates who had shown themselves so ungrateful for all the benefits bestowed on them by the Apostolic See.[25]

These letters were never officially received. The king ordered the arrest of the papal messengers before they arrived at their destinations and had the letters confiscated. To this Philip added the precaution of renewing his edict against the departure of the clergy from France,[26] though he made no move to stop Jean Lemoine, who quietly returned to Rome[27] to avoid being caught in the approaching storm. Simultaneously, Nogaret began his own ambiguous and mysterious movements in Italy.[28]

23. *Reg. Bon. VIII*, 5344.
24. *Ibid.*, 5341, 13 April 1303.
25. *Ibid.*, 5343, "Ipsi namque, qui ab Apostolica Sede tot receperunt beneficia et honores, urenti ingratitudinis vento pleni, sunt eo acrius de inobedientia puniendi, quo erant amplius ipsi Sedi ad exhibitionem obedientie ac reverentie debitores."
26. Dupuy, *Histoire du différend*, 99.
27. One anonymous chronicler, *Rec. Hist. des Gaules et France*, XXI, 640, claimed that he made his departure secretly and at night to avoid the king's guards.
28. Holtzmann, *Wilhelm von Nogaret*, 45.

It is not impossible that Philip deceived his councillor and kept from Aycelin all knowledge of the pope's final offer of a chance to repair his situation. But the archbishop's active involvement in the later development of the French offensive suggests that he knew his bridges were burned forever. Philip had certainly never had any cause to doubt the loyalty of Aycelin in any matter involving the pope. It is therefore more likely that he informed Aycelin privately of the contents of the letters. The archbishop could easily have calculated that there was very little likelihood that he could be effectively deprived of his position as long as he had the king's protection. More important, it would be unfair to assume, in the absence of evidence to the contrary, that Aycelin did not sincerely believe the king to be in the right or approve the policies that had brought him to this impasse.

But the pope's power could not be wholly disregarded. No one in France could have desired a schism with Rome. The French policy of trying to discredit and depose Boniface VIII without challenging the power and prestige of his office was the only possible method by which Aycelin could hope to get clear of the condemnation issued against him in April. This consideration must have gained weight when reinforced by the suspicions raised in the past by Beaulieu and Hugh Aycelin. Nor can we forget the grief Aycelin must have felt for Pierre Flote and his indignation over the pope's condemnation of his dead friend and his sons.

In any case, the Archbishop of Narbonne made no reply to the pope's new citations. In June, as spokesman for the French clergy, he stood forth boldly against Boniface at the great public meeting held at the Louvre. On 14 June Nogaret's deputy, Guillaume de Plasians, read a list of thirty specific charges against Boniface that included every scurrilous accusation that rumor, exaggeration, or sheer invention had circulated over the years, some of which may have been collected in earlier times by the defunct Flote.[29]

29. Dupuy, 100ff. Among the charges that sound as though they had been garnered as the fruit of Flote's personal arguments with the irascible pope when he and Aycelin were at the Curia are No. 2, that he did not believe in the immortality of the soul because he stated that he would rather be a dog or an ass than a Frenchman—proving that he did not believe that the French had immortal souls; and No. 7, that he swore that he would bring himself, the whole world,

Plasians ended with a new appeal to the king to take action. When he had finished, Philip with great propriety expressed his long-standing unwillingness to believe such charges against a reigning pontiff and to create a scandal in the Church. He then modestly asked the assembled clergy for their advice. As their designated spokesman, the Archbishop of Narbonne stepped forward with a different list of charges.[30]

All ten of these charges were included usually with more lurid details, in Plasians' indictment. Aycelin, however, introduced some interesting innovations. The charges for which he gave concrete details (numbers 6 and 7) are those which he might have received first-hand from his brother Hugh. Later testimony related that Boniface made his remark about the mortality of the soul to the cardinals who had gone to condole with him on the occasion of his nephew's death in 1296. Hugh Aycelin was probably one of these. Likewise, the story of the Spanish bishop sounds like one garnered directly from curial gossip.

Aycelin's charge, if it can be seriously called a charge, that Boniface granted tenths to Edward of England to support his war against France is more reasonable than Plasians' corresponding charge that the tenths were granted to England *on condition* that Edward make war on France. On the other hand, Aycelin's final charge that Boniface bribed the Saracens is far more outrageous than Plasians' allegation that he prevented the recovery of the Holy Land by keeping the crusade money for his own purposes. Plasians' version, however, was open to the countercharge that the King of France had done the same thing. In general, too, the lack of detail

---

and the Church itself down in ruins if it would help him to destroy the French and humble their pride.

30. Baillet, *Histoire des démeslez, preuves,* 29–30. Aycelin's list was reduced from Plasians' thirty to ten charges: (1) that Boniface was a simoniac; (2) that he was known to have said it was impossible for a pope to commit simony; (3) that he was a homicide; (4) that he was a manifest usurer; (5) that he did not hold orthordox views on the question of the Eucharist; (6) that he said the soul was mortal and there is no other joy than in the present life; (7) that he revealed confessions:". . . nam coegit quemdam Cardinalium ut confessionem a quodam Hispaniae presbytero sibi factam revalet, qua cognita episcopum loco movit sed post pecunia placatus Papa eumdem restituit"; (8) that he had known his two nieces carnally and had sons by both of them— "O foecundum patreml"; (9) that he conceded all the tenths on ecclesiastical goods to the King of England to subsidize him in the war against France; (10) that he offered bribes to the Saracens to invade Sicily.

provided by Aycelin is far more effective than Plasians' highly descriptive charges, since the latter included so much that even the most gullible listener could hardly have accepted. It would appear that Aycelin's list, rather than that of Plasians, was the official indictment circulated after the assembly, since the only chronicler who went into detail about the charges listed those made by the archbishop almost verbatim.[31]

Aycelin concluded by saying that since the Apostolic See was vacant, the charges must be left to the judgment of a council and a future pope and urged the clergy to appeal for such a council. Under his direction, the prelates then withdrew for private consultation. On their return, they issued a formal statement calling for the general council. With a dispassionate show of impartiality they included a statement that, beyond recognizing that the charges must be answered, they did not intend to take sides in the matter and trusted that Pope Boniface would be vindicated. Moreover, though he might punish them to the full extent of his papal power, they would hold to their resolve to pursue the matter and leave their own vindication to the council and a future pope.[32] This proviso not only served to give them some protection from the results of their rebellion but presumably could also be made to cover the excommunication and deposition threatening most of them for their failure to go to Rome.

After the June meeting, France began to mobilize for the last stage of the struggle with Boniface VIII. From this point, however, it was a matter for the laity. Nothing further was asked from the clergy, and Aycelin turned his attention to the relatively innocuous task of raising new armies and subsidies for the Flemish war. His name does not appear again in connection with the affair of Boniface VIII; he might have been the prelate assisting in the king's council who detained Pierre de Paredo as he was leaving to meet Nogaret in Italy, saying that it would be a good work to rid the world of so dangerous an evildoer and heretic as Boniface VIII.[33]

31. Johannes Victorienses [or Victring] Chronicle, 346.
32. Dupuy, Histoire du différend, 66.
33. Höfler, Paredo's testimony (p. 73): "Et dum praedicta mihi injungerentur

The summer and fall of 1303 were a period of tension and difficulty for anyone with any involvement in the great affair. It must have been particularly trying for Aycelin to support a position of such sharp commitment, so foreign to his customary prudence. Of all the major prelates of France, he was then the one most deeply bound to the proposition that Boniface was guilty. Nogaret's bullying at Anagni, the slapping of the pope by Sciarra Colonna, the resultant uprising by the outraged citizenry against Nogaret's troops, and Boniface's death only a month later brought both Philip and Aycelin to the realization that reputation and good character were staked on the chance of proving that the attack on the pope was justifiable.

But in the aftermath of Anagni, Aycelin was silent. Unlike many of his fellow councillors and prelates, he was never inclined to pursue the matter once Boniface himself had vanished from the scene. Through the years when Nogaret was straining every nerve to clear his king and justify himself, Aycelin said nothing. Although he unquestionably had evidence to submit, he made no appearance at the hearings of 1309 on the question of Philip's good faith. Prominence of that sort, public testimony of any kind, was foreign to all that we can discern of his character.

Perhaps Anagni horrified him; perhaps he did not know—or hid from himself—the significance of Nogaret's preparations in Italy. Perhaps he knew entirely too much to be willing to perjure himself in testimony. He never disavowed the charges he made in June 1303, but he never defended them either. From 1309 to 1311 he took over the seals in trust from Nogaret when that gentleman was occupied in pressing the charges against the deceased Boni-

---

unus magnus praelatus de assistentibus in consilio Regis dixit mihi ista verba: Prior de Cesa [Paredo], tu scis quam malus homo est ille Bonifacius et quod est haereticus et quod multa mala fecit et multa scandala suscitavit et adhuc pejora si vixerit; dico tibi quod in conscientia mea, quod tu bonum opus facies si interficias eum et interficias eum, scave in periculum animae meae; et tunc dictus Dominus Rex ad haec verba respondit ore proprio; Non faciet si Deo placuerit, quia adhuc posset esse idem prior Episcopus vel Papa. Sed eatis Prior et faciatis prout est vobis injunctum et prout injungent vobis isti duo Praelati de consilio meo, quos scitis, qui sunt fideles homines et bene litterati et constantes. Que Praelati mihi injunxerunt, ut erat injunctum mihi in praesentia Domini Regis et nihil amplius."

face at Avignon. But, lest this imply approval, it must be noted that on 9 July 1309, at the beginning of his term as guardian of the seals, he established a memorial mass in the Cathedral of Narbonne for himself and for the soul of Boniface VIII.[34]

34. Delisle, "Gilles Aicelin," 494.

XII

Recovery and Reform

The years from 1302 to 1304 marked a turning point in the reign of Philip the Fair. With the defeat in Flanders so profoundly intertwined with the pope's mounting offensive, the king demanded much and received much from his subjects. But he did not repeat the aggressive tactics of his youth when the passage of the *maltôte* had driven people of every class into open defiance. The great public meeting of 10 April 1303 set the tone for the royal program in the years that followed, coupling his request for increased monies and moral support with a broad program of domestic reform.[1] In return for their abandonment of the pope, for example, the clergy was tactfully promised reforms of royal abuses and guarantees of their liberties. Aycelin's charter for Narbonne was but one of the concessions offered the clergy at this time.

Aycelin and the other councillors distinguished themselves during this time of trouble by their inventiveness and loyalty. The Archbishop of Narbonne not only undertook the extensive diplomatic tasks necessary to prevent the formation of new foreign coalitions in the French moment of distress, but also busied himself in the solution of the domestic crisis. As we have seen, in 1303 he assisted in the mobilization of the French clergy against Boniface VIII. At the same time he was instrumental in the effort to secure new financial subsidies for the Flemish campaigns. As the Aragonese ambassador attested in 1304, his preeminent place in the councils of the king was never more secure.[2]

Our examination of the quarrel between Aycelin and the Vis-

1. Strayer, *Studies in Early French Taxation*, 34, demonstrated at some length the connection between the Grand Ordinance of 1303 and Philip's request for further subsidies.

2. Reporting to James II that he expected a successful outcome for a certain marriage proposal, the ambassador stated that his suggestions had received a friendly reception from the Archbishop of Narbonne, "the principal councillor of the King of France." *Acta Aragonensia*, III, 116.

count of Narbonne has illustrated some of the concrete details of Philip the Fair's relationship with the magnates of the kingdom. In this case at least, it is clear that he did not make use of courts or lawyers to pursue an "anti-feudal" policy. At most, the treatment of the case in the Parlement of Paris might be construed as an effort to perfect the feudal hierarchy by strengthening the king's own position at its peak—a policy confirmed by Philip's famous pronouncement that it was contrary to custom for the king of France to do homage to his subjects.[3] It was the policy of Philip the Fair, insofar as he ever expressed policy statements publicly, to act toward his subjects as a good lord should, representing their rights and the customs of the land as sacred to him. This was the stated goal of his great organizational reforms, particularly of the Grand Ordinance of 1303.[4]

Strayer has recently shown Philip as a monarch devoted to the traditional ideals of the French monarchy.[5] Previously, only a few historians attempted to view him in this light. Ducoudray described him as a product of a feudal age,[6] and Lévis-Mirepoix[7] contributed the important point that the initiative which resulted in the loss of seigneurial jurisdiction was frequently taken by the lords themselves in their constant need to relieve their financial needs. Or they found that the complexity of government in this period presented too formidable a task for them to undertake independently. Again, as we have seen in the case of Amaury of Narbonne, they might prefer direct homage to the king of subjection to a more immediate lord. To great noblemen like the Duke of Burgundy, the royal court offered a greater scope of activity than the government of their own lands. Forces were clearly

3. The rule is expressed in the Grand Ordinance of 1303 and repeated in an arrest of the Parlement of 22 October 1314, *Les Olim*, II, 616. For further discussion of this point, see Lot and Fawtier, *Histoire des institutions*, II, 21.

4. Ordonnances, I, 354ff.

5. Strayer, "Philip the Fair—a 'Constitutional' king," in *Medieval Statecraft*, 195ff.

6. Ducoudray, *Les origines du Parlement de Paris*, 61: "Philip was a true baron of the middle ages who did not dream of breaking the church, though he insulted the pope, or destroying feudalism, whose prejudices and customs he shared. He only sought to make his authority felt and to collect money. Supple and despotic, he was a prince who adjusted himself to changing circumstances which he had neither the will nor the force to break."

7. *Philippe le Bel*, 31.

in operation to bring the magnates of France into a nearer relationship with their sovereign without any serious display of aggression on his part.

To be sure, Philip the Fair was frequently aggressive in the extension of what he believed or declared to be his legitimate rights,
as events in Aquitaine, Flanders, and even Bigorre amply demonstrate. Far more commonly, however, he did not attempt to interfere with the independent jurisdiction of his subjects but used his
authority more modestly to bind their interests to his own, as exemplified by his delays and counterpressures in the case of Narbonne. The French nobility made increasing concessions to the
authority of the crown in these years but, by and large, they did so
because it was advantageous to themselves.

Philip the Fair was not a tyrant. Like all competent rulers, he
was an opportunist. But he was careful, particularly in his later
years, to keep public opinion on his side. When he struck ruthlessly, as he did at the Lombards, the Jews, and the Templars, he
chose victims whose fate was of little concern to most Frenchmen.
Even then, he was willing to make practical concessions. When
the Archbishop and the Viscount of Narbonne made a joint protest against his attempt to confiscate the property of the Jews of
Narbonne, claiming it as their right, he recognized their claims
and yielded. Discussing the record of Aycelin's protest in the
Parlement of Paris in this case,[8] Pegues argued that he was motivated only by a conservative regard for correct legal form[9] but,
as we have seen the case develop, he was actively opposing the
king in order to protect his own interests. Once he and Amaury
had demonstrated that the two *juiveries* in the city were not in
the bourg,[10] where the king's agreements with the consuls gave
him some rights, the two lords were able to secure the property
for themselves.

Not only did Philip recognize the right of his subjects to exercise their local jurisdiction independently but, at least in the second half of the reign, he showed an increasing willingness to con-

8. *Les Olim*, II, 507.
9. *The Lawyers of the Last Capetians*, 125.
10. Boutaric, *Actes du Parlement of Paris*, n.3419e.

sult with them on matters that concerned the realm as a whole. In 1302 and 1303, on the great question of the rupture with Boniface VIII, and again in 1308, on the subject of the condemnation of the Templars, Philip held great consultative assemblies to which barons, prelates, and representatives from the towns were invited. The tradition has long persisted that these meetings represent the first appearance of the Estates General in France. Though this view has recently been challenged,[11] it has never been denied that they represent a genuine attempt to consult directly with representatives of public opinion in France and to gain popular support for the king's policies.

The crucial test of the representative idea is in the area of taxation, where Philip the Fair's contemporary, Edward I, achieved such successes with his parliaments. Conditions in France were vastly different from those in England, but it can easily be shown that Philip also acted increasingly on the representative principle in his requests for fresh subsidies from his subjects. In 1302, when he was desperately in need of fresh methods of raising subsidies without provoking resistance, he convoked the *arrière-ban* for the first time.[12]

This version of a general property tax levied in terms of specific military needs was more acceptable than the *maltôte*. Nevertheless, its collection—especially after Courtrai—demonstrated a care for public opinion that Philip had not shown in earlier years. The levy of February 1303 was passed only after consultation with numerous prelates, barons, and members of the royal council. The instructions to the collectors warn them to proceed with caution, calling the leading men of each town together and explaining to them the purposes of the ordinance. They were to demonstrate how merciful the proposition was to the poor and be "courteous" to those who could afford to pay. Royal officials were to speak sweetly, condemning the Flemings and explaining the expenses involved in a new expedition against them. Moreover, they were

---

11. Lot and Fawtier, *Histoire des institutions,* II, 553, question whether these assemblies can be called Estates Generals on the grounds that they deal with the question of relations with the pope and do not involve discussion of monetary matters.

12. *Ordonnances,* I, 345.

to take no action against anyone who resisted without specific instructions from the king.[13]

A second requisition was formulated in October 1303. At that time even greater care was taken to give at least an impression of popular consent. A select group of trusted prelates and barons was gathered at Chateau-Thierry to study the proposal, and the king promised to undertake separate negotiations with representatives of the Third Estate after their meeting. The resultant call for the *arrière-ban* purports to have been drawn up "with the consent of the prelates and barons of the realm."[14] However, the appended letter to the Bishop of Paris, demonstrates how limited this council was in fact:

> Because we could not have our other prelates and barons of the realm at this deliberation, so quickly was it necessary to act, this was done with the deliberation and council of our friends, the Archbishop of Narbonne, the Bishop of Auxerre, the Bishop of Meaux, the King's brothers and several noblemen who customarily attend the council.[15]

Even with so limited and friendly a representative body, Philip had apparently felt the need to promise reforms in exchange for the desired subsidy. The call to arms was coordinated with a plan to reform royal monies. This was a reversal of the long policy of debasement which so angered the Count of Flanders and caused Bernard Saisset to call the King of France a counterfeiter.

Personally, Aycelin was well rewarded for his cooperation at this meeting and for his future assistance in collecting subsidies from the clergy. At that time he received an important concession of privileges for his own churches. In 1304 he was given charge of the collection of a new *decima* from the clergy designed to relieve the king of the burden occasioned by the monetary reform,[16] an assignment which was repeated in 1307.[17]

13. *Ibid.*, 369–71.
14. *Ibid.*, 408.
15. *Ibid.*, 383.
16. D'Achéry, *Spicilegium sive Collectio Veterum Aliquot Scriptorum*, III, 703. Although Clement V was persuaded to revoke *Clericis Laicos* in 1306, Philip never taxed the clergy again without seeking papal approval and assistance in the collection of the subsidies. This method proved far more effective and efficient than his earlier reliance on the cooperation of provincial councils.
17. *Ibid.*

By 1304 the French had almost entirely recovered from the setbacks of 1302. The successes of Charles of Valois in Italy, combined with the diplomatic efforts of Boniface VIII, had resulted in a relatively permanent peace in Sicily in 1302. The alliance of Vaucouleurs, added to the Burgundian marriage of Philip's heir, created a stable position in the east. The question of Aquitaine had been temporarily settled by the betrothals of 1303. On 18 August 1304 the French achieved a crushing victory over the Flemings at Mons-en-Puelle, and Aycelin was instrumental in forging the Treaty of Athis—the "Treaty of Iniquity" as it became known in Flanders in the years that followed.

Ten years after the conclusion of the treaty, Robert of Bethune blamed Aycelin personally for all the difficulties that resulted from the inability or unwillingness of the Flemings to respect its terms. He claimed that when he surrendered at Lille in 1304, the French had agreed that they would confine their choice of negotiators to "knights, resolved to negotiate in a loyal manner, eschewing all ruses, machinations, cavillations, and subtleties and, to this end, we closed the deliberations to all clerks and men of law. But the French joined to their delegates the Archbishop of Narbonne and the Bishop of Auxerre, masters of law, and other astute men of the king's council who circumvented and fooled the Flemish negotiators, who were simple and upright men."[18]

Indeed, the Treaty of Athis gave the French all the revenge they could have wanted for the Matins of Bruges and the loss of Pierre Flote. The Flemings were forced to agree to an enormous idemnity in addition to pledging their future military service to France. Three thousand burghers of Bruges, personally chosen by the king, were to make an expiatory pilgrimage—a thousand of them to go overseas. The fortresses of Bruges and other strongholds were to be demolished. Only when all this had been accomplished would the king be willing to free Count Guy and his sons and restore the rebels to their estates. Ten years later Count Robert claimed that the tricky French lawyers so twisted and turned the question of sureties that they were able to detain the old count in prison until he died, and to bind the new count

18. Limburg-Stirum, *Codex Diplomaticus*, II, 267.

with excommunication because the Flemings could not fulfill the terms of this atrocious treaty.

After 1304 Aycelin spent very little time on diplomatic activity, but he continued to press the fulfillment of the Treaty of Athis to the end. On 7 June 1307 he extorted its confirmation from Clement V at Poitiers, with a rider that the Flemings would be excommunicated automatically if they failed to meet its provisions (the excommunication that later fell on Count Robert).[19] In 1309 he was with the king in Paris to witness the further humiliation of the Brugeois, who were forced to go into France to renew their oaths to observe the treaty.[20] In 1313 he accompanied Enguerrand de Marigny on a military expedition into Flanders to force a new confirmation of the treaty.[21]

Negotiations with England also dragged on through the years though they did not build to any new crisis. In January 1308 the marriage arranged by Aycelin between Edward II and Isabella was finally celebrated and a new series of discussions on the question of Aquitaine was begun with the pope at Poitiers. The English claimed that settlement was never reached because the French refused to make any concession in recognition of Edward II's claim to the duchy. (Despite the provisions of Montreuil, which secured the duchy to the eldest son of Edward's French wife, Edward—just before his death in 1307—had invested the Prince of Wales with the duchy). In 1311 the English claimed that the French had made a previous agreement with Edward I at Boulogne to submit the entire question of the jurisdiction of Aquitaine to a joint commission of English and French negotiators. But in 1311, when a new delegation of English recalled this agreement, "the Archbishop of Narbonne and others of the council who were present at Boulogne, testified in the presence of the king, where we were, that nothing was said at Boulogne about this joint inquiry except for things done during the war and the truce. And it seemed to them that nothing should be done jointly with the King of France concerning things pertaining to him

19. Funck-Brentano, *Philippe le Bel*, 554.
20. *Ibid.*, 570.
21. *Ibid.*, 634.

and his jurisdiction as between equals."[22] This incident hints at a history which has largely been lost, of fruitless negotiations during which the Archbishop doggedly pursued the line of conduct he had laid out in the note he appended to the Treaty of Montreuil in 1299, denying Edward I's claim to the lordship of Aquitaine.

Aycelin's final diplomatic service to Philip the Fair was the completion of a treaty with Henry of Luxembourg, 20 July 1311, at which the Emperor ceded the rights over the disputed city of Lyon to France.[23]

Like the king, the archbishop's attention and energies were increasingly withdrawn from problems of foreign policy, partially because the successes he had achieved lasted out his lifetime and partially because of the growing recognition of the need for administrative reforms at home. The focus of interest was on the judicial rather than the legislative powers of the king. In France, royal power to legislate was generally still considered an extraordinary one, and it was never exercised by Philip without the advice and consent of a council which included a number of the magnates without whose cooperation no enforcement could be expected.[24] Most commonly, the ordinances took the form of charters redacting local customs—a practice which operated to transform them into royal laws.[25]

Aycelin's activities in the provinces of Narbonne and later in Rouen, important as they were in giving practical application to the policies of the crown at the local level, were by their nature essentially narrow and limited in scope. Their importance is heightened, however, by the fact that Aycelin was also an active participant in the royal government at its highest levels, sitting with the royal council and assisting in the formulation of broad policies which were to be applied in the lands under his jurisdiction. This coincidence of interest in the central and local gov-

22. Chaplais, "Règlement des conflits internationaux franco-anglais au XIV° siècle," 298–302, letter of the Bishop of Norwich to Edward II.

23. Leroux, *Recherches critiques sur les relations politiques de la France avec l'Allemagne, 1292–1378,* 137ff.

24. Lot and Fawtier, *Histoire des institutions,* II, 292.

25. *Ibid.,* 294.

ernments goes far to explain the lack of friction between the king and his magnates in this crucial period of centralization.

For the twelve years preceding 1302, whenever he had not been absent from court on the king's service or attending to the affairs of his church of Narbonne, Aycelin had been participating in the meetings of the Parlement of Paris, adding practical experience to his early training in the law. There can be little doubt that he was one of the king's major advisors in the formulation of the great reform edicts of 1302–1303, especially the Grand Ordinance of 23 March 1303, which outlined the program of administrational reorganization and reform which would be pursued in the years that followed.[26]

As was customary with the French monarchy, Philip did not incorporate any new laws into the Grand Ordinance but presented the document as a statement of the traditional rights of barons and prelates which were to be fully restored as they existed in the days of Saint Louis. A separate set of ordinances for the bourgeoisie was appended. Guarantees were provided for the observance of these customs in the extensive controls on the activity of local royal officers, who were placed under the jurisdiction of the royal council. The council itself was generally to be composed of the princes of the blood, the great nobles, and the great prelates of the realm, many of whom, like Aycelin, had won their positions because of their legal expertise, but who nevertheless took seriously their duties as protectors of their churches and the feudal rights that pertained to them.

As Lot and Fawtier have pointed out,[27] the Grand Ordinance is an important document in the history of France because it is the first time a king of France undertook a general reform of his government by ordinance. It was not, however, intended as a change in the machinery of government itself. Rather, Philip's intent was, with the help of his councillors and the customs in force under Saint Louis as guides, to perfect the government already in existence by instituting greater controls over the agents assigned to carry out the law. This over-all renovation of the government was complemented by the series of local charters issued in the same

26. *Ordonnances*, I, 354ff.
27. *Histoire des institutions*, II, 554–55.

years and even, we might suggest, by those issued as a result of the pressures of the leagues of 1314–1315.

To provide a mechanism for the enforcement of his reforms, the Grand Ordinance provided the first step in the reorganization of the royal system of justice. It was the judicial rather than the legislative role of the monarch which provided the main source of his power. The chief aim of the king was the extension of his right to receive appeals over the entire kingdom—an aim that was already near fulfillment by the end of the thirteenth century. By that time only three barons still retained the right of high justice,[28] and the appellate jurisdiction of the Parlement of Paris as a court of peers had been recognized even by the Count of Flanders in his various appeals to its authority. Here, if anywhere, the historian must seek the traces of the influence of the lawyers in the government.

The royal court, called the Parlement of Paris since the minority of Saint Louis, was only gradually distinguished from the meetings of the royal council in extrajudicial matters. By 1282 it had become customary to convene the Parlement for judicial hearings twice a year. The official registration of its judgments had been fairly continuous since 1254.[29] From this date onward there was a steady but inconsistent trend to settle the royal court at Paris and to separate it to some extent from the king's person. By the beginning of the reign of Philip the Fair, according to Langlois, the Parlement was on the verge of becoming a fully autonomous unit. Far from following the traditional idea of recognizing the Grand Ordinance as its charter of foundation, Langlois criticized Philip for failing to undertake the final steps in its development.[30]

The first known constitution of the court is an ordinance of Philip III, in 1278, containing general recommendations for the conduct and procedure of its meetings. Recognizing the new needs resulting from the reversion of the south to the crown, he recommended that special judges be appointed to hear cases of

28. Ordinance on the local courts of 1298, Langlois, *Textes*, 95, no. lxxii.
29. The history of the Parlement of Paris before Philip the Fair is outlined by Langlois, *Revue Historique*, XLII, 90ff.
30. *Ibid.*, 102.

"written law." This was not, however, the thin edge of the wedge which would open the way for the relatively absolutist legal system of Roman law. Philip III specifically disapproved its use in cases involving men from the lands of customary law—a policy which was strengthened by his son's charters. Specific instructions concerning the personnel of the court and the ground rules for its hearings were reserved for Philip the Fair in his ordinance of 1291.[31]

Even though Article 62 of the Grand Ordinance did not represent the establishment of the Parlement, it was still important for the creation of a set of rules to govern the operation of the royal court. It appeared to be intended to protect an older system of separate judicial hierarchies,[32] since it was supported by provisions protecting the local jurisdiction of barons and prelates so long as they executed royal laws. All subjects were thus seemingly guaranteed trial in their own land by their own law. In addition, restrictions were placed on the behavior of royal advocates and judges, setting their salary scale and placing controls on them designed to prevent bribery.

By this recognition of the authority of provincial courts of appeal already in existence, the Grand Ordinance seemed to place the royal seal on a separatist system of justice. The Exchequer of Rouen—maintained after the French conquest of Normandy as an independent body to receive appeals from baronial and royal bailli sentences alike—with its sister courts was highly prized by provincial subjects. Their insistence on including guarantees for these courts in their various charters of liberty suggests that they saw them as a defense against the development of a monolithic form of royal justice. Repeatedly, Philip and his sons were obliged to promise that they would not allow appeals from these courts to Paris.

In fact, the separation was only nominal. Philip the Fair found a method to make the local courts *de facto* extensions of the court

---

31. *Ordonnances*, I, 320ff.

32. *Ibid.*, I, 355: "Praeterea propter commodum subjectorum nostrorum et expeditionem causarum, proponimus ordinare quod duo parlamenta Parisius et duo Scacaria Rothomagi et dies Trecenses bis tenebuntur in anno, et quod parlamentum apud Tholosam tenebitur, si gentes terre predicte consentiant quod non appelletur a presidentibus in parlamento predicto."

of Paris by naming members of the Parlement of Paris to conduct their sessions.[33] Thus, in 1306, after the Parlement of Paris adjourned, the Archbishop of Narbonne and Enguerrand de Marigny were appointed to sit at the sessions of the Exchequer of Rouen and similar appointments were made for other local courts.[34] In addition to hearing routine cases, they undertook at that time to reform and define the functions of royal baillis in the province, following the model set in the Grand Ordinance.[35]

Granting that there was an active desire on the part of the king and his councillors to bring the various courts of the land into some uniform system, this does not necessarily lead to the conclusion that the king and his lawyers were conspiring to destroy the nobility and clergy as powers in the land. In studying the records of arrests by the Parlement of Paris, Lot and Fawtier concluded that they yield no evidence that a "legist spirit" was guiding its decisions.[36] On the contrary, they point out, the personnel of the Parlement was still largely aristocratic—both lay and ecclesiastical—and thus naturally opposed by their own interests to an overly strenuous extension of royal power. If there was in fact a legist spirit at work, it would best be found among those provincial officials, like Pierre Dubois, against whom so many complaints were lodged. According to the Grand Ordinance, however, it was a chief function of the Parlement of Paris—where the greatest lawyers of the realm sat in attendance—to redress these grievances.

The real work of Philip's lawyers is, then, not to be found in the aggressions of local officials or in the spectacular deeds of Nogaret, but in the quieter careers of men like Gilles Aycelin. His

33. Lot and Fawtier, *Histoire des institutions*, II, 491, have noted that the continuation of this practice, even after the Norman charter of 1314–1316 once more prohibited appeals from the Exchequer of Rouen to Paris, represented a steadily undermining factor against the independence of this court.

34. Floquet, *Histoire du Parlement de Normandie*, I, 94ff., points out that in addition to this practice, which in fact took the conduct of the court out of the hands of the local nobility, Philip continued to entertain appeals from its judgments to Paris, a practice which undoubtedly was not seriously protested by Aycelin and Marigny.

35. Soudet, *Ordonnances de l'Eschiquier de Normandie aux XIVe et XVe siècles*, 225.

36. *Histoire des institutions*, II, 358.

legal expertise was acknowledged by such diverse persons as Nicholas IV, Boniface VIII, and the Count of Flanders. Philip the Fair actively acknowledged it in the uses he made of it. He was one of the most prominent figures in the Parlement of Paris after 1302. Yet there is no evidence that he experienced in this work any conflict with his responsibilities and interests as a feudal lord and prelate. In his own person, Aycelin proves Lot and Fawtier's contention that the prestige and authority of the Parlement are largely owed to the fact that its members acted as representatives of the nation as well as of the crown.[37] Philip the Fair's early ordinances were in no sense designed to exclude from his courts the prelates who played so important a role in his council. Nor did he intend to use the courts as a means of attacking their privileges. Philip's policy was less to attack the jurisdiction of the prelates and barons than to regularize it and put it in its proper place in a well-ordered kingdom. The ordinances of 1302–1303 confirmed the immunities of clergymen "who live clerically."

Indeed, a similar clarification of the role of the greater subjects was the purpose of all legislation relevant to the Parlement after 1303. For all his show of tender concern for the rights of his prelates and barons, the king was naturally desirous of enforcing his own right to submit them to his primary appellate power. The Grand Ordinance was intended to make royal justice attractive to his subjects. Second, Article 56 created an alliance of the king and the magnates of the realm since the Parlement was constituted as a court of peers by assuring the presence at its sittings of two representatives of the nobility and two from the higher clergy.[38]

In studying the registers of the Parlement, Beugnot came to the conclusion that these early ordinances on the establishment of the court were not designed to destroy any particular class, though they were designed to weaken the effects of independent jurisdiction by making Parlement the ultimate court of appeals for the entire realm. Moreover, he believed that the clergy played an

---

37. *Ibid.*, II, 506.
38. *Ordonnances*, I, 355: "Quia vero multa magne cause in nostre parlamento inter notabiles personas et magnas agantur, ordinamus et volumus quod duo prelate et due alie bone et sufficientes persone laica causa audiendi et deliberandi dictas causas, continue in nostris parlamentis existant."

indispensable role in this effort.[39] Most of the necessary precedents can be traced to canon law and were probably provided by men like Aycelin who had training in canon as well as Roman law, in addition to their experience in the customary courts.

Gilles Aycelin was clearly the prelate Philip preferred for the extension of his plan. The fragmentary list of the presidents of the Parlement of Paris during his reign indicates that at each sitting this position was conferred on one prelate and one great lord. Whenever possible, the Archbishop of Narbonne was the prelate employed.[40] In 1304–1305 he was specifically named by the king as one of the prelates whose presence would be considered indispensable to a meeting of the Parlement.[41] This policy was continued after the death of Philip the Fair. In July 1316 Philip V appointed Aycelin, then Archbishop of Rouen, as one of the four presidents of the Parlement and named him again the following November, though he was subsequently replaced, "because he could not come."[42]

The special value of men like Aycelin in this context can hardly be overestimated. If the lawyers of Philip the Fair are to be given any of the credit for the accomplishments of this monarchy, Aycelin's share would be obvious if it were only limited to his routine work in presiding over the meetings of the royal court. More important, however, is the fact that he acted not as a lawyer with an aggressive "secular" point of view but officially as an archbishop. His legislation in Narbonne had contributed to the general effort of clarifying the line that separated the competence of lay and ecclesiastical courts at the local level. The problem of appealing cases involving the clergy to a higher court was still a vexatious one. As early as 1288, the Parlement—representing the king—had tried to maintain that the monarch was the highest source of justice in the kingdom. At the synod of Sainte Geneviève in 1290, the future Boniface VIII himself recognized that the king was the holder of ultimate jurisdiction over all cases involving the temporals of prelates. In return, the king recognized

39. *Les Olim*, Introduction, III, liii.
40. Ducoudray, *Les origines du Parlement*, 156.
41. *Ordonnances*, I, 547.
42. Lot and Fawtier, *Histoire des institutions*, II, 336.

the jurisdiction of the Church over actions regarding clerks.[43] A practical solution to this problem lay in the royal policy of using prelates as a court of peers in cases involving ecclesiastical personnel and combining such hearings with the sittings of the Parlement of Paris.

Moreover, the Parlement had a special advantage resulting from its mixed composition. It could act, as could no other court, in cases involving both lay and ecclesiastical lords because it represented both. As early as the twelfth century the king's court had been established as a court of peers for the lay nobility,[44] and had begun to act in a similar capacity for prelates by entertaining the appeals of bishops and abbots against local lords. Later the claim was made that persons coming to plead before the royal court must be present in person to defend themselves in pleas against them.[45] In the same tradition, Philip the Fair, in an ordinance of 1290 outlining the immunities of the clergy, included specific assurances designed to encourage their use of the Parlement as a court of appeals.[46]

Clearly, this was no anticlerical ordinance. In the same fashion, the famous ordinance of 1287, which Michelet interpreted as an attempt "to render the Parlement totally laic—the first separation of the civil and ecclesiastical orders . . . the foundation of the civil order,"[47] should rather be seen in a more conservative tradition of attempting to clarify a separation already in existence and desired by both parties[48]—not as a "cleansing of foreign elements"

43. Gaudemet, in *Histoire des institutions,* III, 329ff.
44. Langlois, *Revue Historique,* XLII, 85.
45. *Ibid.,* 87.
46. *Ordonnances,* I, 318–19. Clergymen were given the right to send procurators rather than appear personally in a secular court at the demand of a lay judge. They were not to be compelled to plead in any lower secular courts, but the Parlement of Paris was to be open to them not only for appeal in cases involving themselves but also for cases judged in their own feudal courts. Their jurisdiction over wills, pious legacies, and dowries, and over all ecclesiastics who committed crimes was confirmed. The same ordinance confirmed the immunity of ecclesiastical goods from the *taille* and from any depredations by royal officials.
47. Michelet, *Histoire de France,* III, 28.
48. *Ordonnances,* I, 316–17. Anyone having temporal jurisdiction in the kingdom of France was ordered to employ laymen as procurators, replacing all clerks then occupying such positions whose immunities made it impossible to subject them to professional discipline.

preliminary to the great aggressive movement of the lawyers. It is not, however, generally accepted that the ordinance was simply a move to bring those procurators under the jurisdiction of the secular courts where they could be made vulnerable to charges of malfeasance. Likewise, the ordinance of 1288, which forbade clerks to hold secular offices in the towns,[49] was not an attack on clerical immunities so much as an effort to make them workable by separating them from the necessary sphere of secular authority.

Neither ordinance represents a serious move to bar the clergy from the judicial life of the nation. The ordinance of 1291, assigning the judicial authority of the court to members of the royal council,[50] was not designed to create a court cleansed of the "foreign element" of the clergy, since prelates like Aycelin were consistently included in the number of councillors. Further, an ordinance of 1296 granted entrance to the meetings of the Parlement to additional "privileged persons," like the Abbot of Cîteaux.[51] Finally, the vast majority of the famous lawyers in whose hands the whole movement was placed were actually prelates.

Thus, rather than attacking his barons and prelates, Philip sought to put himself at their head, strengthening his own authority by his protection of theirs. Beugnot remarked that the addition of the two prelates made it possible for the Parlement to be treated as an ecclesiastical court of appeals when the occasion demanded, thus bringing the jurisdiction of the Church under the ultimate authority of the crown.[52] At the same time, however, it ensured the French clergy the protection of members of their own class who had the firmest confidence of the king. Thus, Aycelin and his fellow prelates—lawyers like Pierre de Belleperche, Pierre and Etienne de Mornay, Etienne de Suizy, Pierre de Latilly, and others—assisted in giving the development of the French monarchy that special tone of consensus which always distinguished its greatest periods.

49. *Ibid.*, I, 317.
50. *Ibid.*, I, 320ff.
51. *Ibid.*, 317.
52. *Les Olim*, III, xxx.

XIII

The Destruction of the Templars

When Boniface VIII died in 1303, Aycelin must have been at least technically under the papal ban of excommunication as a result of his failure to obey the pope's demand that he appear in Rome. He shared this ambiguous and uncomfortable situation with Philip the Fair, whose excommunication Boniface had published just prior to Nogaret's attack on Anagni. Everyone affected, from the king down, behaved as though the sentences had never been issued. Benedict XI hesitated to confirm them and finally sought a more solid base of action, attempting to isolate the offenders who had perpetrated the actual attack on his predecessor by effecting a reconciliation with the king and other French officials who had not personally participated in the outrage.

Until 25 March 1304 the new pope tacitly upheld Boniface's excommunication of Philip the Fair, refusing to communicate with him even to the extent of omitting a formal announcement of his election.[1] During this period the Archbishop of Narbonne was subjected to the same treatment. The pope's correspondence on the construction of the new cathedral in Narbonne, a subject which had previously been handled exclusively by the archbishop, was addressed to the archdeacon and chapter, presumably because Benedict wanted to preserve the possibility of considering the archbishopric vacant.[2] His first direct communication with Aycelin was on 30 March, after the decision represented by the letter of 25 March to King Philip. Moreover, this first letter to Aycelin reflected the pope's decision to pursue a path of reconcilia-

1. Holtzmann, *Wilhelm von Nogaret*, 120, draws this conclusion from his analysis of Benedict's correspondence. Before his letter of 25 March formally removing the ban from the King and his family (*Reg. Ben. XI*, 1311), he avoided every communication with Philip. This conclusion was upheld by Digard, *Philippe le Bel*, II, 191.
2. *Le registre de Benoît XI*, 52.

tion by providing the archbishop with the power to absolve those officials in his diocese guilty of laying violent hands on ecclesiastical persons.[3] This privilege might have been utilized either in connection with a newly impending settlement with the viscount or to settle the last repercussions of the Saisset affair. Within a few days Benedict addressed four additional bulls to Aycelin, obviously to soothe the feelings of the archbishop and effect a full reconciliation with him.[4]

Further, Benedict reversed Boniface VIII's prohibition on the archbishop's proposed reconciliation with Amaury of Narbonne and sent formal approval of the settlement of 1300.[5] Within a year Aycelin received the viscount's homage, and the question of the jurisdiction of Narbonne was effectively settled.

On 13 May 1304 the pope issued a series of bulls granting more specific absolution to those who suffered under the sentences of Boniface VIII. Pierre Flote and his sons were released from the papal sentence of damnation.[6] All sentences against prelates who had failed to attend the Roman council were revoked,[7] along with all sentences which any ecclesiastics, nobles, or laymen of France might have incurred because of the process against Boniface.[8] Restated by Clement V in February 1306, these bulls effectively freed Aycelin from any further involvement with the affair.

Benedict had laid out the lines of papal policy for the future. The prelates and the king were assumed to have acted in good faith in calling for a council to judge Boniface. Nogaret and his confederates were isolated, and the attack would henceforth be concentrated on them alone. On the French side, though they were never repudiated by the king, they were generally left to

3. *Ibid.*, 748.
4. *Ibid.*, 747 gives the archbishop full power to dispose of benefices in his diocese, even when they were formerly reserved to the pope; 750 confirms Boniface's privileges allowing him to endow two prebends; 751 provides permission to give revenues of benefices to three of his clerks or domestics while they remained in his service; 808 dispensed Aycelin's procurator, Andreas of Saint Flor, from his visitation duties in the church of Clermont because of his commitments to Aycelin.
5. *Ibid.*, 749.
6. *Ibid.*, 1260.
7. *Ibid.*, 1259.
8. *Ibid.*, 1253.

carry on the case against Boniface without active assistance from the king or his other ministers. It is likely that the archbishop of Narbonne was one of the "prelates, clerks, and others specially gathered" in the Cathedral of Notre Dame in Paris on 28 June 1304 to hear the entire bundle of letters of absolution read publicly to the royal family.[9] Then, before he could begin the pursuit of his vengeance against Nogaret and his confederates, Benedict XI died suddenly—some said mysteriously—on 18 July 1304.

For a year thereafter the cardinals sat deadlocked in conclave while the French exerted themselves to procure the election of an even more amenable pope. With the election of Bertrand De Got, Archbishop of Bordeaux, as Clement V, they secured a pontiff who could be coerced into allowing the fulfillment of some of the most ambitious undertakings Philip the Fair and his councillors had yet conceived. For centuries, Clement's helpless acquiescence to French demands has convinced historians that the true story of his election was to be found in the romance concocted by the Italian chronicler, Villani.[10] His was a gripping tale of secret meetings in the dead of night between the King of France and the Archbishop of Bordeaux. There, in the woods near Saint Jean d'Angély, Philip was said to have extorted a series of commitments from de Got in return for which he guaranteed his election to the papacy.

This story was thoroughly discredited by an examination of the itineraries of the two principals during the crucial months.[11] Nevertheless, the fact that the two never met in person at this period does not rule out the possibility of their having reached an agreement by more traditional channels of communication. There is, in fact, every reason to believe that at least some of the early acts of Clement V favoring the French represent the price he paid for his election.[12]

De Got was on a tour of visitation in the vicinity of Poitiers on 23 July 1305 when he received the cardinals' letter notifying

9. Frachet, *Chronicle*, 23; Guillaume de Nangis, *Chronique latine*, 342.
10. *Istorie Fiorentine*, 159–63.
11. Rabanis, *Clement V et Philippe le Bel, passim.*
12. This proposition is accepted by the most recent authors on the question, Lizérand, *Clement V et Philippe le Bel*, and Finke, *Papsttum und Untergang*, I, 89.

him of his election. A suspiciously large delegation of French notables happened to be with him during these routine travels, including the king's brother Louis, the Archbishop of Narbonne, the Duke of Burgundy, the Count of Dreux, Pierre de Latilly, and Pierre de Belleperche. It is not known at what date they joined him, but the fact that they were already there before de Got had been informed of his election indicates that they had been undertaking some preliminary negotiations with him. They stayed glued to his side on his return to Bordeaux even though their entry caused the citizens to riot in the streets "because of their malevolence toward the king of France, who had called them to arms for his war," obliging the English seneschal to post guards in the city for the length of the pope's stay.[13]

Even passing over the signs that the French had anticipated the news without questioning their implications, we must recognize that this embassy to the new pope was no simple visit of congratulation. On 13 October 1305, when Clement V was writing to Philip about the plans for his coronation, he added his apologies for omitting to notify the King formally of his election on the ground that he had assumed that the Archbishop of Narbonne and Pierre de Latilly, Bishop of Châlons, had kept him fully informed. At the same time, he indicated his willingness that the king disclose "certain secret things" which Clement had discussed with the two royal representatives to three or four additional members of his council, confiding in Philip's circumspection to keep the secret from becoming general knowledge.[14]

At the very least, these discussions must have included a demand for the revocation of Boniface's anti-French bulls, the reconciliation of the king's servants and friends to the Church, and the restoration of both Colonnas to the cardinalate, since Clement V took action on those questions as soon as he was crowned. He resisted only in his stubborn refusal to give absolution to Nogaret. It is probable that the secret discussions proceeded at least as far as an initial presentation of some of the French aims to be pursued

---

13. The entire account of this journey is from the report of the English seneschal in Gascony: Langlois, "Documents relatifs à Bertrand de Got (Clement V)," 52.

14. Baluze, *Vitae Paparum Avenionensium,* III, 48.

during the next five years. The question of the charges against
Boniface VIII would have been an obvious point of discussion.
And several years later, in the bull *Faciens Misericordiam*,
Clement V himself suggested that the question of the Templars
was first raised at that time.[15]

Dispensing with romantic skullduggery in the midnight forest,
we are left with the same results that Villani suspected. In the
plain light of day, a French embassy headed by Gilles Aycelin
negotiated their demands with the Archbishop of Bordeaux before
and immediately after his election to the papacy. Beyond the
immediate acts of restoration to grace of most of the enemies of
Boniface VIII, it is not clear how far he acquiesced at that time—
but he must have been given a reasonably plain picture of what
the French would demand in the years to come.

Aycelin's name was not recorded among the luminaries assembled at Lyon for the coronation of the new pope in November.
But, in the absence of any indication that he was elsewhere, it is
probable that he was one of the councillors with the king. His experience would have been particularly useful in the final extension
of royal jurisdiction over the city of Lyon which was achieved
during this visit. Moreover, the archbishop was given charge of
the ceremonies for the translation of the head of Saint Louis to
the royal chapel in Paris the following spring, a privilege conceded
to the king during his stay in Lyon.[16] The Aragonese observer
noted that the new pope was constantly occupied with the French
king and his councillors, discussing the affairs of that kingdom.[17]
It is hardly likely that the king had dispensed with the advice of
Aycelin, who was certainly one of the best informed and most
experienced of his councillors and who had been so recently in
contact with the new pope.

15. *Regestum Clementis Papae V*, 3402: "Sane dudum circa promotionis
nostre . . . etiam antequam Lugdunum, ubi recepimus nostre coronationis insignia,
veniremus, et post etiam tam ibi quam alibi secreta quorundam nobis insinuatio
intimavit, quod magister, preceptores et alii fratres ordinis militie Templi Jero-
solimitani et etiam ipse ordo, qui ad defensionem patrimonii ejusdem domini nostri
Jhesu Christi fuerant in transmarinis partibus deputati, contra ipsum dominum in
scelus apostasie nephandum, detestabile ydolatrie vitium, execrabile facinus
Sodomorum et hereses varias erant lapsi."
16. Bréquigny, *Tables chronologiques*, 80–81.
17. Finke, *Papsttum*, II, 7–9.

Since Clement V remained within easy reach of the king throughout his pontificate, the need for diplomatic missions such as those Aycelin had performed in the past was obviated. In general, Philip personally headed important embassies in those years. As a result, Aycelin's role is less readily discernible but he was mentioned frequently in connection with the confrontations between the pope and the French. He was at the Curia in June 1307 to secure the pope's ratification of the Treaty of Athis. Thus, though his name was not mentioned in other reports, he probably participated in the discussions opened by the king at that time on the reorganization of the military orders.[18]

That question certainly came to preoccupy him incessantly over the years that followed. The evolution of the French offensive against the Templars was accomplished in entire secrecy before their arrest in October 1307. But if we assume that discussions on the subject with the pope were opened at Bordeaux in 1305, Aycelin was privy to them from their inception. Boutaric's thesis that he opposed their arrest in October 1307 was based entirely on his erroneous belief that Aycelin resigned the seals at that time, and is therefore entirely without foundation.[19]

Philip the Fair's order for the arrest of the Knights Templar stated that he was acting with the advice of the "prelates and barons."[20] Though the document gives no specific names, Aycelin's active participation in the mobilization of French opinion against them indicates that he was one of the advisors. Philip was anxious to have at least the appearance of full support from the clergy. To this end, he requested each of the French prelates personally to attend a great public assembly on 25 May 1308.[21] The invitation was modified by his advice that each province hold a synod two weeks in advance of the scheduled meeting at which those unable to attend would elect representatives. Similar suggestions to the

18. *Ibid.*, II, 33–36.
19. "Clement V, Philippe le Bel et les templiers," 326. His acceptance of this theory led Schöttmüller, *Der Untergang des Templerordens,* to misinterpret Aycelin's role in their destruction as that of a well-intentioned dupe. The question of Aycelin's holding of the seals will be discussed in the following chapter.
20. Boutaric, *Ibid.,* 327–38.
21. Picot, *Documents relatifs aux Etats Généraux,* Introduction, xlvi.

members of the other two estates hint that Philip was less than anxious to inspire a national debate on the topic.

This suspicion is amply borne out by the frequency with which the lords of Languedoc "appointed" Guillaume de Nogaret to represent them in the assembly.[22] Likewise the clergy, of Rouen and Rheims—among the few provinces which can actually be shown to have held a meeting at all—contented themselves with sending a single representative. From Rouen, they appointed the Bishop of Bayeux, one of Philip's trusted councillors who would later be a reliable assistant to Aycelin in his prosecution of the case. The Archbishop of Narbonne was at Paris at the time and did not even undertake the formal convocation of a provincial council. Instead, he simply informed them that he had already received the king's permission to act, with the Bishop of Toulouse, as representative of the province.[23] It seems apparent that what the king really wanted was an impressive list of names supporting him, and that Aycelin was assisting him in the organization of a great show from which nothing could result but mere formal approval of the royal propositions.

On the basis of John of St. Victor's remark that the laity procured the condemnation of the order,[24] Hervieu[25] thought that some of the clergy must have protested the action against the Templars. There is no evidence to support this contention, and the fact that most of the important prelates were content to send

22. Renan, *Etudes sur la politique religieuse*, 113.
23. Picot, 492–93. The king's summons to Aycelin was dated 2 April, suggesting that he handed it to the prelate personally, they discussed it together, and then Aycelin wrote his letter of 4 April. The letter itself presents a special puzzle in that it directed those of Aycelin's suffragans who wished to attend the meeting personally to go to Poitiers, where the pope was in residence, instead of to Tours where the meeting was to be held according to the convocations of 24 March. This was later corrected by a counterorder which did not reach all the deputies. Picot, Introduction, p. xlix, found seventeen false directions to deputies, most of whom came from Narbonne, and suggested that the confusion resulted from a change in the king's original plan to frighten the pope with a flood of deputies. But it is also provocative to note that one of the few dignitaries who came from Narbonne on his own account, the Abbot of Valmagne, gave up the project altogether when he arrived at Poitiers only to discover that he was expected to go on to Tours.
24. *Excerpta e memoriali historiarum*, 651.
25. *Recherches sur les premiers Etats Généraux*, 94.

representatives rather than attend personally argues against it. It
would have been a hardy soul indeed who could have attended
the meeting of 1308 with the purpose of defending the order. The
king had no intention whatever of admitting debate on the subject of their guilt, as the language of the summons plainly indicates. After a lengthy statement of his conception of his own duty
as king of France to suppress heresy with all his strength, Philip
cited the errors of the Templars as though they had been proved
by their confessions, and asked help and council from the representatives of the nation only on the question of how he should
present the case in his forthcoming meeting with the pope. For,
with his accustomed modesty of demeanor, Philip admitted his
inability to carry the case beyond the boundaries of his own kingdom, though his information clearly exposed the universality of
the heresies.[26]

Since many of the representatives present at the meeting accompanied the king on his subsequent journey to Poitiers, it may
be that the only serious result of the assembly was to organize a
show of strength for the pope's benefit. It cannot, of course, be
proven that the members of this delegation were deliberately acting
in bad faith; the question of the guilt or innocence of the Templars
remains a subject of debate to the present. To this extent, Pegues'
argument that by 1308 Aycelin was fully convinced of the guilt
of the knights and supported their condemnation in good faith is
as feasible as any other interpretation of his conduct.[27] But it may
with equal likelihood be extended to cover the actions of Clement
V, Philip the Fair, and Nogaret. Aycelin certainly knew as much
as they did about the affair and there is absolutely no reason to
suppose that he was more naive than any of them.

On 26 May 1308 he accompanied the king and other prelates
and barons of the council to Poitiers to confer with the pope on
their great affair. On 29 May the formal consistory opened at
which the condemnation of the order was to be discussed. The
Aragonese ambassador described the papal palace as being filled
with French dignitaries from all three estates who had come with

26. Picot, *Documents relatifs aux Etats Généraux*, 487–88.
27. *The Lawyers of the Last Capetians*, 96.

the king from Tours.[28] The meeting opened with an exhaustive exposition in French by Guillaume de Plasians speaking in the king's name—an ominous repetition of the sequence of events at the Louvre five years before which had launched the attack on Boniface VIII.

Beginning with praises for the piety and devotion to duty which distinguished the King of France and a description of his long-standing unwillingness to believe the charges against the Templars, Plasians recounted the investigations which had been undertaken with the pope's authorization and in the king's own capacity as "vicar of God in his realm in temporals."[29] He denied the king had acted from avarice or any of the other unworthy motives of which the whispers started by the malevolent Templars had accused him. Twice Plasians stated that it was God who brought Jacques de Molay, the Grand Master of the Order, to France in time to be taken up in the general arrest, though in fact it was the pope and the king who had summoned him to a conference in 1307. Plasians also asserted that de Molay had confessed without torture. Finally, he exposed a legal technicality which would play an important part in Aycelin's later conduct of the investigation against the order. He asked that proceedings against individual Templars be begun immediately because their cases were not all the same—some of them were open to charges as relapsed heretics.[30]

When Plasians had concluded, the Archbishop of Narbonne rose to make a brief but chilling statement. Comparing the Templars to the Midianites who had perverted Israel, he declared that there was never a more perverse group than theirs; even the pagans and other heretics who denied that Christ was God conceeded that he was a prophet and a holy man. But the Templars denied that he was God, and branded him a false prophet as well. Anyone who should neglect to root out such manifest heresy when

---

28. Finke, *Papsttum*, II, 140–50, includes a verbatim report of the speeches given at the meeting.

29. *Ibid.*: ". . . regem Francie qui in regno suo est Dei vicarius in temporalibus."

30. *Ibid.*, 146: "Non enim omnes sunt in eadem culpa. Quidam enim sunt relapsi, quidam coacte confessi, quidam vero sponte confessi et penitentes, cum quibus mitius erit agendum, cum ecclesia non claudat gremium redeunti."

given the opportunity must share in their guilt. And this particularly applied to prelates who were in a position to correct them.[31]

Following as it did a campaign of whispered rumors about Clement's orthodoxy, which had been circulated throughout France that spring, Aycelin's remarks had an especially ominous ring. The threat would have been chilling enough had he been content to "whisper slyly" into the pope's ear, as Mollat described the scene,[32] but he was speaking publicly. Anyone who remembered Boniface VIII—and Clement V was never allowed to forget him for very long—must have been struck with dread by the archbishop's speech.

Aycelin's remarks were followed by a numbing display of Gallican unity. The Archbishop of Bourges, Gilles de Rome, who had formerly stood alone in support of Boniface VIII, spoke against the order. He was followed by a procession of barons, citizens of Paris "pro lingua Gallica," and citizens of Toulouse and Montpellier "et tota lingua Occitana" with petitions supplicating the pope to proceed without further delay.

The pope hestitated, made a show of reluctance, but finally gave way and agreed to appoint a special commission of cardinals to interview some of the accused Templars.[33] In return, Philip

31. *Ibid.*, 147: "Hec fuit in suma proposito facta nomine et pro parte regis Francie per dictum Guillelmum de Plasiano, sed tamen in vulgari. Post quam propositionem surrexit archiepiscopus Narbonensis et assumens quandam auctoritatem de Madianitis, qui pervertebant Israel, comparavit illos ipsis Madianitis et prosequens de ipsorum Templariorum errore dixit, quod perversior heresis nunquam fuit. Nam et si aliqui negaverint et negent Ihesum Christum fuisse Deum, sicut fuerunt aliqui heretici et hodie sunt pagani, tamen dicebant et dicunt illum fuisse prophetam et sanctum hominem. Sed isti negantes eum esse Deum dicunt et mentiuntur eum fuisse pseudoprophetam. Allegavit etiam, quod facientis culpam obtinet, qui manifesto errori negligit obviare, cum possit et quod istud signanter intelligebatur de prelato, qui obviare poterat et corrigere. Conclusit pro celeri expeditione allegans pericula, que ex eorum . . . provenire poterant et inducens exemplum de scintilla Arrii, que orta est in Alexandria, que, quia in continenti non fuit extincta, crevit in maximam flammam que quasi totum mundum accendit."

32. *Les Papes d'Avignon*, 236.

33. Schöttmüller, *Der Untergang des Templerordens*, II, 13–71, gives the text of the hearings they conducted. Their results were highly suspicious, however, due to the composition of the commission: Berengar Frédol, Étienne de Suizy, and Pierre de la Chapelle had formerly been members of Philip's council; Thomas

obliged the pope with a public declaration that he was only holding the Templars in the pope's name and their goods were being guarded pending a future decision on the disposition of the order. This seeming concession, however, was balanced by a new series of demands by Plasians on 6 July.

Most of Plasians' requests were probably intended to stimulate the pope to quick action. He wanted the permanent establishment of the Curia in France; convocation of a general council to deal with the Templars which would be held in France; the canonization of Celestine V; the condemnation of Boniface VIII and the burning of his body; and Nogaret's absolution.[34] Clement offered tentative agreement to the second and third points, but continued to insist that he and the Curia must remove to Italy because of their financial position. He could not show himself to be intransigent on the canonization, but was well aware that the intention of the demand was linked to the idea that the former pope had been a martyr to the ambition of Boniface VIII and therefore avoided a promise; he absolutely refused the last two demands. Probably the French had not expected any better result. Their exorbitant demands had secured the two most immediately important points. However, this does not imply that they were not serious about the remainder of the program—the French representatives would hound Clement for its fulfillment for the rest of his life.

By 20 July the pope had been subjected to sufficient pressure to give King Philip a sense of security for the immediate future. Having won the battle—at least in principle—he left Poitiers. But the pope was to have no peace yet. Plasians, Nogaret, and Aycelin stayed behind to continue the application of pressure for a final proceeding against the order. Presumably, they performed a three-way variation on the game Flote and Aycelin had played so effectively in former years. Plasians and Nogaret, to whom Clement resolutely refused to speak, concentrated on threatening the pope with a reopening of the affair of Boniface VIII. Aycelin, perhaps playing the role of the sympathetic and moderate party,

de Ocra was a Celestinian cardinal. Landulph and Pietro Colonna were similarly tied to the French.
34. Finke, *Papsttum*, II, 123.

arranged the concrete details which would destroy the Temple. The Aragonese ambassador wrote that the three Frenchmen pursued Clement with the French king's complaints more persistently than they had done when Philip was there, and predicted that they would continue to monopolize the pope's time until his departure from Poitiers on 13 August.[35] Thus, even before the cardinals had reported the results of their investigations, Clement was yielding to the pressure of Aycelin and his colleagues.

The major problem concerning the pope at this point was the question of the fate of the order as a whole, as opposed to the condemnation of individual Templars. A sufficient number of confessions had been obtained by that time to justify widespread action against individuals, but these did not in themselves provide a reason to destroy the order as a corporate body, which was the real desire of the French. Clement seemed inclined to let the individuals go, with the exception of the highest officers who were to be reserved for his own judgment. But he was determined to uphold his exclusive right to decide the future of the order. The French were equally determined to make good their argument that the crimes of the individuals stemmed from the crimes of the order as a heretical sect. They demanded its dissolution and the confiscation of its goods.

Though he continued to retain the illusion of control, the pope surrendered the substance with a series of bulls issued between 8 and 12 August. Reserving the right to judge the order as a whole, he appointed a special committee of investigation to act in his name. But the membership of the commission was solely drawn from among the French bishops trusted by Philip the Fair, and it was to be headed by the Archbishop of Narbonne. In effect, he had abandoned the order, for it passes the bounds of the imagination to suppose that Clement could by that time have been under any illusions about the impartiality of that prelate.

The terms of the appointment were laid out in the bull *Faciens Misericordiam*, giving a history of the case, and including a record of the confessions of individual members of the order. The commission was instructed to meet and read the bull publicly, con-

35. *Ibid.*, I, 156.

voking all who had any testimony to present about the order as
a body, holding hearings, recording their findings, and trans-
mitting them to the pope for final judgment.[36]

Faciens was supplemented by a request to the French prelates
to undertake preliminary investigations in their own provinces and
a series of bulls on the subject of a new crusade. The Archbishop
of Narbonne and the other prelates of France were instructed to
take over the guardianship of the goods of the Temple for this purpose.[37] Finally, on 12 August, the bull convoking the Council of
Vienne was issued.[38]

As the pope left Poitiers, Aycelin could return to the king with
a fully satisfactory report of his accomplishment. The persons of
the Templars, their goods, and the ultimate power to dispose of
the order were now firmly in the king's hands, despite the technicality that he held them in the name of the pope. Until this time,
the French had pressed mercilessly for haste in dealing with the
case. From August 1308 until August 1309 they now took no action
at all. The reasons are not overly difficult to discern. The longer
the Templars lay in prison while the assumption that they were
guilty was allowed to take root in the popular mind, the easier
it would be to condemn them in the end. Even more important:
until the order was finally judged, the goods were in the king's
custody. To be sure, he was technically only to guard them until
some means of utilizing them for the assistance of the Holy Land
could be devised. But the long history of Philip the Fair's abuses
of his regalian rights in the French churches is sufficient illustra-
tion of the means by which his agents were able to make such
guardianship profitable. And this was a case in which no one had
an interest in securing the application of the terms of the Grand
Ordinance against the king's officials. Clement V knew this as
well as anyone, and made a feeble effort to prevent the dissipation
of the goods by placing them in the hands of the Church. Again,
however, he retained only the shadow of his rights, having been
induced to appoint a board of French prelates "in whom the king
had special confidence" as the administrators of the property.

36. *Reg. Clem. V*, 3402.
37. *Ibid.*, 2987–89; 3400–3401.
38. *Ibid.*, 2628.

The board was headed by the ubiquitous Archbishop of Narbonne.[39]

The date of this appointment is unknown, but Philip referred to such an order to "certain prelates" in his letter of 6 May 1309, complaining that recent communications from the pope had implied that he had seized the goods of the order and asking for a public recognition that he never held them at all except as custodian. Finally, Philip demanded that the public be made to recognize his own disinterestedness in the entire affair.[40]

The same letter described in some detail the methods by which the king had supposedly attempted to bring the case to a conclusion. Philip blamed the pope for the delays resulting from certain confusions in procedure caused by the pope's decision to conduct the trials of individuals who, believing that the pope's bulls made a difference in their own position, he revoked their confessions and thrown themselves on the mercy of the Church.

The pope in turn defended himself from these imputations by putting the blame on the French prelates, who delayed local prosecution on various pretexts, sending nuncios to him in the Toulousain to require clarifications of his instructions.[41] They pretended that letters ordering provincial investigations had not been sent to certain dioceses, including Narbonne, although the pope maintained that they had all been sent out together. This assurance that he had informed the province of his wishes, was written by the pope on 6 May. On the day before, 5 May 1309, Aycelin had finally gotten around to writing to the bishop of Nîmes from Paris, instructing him to proceed with the desired investigations.[42] Meanwhile, the prelates on Aycelin's commission had delayed meeting until the pope could reply to their request that they divide into small groups to go to each province for the collection

39. This appointment was revealed only in a letter of 12 May 1311, *ibid.*, 6816, describing the methods to be employed in the accounting, probably preparatory to their presentation in Vienne. The pope does not reveal the date at which the board was appointed except that it had occurred some time in the past.

40. Finke, *Papsttum*, II, 189–201.

41. *Ibid.*, 189–201. In February 1309 the pope was with Aycelin at his chateau in Narbonne, presumably conferring on this business, De Vic and Vaissette, *Histoire de Languedoc*, 311.

42. Ménard, *Histoire civile, preuves*, n.cxxxv ff.

of the evidence. The pope replied that they could not, since they would then be likely to disagree on their conclusions.

For a year this smoke screen of confusion and conflicting directions delayed the process. The same man who had hounded the pope so pertinaciously in Poitiers until he had gained his master's ends now found himself utterly "unable" to organize the logistics of the investigation upon which he had so urgently insisted. Philip the Fair, supposedly prey to daily pangs of conscience regarding the order, survived this delay remarkably well and even found occasion to show new marks of his trust in Aycelin. When the commission finally began its meetings, Nogaret went to Avignon for the express purpose of diverting the pope's attention with a renewal of the charges against Boniface VIII and a new demand for his own absolution. While he was absent on this project, he resigned the office of guardian of the seals to the Archbishop of Narbonne.

XIV

Guardian of the Seals

Shortly after Aycelin's commission finally began to do its work, the archbishop was appointed chancellor, or guardian of the seals,[1] ostensibly at least to fill in for Nogaret during his absence at Avignon. The holder of this office was generally considered the principal member of the king's council, but the exact definition of his duties was not yet clear. The council itself was still a rather informal body, consisting of those men whom the king wished as advisors at any given moment. Its meetings were generally secret and only rarely did a faint whisper of their discussions emerge in public. It is not generally clear why certain men held the seals at various times. Perrichet[2] attributed the difficulty of establishing who actually held the title at various times to this rather casual policy of convenience. However, he also noted that at most periods the office appeared to be conferred on the councillor most closely associated with the policies being pursued at the moment.[3] In that connection, he believed that Aycelin's tenure was related to his prosecution of the Templars rather than to Nogaret's absence.

Boutaric's study of the office was based on the fact that, theoretically at least, it was revocable.[4] As it happened, there was a succession of guardians of the seals after Flote's death, but in each case their resignation has some explanation other than a change in royal policy: de Suizy was promoted to the cardinalate; Pierre de Mornay died in 1306, and Pierre de Belleperche resigned because of ill health in 1307 (and died in 1308). Boutaric's entire argument depends on the circumstances under which Gilles Aycelin held the seals. He believed that they were in the hands of

1. Perrichet, *La grande chancellérie*, 154ff., discusses the ambiguity in the title of this office.
2. *Ibid.*, 178ff.
3. *Ibid.*, 188ff.
4. *Rev. Quest. Hist.*, X, 326.

the Archbishop of Narbonne when the king's council met at Maubuisson on 23 September 1307 to decide on the arrest of the Templars. Accordingly, Boutaric proposed a mild sort of palace revolution in which Aycelin, who supposedly flinched from the attack on the order, was asked to resign and the seals were given over to Nogaret who was prepared to carry out this extreme undertaking. The entire story, however, has been amply disproved by later commentators who show that Nogaret got the seals at this time because of the resignation of the ailing Belleperche.[5]

The only remaining evidence that Philip ever utilized his power to revoke the seals comes from Nogaret himself, and in very special circumstances. In 1309–1310, when he resigned the seals into the hands of Aycelin, he may have done so because of his inability to carry out the duties of his office *in absentia*. But the same argument never seems to have induced Pierre Flote to resign even temporarily.[6] Nogaret's action was probably part of his general policy of keeping the king, and himself as a royal official, clear of the more dubious undertakings of his career. Thus, he could state clearly in his apology of 1310 that he was acting only as a private person. He then defined his office as a revocable one, which he exercised only when he was with the king.[7] The fact is that Philip the Fair was remarkably loyal to his councillors and cannot be shown ever to have revoked the appointment of his chancellors for motives of convenience.

Aycelin held the seals during Nogaret's absence and it was fairly clear that he was acting as a substitute. Holtzmann[8] dated

5. Boutaric supported his entire argument on a single document from the National Archives which stated only that on 13 September the king transferred the seals to Nogaret, who then authorized the arrest of the Templars. There is no mention whatsoever of Aycelin. Holtzmann, *Wilhelm von Nogart,* 142, has ably refuted Boutaric by showing that the report of Belleperche's death in De Vic and Vaissette, *Histoire de Languedoc,* for 17 January 1307 follows the old style and that in fact he still held the seals until his resignation in September, followed by his death 17 January 1308. It remains possible that his decision to resign because of ill health was strengthened by a personal unwillingness to involve himself in the affair of the Temple, but this does not mean that the seals were taken from him.

6. Perrichet, 180.

7. Dupuy, *Histoire du différend,* 518, Renan, *Etudes sur la politique religieuse,* 123, bases his argument that the office was treated as revocable on the same text.

8. *Wilhelm von Nogaret,* 142.

the beginning of Aycelin's tenure as 27 February 1310, but the end of his term is unknown. Père Anselme[9] thought he held the seals until 1314 when they were given to Pierre de Latilly, but in that case his deprivation would be unaccountable. Moreover, Norgaret's statement that he held the office when he was with the king implied that he expected to take it up again on his return. Assuming he did so, Aycelin would have restored the seals to him sometime in 1311 or 1312 and the appointment of de Latilly would follow the death of Nogaret. What connection, if any, Aycelin's period of office had with the meetings of his commission on the guilt of the Templars, which was meeting through that time, has been obscured by time and his own deviousness.

The commission began its meetings at Sainte Geneviève in Paris on 7 August 1309. Although they are easily obtained, the records of Aycelin's hearings have not been very widely studied by the authors interested in the problem of the Templars.[10] Those who have discussed Aycelin's role tend to isolate it from the activity of the rest of the French, viewing him as a relatively impartial, though timid, arbiter.[11] Occasionally, harsher judgments have been passed against the commissioners in view of behavior during the commission sessions.[12] Only Pegues, however, has made any effort to view Aycelin's role on the commission in the broader framework of his position on the king's council. His treatment is cursory, however, and his interpretation is based on his own commitment

9. *Histoire généalogique,* 275.

10. Michelet, *Procès des templiers,* is a day-to-day transcript of the proceedings.

11. Lizérand, *Clement V,* 148, analyzed the relations of Philip and the individual commissioners, but treated the body as though it was acting independently and without interference until the Archbishop of Sens burned some of the witnesses. He believed that Aycelin was intimidated by this action and made no further effort to bring his investigations to a successful conclusion. Langlois, *Saint Louis,* 188, described the commission as "a company of moderate men, relatively independent, covered by the prestige of the holy see, hostile to the use of torture, viewed by the king's councillors with distrust." Again, he believed that the action at Sens intimidated them and made further investigation impossible.

12. Mollat, *Les Papes d'Avignon,* 237, accused them of being lax in their duty because they allowed officers of the king to be present at interrogations, and failed to respect the secrecy of depositions made to them. Héfèle and Leclercq, *Histoire des Conciles,* VI, 583, noted that they persisted in remaining close to the king at Paris, having witnesses brought from the provinces to them there. Further, this is the only notice of the fact that the earliest meetings were only a mummery to which the commission must have been a party.

to the view that Aycelin represented an independent and conservative force among the king's more radical lawyers.[13]

The actual records of his behavior shows something quite different. Aycelin was not acting as an intimidated or naive man, but
as a very competent judge who knew exactly what the king
wanted. The course of the hearings moved in stately fashion; the
outward forms of the law were treated with grave deference; but
it was clear that Aycelin's deliberate paces were directed toward
an inevitable end. He had no need to act violently or illegally. He
never publicly disapproved the menacing behavior of Nogaret and
his associates, but his own style was more than sufficient for the
same end. He had known since 1305 what Philip the Fair wanted.
He may well have been the first of the councillors to know. His
display of legal niceties and moderate impartiality was exactly
suited to the legal comedy that was being played with the Knights
of the Temple.

At their first meeting the commissioners prepared letters to the
prelates in France, asking them to circulate a citation to the Templars in France directing them to present themselves at the episcopal court in Paris on 12 November to answer charges against
the order. The letters concluded with the ominous warning that
the commission would proceed with its investigation even if the
Templars did not appear. Haste, they claimed at this late date,
was indispensable because the affair presented such grave dangers
to the faith.[14]

This letter suggests that the first impulse of the commissioners
was to try and condemn the Temple out of hand, without any
testimony from the knights themselves. The archbishop and his
fellow commissioners knew as well as anyone that the Templars
were in prison and could not be expected to appear without some
assistance. That they provided no instructions to procure their
presence beyond a request that the prelates publish their an-

13. Pegues, *Lawyers of the Last Capetians*, 96.. "Whatever hopes Philip had
of collaboration from Aicelin in this position were disappointed. The archbishop
evidently expected to find honest and convincing proof of the Templars' guilt,
and when it didn't come, he acted as though he were unconscious of the king's
ultimate aims. His behavior was an impartial and independent as it had been in
Saisset's case."
14. Michelet, *Procès*, I, 11.

nouncement and circulate it among all the people who should
know about it, hints at such an intention.

On the appointed day and on each day for the following week,
the commission solemnly assembled at the place and hour cited
in their letters. For two hours after having their presence there
cried publicly, they patiently awaited the appearance of witnesses
whom they must have known could not possibly appear. At the
end of that time, they summoned public notaries to record their
presence and the fact that they had their citation repeated publicly
on that day. Each of the meetings concluded after the commission
caused a summons for the next day to be read.[15]

On 18 November they read into the record the assurances of
various prelates that the citation had indeed been published in
their respective sees. They then sent new letters with the same
message to the Bishop of Paris and others from whom they had
received no answer, repeating that they were commissioned only
to investigate the order as a whole and therefore no individual
was bound to come before them unless he should desire to speak
for the entire body.[16]

It would seem that some unrecorded event made them decide
at this point to change their tactics and begin a genuine hearing
of testimony. On 22 November the Bishop of Paris, who was
Philip's confessor and had acted as Inquisitor of Paris in the
original arrests and confessions of the Templars, came before them
and stated that he had gone to the prison and read the citation in
French to the Templars there. As a result, the Grand Master, the
Visitor for France, and several other brothers had expressed their
desire to appear before the commission in defense of their order.
Accordingly, the commissioners sent letters to the prison guards
requesting that these brothers be brought before them whenever
they wished to come, though they should be kept under heavy
guard.[17]

Thus, after more than a year's delay and a false start, Aycelin's
work as head of the commission was finally begun in earnest.

15. *Ibid.*, 18.
16. *Ibid.*, 23.
17. *Ibid.*, 25.

From this point, the investigators proceeded with at least the appearance of regularity until their last meeting on 25 May 1311. However, the actual manner in which Aycelin handled the hearings leaves little doubt that he was not acting with an open mind and was never under any circumstances prepared to absolve the order.

The first witnesses were six simple knights, who were questioned separately. The first Templar said that he had come because he understood the edict to mean that the commission wished to know more about the order and he was ready to answer questions concerning it. This would seem to have been a straightforward offer, but after undertaking an examination, the commissioners took pains to explain that their purpose was not the examination of individuals. They told the knight that he need not consider himself bound to testify unless he wished to defend the order as a whole.[18]

After this confusing and perhaps slightly intimidating legal explanation, the knight was asked once more if he wished to defend the order and after some discussion, the tenor of which is not recorded, he withdrew saying he was only a simple knight without horse, arms, or land and did not know how to undertake the defense of the order. The other five brothers were induced to retreat in the same manner. Finally, Hugh Payraud, the Visitor for France, appeared but he refused to make any statement beyond a demand for the protection of the order's goods and a formal statement that he would testify only before the pope and the cardinals.

On the same day, some who wished their names kept secret informed the commission that someone who wished to defend the order was being forcibly detained in Paris. When questioned, the provost of the Châtelet revealed that there were seven fugitive Templars in his prison by orders of "certain members of the king's

18. *Ibid.*, 27: ". . . quod ipsi nullum vocabant vocacione necessaria per predictum suum edictum, nec erat intencio eorum quod aliquis cogeretur venire coram eis ad presens, et quod non inquirebant contra singulares personas, nec de facto singularium personarum, sed contra ordinem, et quod per dictum edictum non vocaverant adhuc aliquos ad testimonium, sed ut venirent, si volebant defendere ordinem antedictum, quia parati erant eos audire, prout racio suaderet."

court." They had come to Paris in disguise with money to hire lawyers for the defense of the order.[19] Precautions had obviously been taken to arrest and detain any Templars who made an attempt to answer the original citation. Considering Aycelin's position on the council, it seems most unlikely that he was unaware of the effort. Perhaps he disapproved of the action strongly enough to have persuaded the king to allow him to secure the condemnation of the order on less questionable grounds than the failure of witnesses to appear, but more than that cannot be said in defense of his innocence. The king must have been willing to follow this new line, for the witnesses could not have been taken from the Châtelet without his permission and it is highly unlikely that their presence would have been made known at all without his cooperation.

The seven witnesses were brought before the commission, but proved no problem when questioned separately.[20] The first witness questioned claimed that he was only a poor man who had come to Paris to make his living. He claimed that he had left the order fifteen days before the imprisonment of the brothers and that he knew no evil of it. Neither he nor his companions expressed any willingness to defend the order though the commissioners kindly said that they were prepared to listen to any defense they cared to make. Probably, after a taste of the royal prison, the poor men were only too glad to have escaped so easily.

Two days went by without any witnesses appearing. Then, on 24 November, Jacques de Molay was brought before the commission. Naturally, he was not so easily dissuaded from undertaking a defense as the "simple knights" who preceded him, but Aycelin's interview with the Grand Master made his intentions fatally clear. De Molay stoutly proclaimed his readiness to defend the order but complained that he had been deprived of counsel and of money to help him in the undertaking. The commissioners answered only that they were ready to listen to his testimony. However, they advised him to think seriously about his position. In matters of faith and heresy, they said, proceedings were plain and simple and no advocates were necessary; but, they pointed out, he should be

19. *Ibid.*, 29–30.
20. *Ibid.*, 30–31.

warned that he must take care that his defense should not constitute a recantation of his original confession. In case he might have
missed the point, they read the transcript of that confession—made
before the cardinals' commission—reminding him that obstinate or
relapsed heretics were customarily relinquished to the secular
arm[21] (an almost sure sentence of death at the stake). To add to
the Grand Master's difficulties, Guillaume de Plasians had been
admitted to the courtroom. Seeing himself caught in a legal trap,
de Molay appealed to him for support as a fellow knight. Plasians
answered laconically that he had better be cautious. Appalled,
the Grand Master said he would take advantage of Aycelin's offer
to allow him to think things over.

When de Molay returned on 28 November, Nogaret was
present. This time the Grand Master took refuge in the statement
that he was, after all, only a poor and illiterate knight and preferred not to say anything more until his case was brought before
the pope. Not content with this withdrawal, the commissioners
reminded him that if he wished to defend the order, he must
testify before them. De Molay answered that, for the sake of his
conscience, he wished only to say that the order was second to
none in the beauty of its altar ornaments and the perfection of its
liturgy. Nor had any order done more works of charity or shed
more blood for the defense of the faith. The commissioners
answered that none of these things helped to save souls when
fundamentals of the Catholic faith were lacking. De Molay only
answered that he personally subscribed to all the articles of the
faith. He was then silenced by Nogaret, who reminded him that
the purpose of the commission was the investigation of the order,
not of his personal orthodoxy. Thoroughly routed, de Molay withdrew, asking to be given the opportunity to attend divine services.
The commissioners granted the request, including in the record
their praise of the devotion "quam pretendabat."[22]

Meanwhile, the commission had heard the testimony of three
Templars who complained of the tortures to which they had been
subjected to secure their confessions. The board members made

21. *Ibid.*, 32–33.
22. *Ibid.*, 42–45.

no response. They were told that thirty-six Templars had already died from these torments in Paris alone, but there was no sign that the commission felt bound to cast doubts on the confessions before them for this reason, or try to prevent a repetition of the tortures. With this kind of information in his possession, Aycelin's attitudes in hearing later testimony cannot be regarded as either unbiased or innocent. Only those blindly committed to acquitting him of guilt in the destruction of the Temple could even suggest that he was intimidated. It is not likely that either Plasians or Nogaret forced his way into the hearings on the crucial days when de Molay appeared. In fact, there is every reason to suppose that Aycelin had informed them on which days these would be, and may even have invited them to appear.

From the French point of view, the hearings at Paris were so successful that the commission decided to extend itself and begin hearing testimony from the provinces. To this effect, after de Molay left them, they issued a new citation to a select group of bishops—including Aycelin's nephew, Arbert, Bishop of Clermont— to undertake preliminary hearings of the Templars in their sees and sort out those who wished to defend the order.[23] Presumably these investigations were intended to follow the pattern laid down by the commissioners who had so successfully discouraged all but one of their witnesses from pursuing their intention to defend the order.[24]

So confident were they at this point that they obtained the king's permission to pay the expenses of the journey for the new witnesses out of the order's revenues. Under these circumstances, local baillis were instructed to bring the witnesses from the provinces to the court in Paris under conditions which would prevent them from communicating with one another, "so that they cannot

23. Prutz, *Entwicklung und Untergang des Templerherrenordens*, II, 327ff., printed the record of the trials in Clermont, with praises for Arbert's gentleness. But Finke, *Papsttum*, I, 245, points out that among the large number of knights from Clermont only a few defended the innocence of the order, and that only after proffering the interesting explanation that they did not expect to be capable of standing up under torture and hoped no one would believe anything they said under those circumstances.

24. Michelet, 36. Ponzardus de Gysiaco persisted in offering himself for the defense of the order, and made a formal complaint against the tortures.

plot together or fabricate any collusions, falsehoods, machinations, or subterfuges."[25]

After these two fruitful weeks the commission adjourned, agreeing to meet again on 3 February 1310. At that time Aycelin was appointed guardian of the seals in Nogaret's absence, and thereafter was more frequently absent "on the king's business" than present at further meetings. Presumably he felt that he laid out the proper pattern of procedure and need no longer concern himself too deeply with the details of the hearings. That he kept in close contact with the process, however, is apparent from the records. Little of importance occurred that he missed.

He looked in on the meeting of 7 February, when the contingent sent by Arbert Aycelin appeared for the first time. After inspecting the group, probably to see who was present, he left before the tedious business of hearing each proclaim himself ready to defend the order was begun. He did not return again until 20 February when the irritating Ponzardus de Gysiaco, who had escaped the original screening, returned to protest the irregularities he had noted in the proceedings of the commission. In particular, Ponzardus claimed that the fact that he had been kept in prison without funds or counsel made it impossible for him to organize a proper defense.[26] Aycelin personally undertook to explain to this fractious knight that the commission had no power to free individuals from prison, being restricted to investigating the order as a whole. Sweetly reasonable to the end, he assured the brother that whenever he wished to appear before them he would be brought in and heard immediately. Aycelin then departed, not to return until 2 March when de Molay appeared again with a request to the commission that they expedite his own testimony before the pope. He was dismissed with a reminder that any defense of the order as a whole must be made before the commission.

In the weeks that followed, while the examination of individual knights arriving from the provinces went forward, Aycelin continued to absent himself. His next appearance was on 28

25. *Ibid.*, 53.
26. *Ibid.*, 81–82.

March, to hear the discussion of procedure for the remaining defenders to collate their case. The knights were told that no business could continue effectively with such a multitude and were induced to elect four representatives to act in their names. Aycelin then adjourned the meetings for several days while the procurators were urged to decide on the line of defense they meant to follow. He particularly urged them to make haste because the date of the general council was approaching, although he must have known that a request had already been made for its postponement, which the pope approved on April 4.[27]

Aycelin stayed with the commission long enough to get the new hearings off to a proper start. When the first group of witnesses appeared, carrying their mantles, the commissioners informed them that they were not to wear their habits in court. With this inauspicious start the hearings began, and the archbishop left his colleagues to their own devices until 15 April, when the four spokesmen appeared to protest against the manner in which the process was being conducted. They declared the testimony to be false and claimed that instead of being assured of protection for their own persons, witnesses were being told that the order had already been condemned and that letters under the king's seal (which was in Aycelin's charge) had been issued promising them liberty and pensions if they would testify against the order. They asked for copies of the proofs, lists of the names of witnesses against them, and, to secure the truth, a promise that all witnesses should be obliged to testify under oath that they had not been suborned and had been assured that their testimony should be kept secret.

Aycelin's only response was to direct the notaries to give the procurators copies of the pope's bulls instituting the commission and listing the charges against the order.[28] He then withdrew, not to return until 5 May when another sticky point was raised. The commission was scheduled to hear a group of witnesses who had not been seen before, except by the pope and cardinals. The representatives objected that the witnesses were not even Templars

27. *Reg. Clem. V*, 6293.
28. Michelet, 202.

and asked for copies of their testimony. The protest was not answered and the hearing of the witnesses was canceled on the pretext that the commissioners had to leave the court.

The pattern of Aycelin's appearances is clear: he never troubled to attend any routine testimony of witnesses for or against the order; he always made it a point to be present whenever procedural difficulties might be anticipated; and he does not appear to have been concerned about the actual evidence which he was supposed to judge.

On the whole, the hearings progressed smoothly through the beginning of May. The Templars were not displaying any stunning successes in defending themselves, but the large numbers of knights wishing to testify made it likely that the hearings might continue for years had they not been rudely interrupted by events taking place in Sens.

On 10 May Aycelin and the other commissioners received the four procurators of the order who informed them that the Archbishop of Sens had undertaken to act independently, condemning as individual heretics a number of the Templars waiting to testify before the commission.[29] They requested that the commission take action to save the condemned and assure the other potential witnesses of protection. Aycelin informed them that none of this pertained to his jurisdiction in the case, although he promised to make inquiries of the Archbishop of Sens, Philippe de Marigny.

No one has ever questioned that Marigny was acting with the full knowledge and approval of his brother Enguerrand and of Philip the Fair. But the general tendency has been to assume that Aycelin, unlike his fellows on the royal council, was innocent of the plan and taken by surprise by the proceedings at Sens.[30] It is unlikely that the king treated his guardian of the seals in so crude a manner. Aycelin's entire defense rests on the fact that he did write a mild letter of protest to the Archbishop of Sens. It is the story of the Saisset case all over again. Legally, he might dissociate himself from the process at Sens, as indeed he did, but the com-

29. *Ibid.*, 260.
30. See above, p. 172, n. 11.

plaints of the procurators were too well grounded to be ignored entirely. If witnesses whose names had already been placed before the commission were to be executed out of hand, then their own investigations clearly could not proceed. If Aycelin were to retain any reputation at all for impartiality he must take some action.

This was the line taken by the representatives of the order, who urged an appeal to the pope to take the defenders under his personal protection. They pressed Aycelin to go personally to Sens and prevent the burning of the witnesses, while issuing a similar appeal to the other prelates of France.[31] Though they did not say so, it is more to the point that he could have gone to Philip the Fair. But when the procurators had read their protest and left and as his colleagues on the commission were beginning to discuss the matter, Aycelin left the room, mumbling that he had to celebrate or hear a Mass.[32]

Those who remained decided to think things over, and sent a message to the waiting procurators that they would receive an answer after the Archbishop of Narbonne could be consulted further. Receiving no encouragement from the commissioners, who continued to explain that the court at Sens was totally separate and distinct from their own, the procurators appealed to the Archbishop of Sens and to Clement V. At last the commissioners were brought to promise to see if they could do anything.[33] Aycelin then disappeared for a week, during which time the Archbishop

31. *Ibid.*, 260–62.

32. *Ibid.*, 262: "Dominus Archiepiscopus dicens se vel celebrare vel missam audire, recessit."

33. *Ibid.*, 263. "Postmodum, eadem die in vesperis, dicti domini commissarii omnes se convenerunt in capella predicta, et fuerunt adducti ad eorum presenciam dicti IV fratres, quibus et aliis fratribus dicti domini multum compaciebantur, ut dixerunt; reponderunt, quod negocium de quo dicti dominus archiepiscopus Senonensis et ejus suffraganei agebant, retractabant in suo concilio, et erant totaliter diversa et abinvicem separata, et quod ipsi nesciebant quid in dicto concilio aliquid agebatur ibidem, et quod, sicut ipsi domini commissarii erant in negocio sibi commisso per Sedem apostolicam deputati, et quod ipsi domini nullam habebant potestatem in eos nec super eos; propter quod non videbatur dictis dominis commissariis prima facie, ut dixerunt, quod haberent aliqua inhibere dicto domino archiepiscopo Senonensi vel aliis prelatis super retardacione processum faciendorum per eos contra singulares personas ordinis predicti; adhuc tamen deliberarent melius super predictis, et facerent quod esset faciendum per eos, precipientes nobis notariis, ut requestam et appellaciones ipsorum fratrum insereremus in processu, loco apostolorum testimonialium exhibendorum eisdem."

of Sens reached out and included one of the procurators in his condemnation.

Clearly some response to this new aggression was necessary. On 18 May Aycelin wrote a friendly letter informing the archbishop that the spokesman was needed if his own investigations were to continue correctly. He did make it clear, though, that he did not want to encroach on the rights of his fellow prelates.[34] The Archbishop of Sens replied that the process had already dragged on too long. He claimed that he could not call his suffragans to council any time he liked. He was not deliberately acting to impede the action of the commission but felt he must continue his own process. Before this answer was received, Aycelin was again incommunicado, and his colleagues felt obliged to write to the Archbishop of Sens that they hoped he would do nothing rash before they could take counsel with the head of their commission.[35]

Hearing that the fifty-four condemned Templars were to be burned at sunrise the very next day, the commissioners sent a second message asking the Archbishop of Sens to give the matter further thought out of consideration for their own proceedings. Some of the fifty-four were in fact scheduled to appear in their court on that very day. The Archbishop of Sens did not respond and, with Aycelin still absent, the commissioners sat the following day, 19 May, to receive a lengthy list of those who wished to re-

34. *Ibid.*, 278 : "Non intendentes dicti domini commissarii, ut dixerunt, propter premissa aliquam inhibicionem facere dominis archiepiscopo Senonensi ejusque suffraganeis et concilio memoratis, nec eorum officium impedire, sed ad eorum dominorum commissariorum exoneracionem, et ut predictorum dominorum veritas eis ignotesceret, significabant predicta, ut predicti domini archiepiscopus Senonensis suffraganei sui et concilium, qui periti erant, deliberarent inter se qualiter haberent procedere in inquisicione contra dictum fratrem Reginaldum qui de eorum esse provincia dicebatur."

35. *Ibid.*, 279–80: "Quod cum, de voluntate et consilio dicto domini archiepiscopi Narbonensis fecissent, absque aliqua inhibicione et precepto, significationem predictam eisdem domino archiepiscopo Senonensi, ejusque suffraganeis et consilio, et dicta significacio clara esset et nullam contineret ambiguitatem, dictusque dominus archiepiscopus Narbonensis absens esset a Parisius, non poterant convenienter, absque ejusdem domini archiepiscopi consilio, declaracionem aliam facere in premissis, sed eo redeunte Parisius, cum ejus consilio declararent eisdem si aliqua erant super hoc declaranda. Addicientes predictos dominum archiepiscopum Senonensem ejusque suffraganeos et consilium a Deo fore peritos quam bene sciebant [sic] discernere quod, ex significacione predicta eis facta, debebant agere in premissis."

move their names from the lists of defenders. They then suspended their meetings for over a week. When they reconvened on 30 May Aycelin was still absent, though he had sent a letter stating that he did not wish his absence to impede them in the conduct of their hearings. He returned the following week to preside over the meeting at which the commission decided to adjourn until the following October or November, at which time they were resolved to press forward even if some members of the commission should be unable to appear.

Before the commission resumed its regular meetings, Aycelin and other members interviewed the two remaining procurators on 17 October and asked them if they wished to persist. They said they did but demanded the counsel of their two companions, who were learned, while they themselves were only illiterate knights. Patiently the commissioners explained that one of the other two had confessed his guilt and then escaped from prison. The other had been reduced to such a state by the Council at Sens that he could no longer be admitted to the defense. The remaining pair then crumbled and renounced any further defense of the order on the ground that in their ignorance they would probably do more harm than good.[36]

The commissioners could now return to their original tactics. On 3 November they met, had the public crier call for witnesses, and directed a notary to record that no one appeared. Then the three commissioners present announced that they could not continue because of the absence of the other members. Since the archbishop was to be out of Paris they decided to adjourn, though they did resolve to pass the time examining a group of prisoners held at the Abbey of Fiscano. There, in January, the archbishop again stopped by to listen to a few witnesses repeat the standard confession. After that, alleging the king's business as his excuse, he left the commissioners to carry on alone through February, March, and April. At the end of May they made an appointment with Aycelin to confer together with the king. Thereafter, on 5 June, the entire commission met for the last time to compile their final report to the pope, ending without a positive conclusion to their investigations.

36. *Ibid.*, 286.

Meanwhile, Aycelin had been translated to the Archbishopric of Rouen, and he appeared at the Council of Vienne in August with that title. He was appointed a member of the conciliar commission to bring the affair of the Temple to an end, a conclusion to his work against the order toward which he had long been aiming. The original bulls of convocation for the council may well have been written under his direction at Poitiers in 1308.[37] He was unquestionably responsible for its frequent postponement while he guided the work of his commission to its predestined end.

He was summoned for the final act in the drama, appearing at the curia in answer to a papal directive on 1 September to participate in the preliminary discussion of procedure for the handling of the Templar affair.[38] The lengthy report of this group comprised the opening business of the council, but no debate was held on the question until the arrival of Philip the Fair in December 1311. At that time the pope submitted the question of whether the Templars should be allowed to defend themselves to the council. Clement felt that they should be, but admitted that such a proceeding posed a grave danger of scandal. The Archbishop of Rouen and others spoke against the proposition and after some resistance and delay they were able to carry their point.[39]

As the Aragonese predicted, the sentence was finally passed without a defense and the prelates of the house and council of the King of France got their way. Everyone saw that there was too much prejudice against the order and that the case had been carried too far to be dropped without scandal. The Bishop of Mende proposed that the council vote Clement the power to

37. This is the opinion of Müller, *Das Konzil von Vienne*, 14.
38. *Reg. Clem. V*, 7518–21.
39. Finke, *Papsttum*, II, 259, report of the Aragonese observer: "L'arabisbe de Roam [Rouen] ab labat de Clunyech [Cluny] et tres bisbes tengren, la dita defensio esser denegadora. Tots les altres tengren lo contari, segons que damunt es dit, e que defenidor devia esser deputat per lo senyor papa. Apres lo senyor papa ordona, que casau metes sa reposta en scrit ab son segell. E han responst. E finalment les responstes, venen e aço, que damunt es dit. Iassia que viam segons que par, que sene altra defensio sera enantar en lo dit fet, esters lo fet se ananta fort a espay, e nol menen axi com a homens, que enantar volen, mas donen aquesta dolor de enantament per tal cor un punt no gosen enantar, que nos sapis lo Rey de Franca, axi que finalment en tot a per tot sic fa axi com el vol. E els fets se tracten es emegen mes que mes per aquells perlats, qui son de sa casa e de son conseyl."

procure a sentence by virtue of his plenitude of power, but no clear decision was taken publicly.[40]

All that Aycelin had done in the service of Philip the Fair was vindicated when the pope, in secret consistory on 12 April, dissolved the order on his own authority. The announcement was made public in the presence of the king and his council. Clement V had been able to save nothing but a shadowy appearance of authority through the device of dissolving the order without a formal statement that the body itself had acually been heretical in its practices.

40. Lavocat, *Procès des frères et de l'ordre du Temple*, 377.

XV

Archbishop of Rouen

In May of 1311, while the affair of the Templars was being brought to its conclusion, Aycelin was translated to the see of Rouen. Despite his years of preoccupation with the great affairs of the realm and his consequent absenteeism, his successor at Narbonne found a well-run and financially sound diocese. Unlike most of the newly appointed prelates of the time, the new archbishop had no need to secure papal permission to make loans to restore the financial condition of his church. Unquestionably, with due regard to Aycelin's own work, this was due in large part to the archbishop's foresight in preventing the exercise of regalian rights by the royal agents in Narbonne. In addition, Aycelin had maintained and strengthened the rights and revenues of that church through his legislation and his securing of the Charter of Liberties of 1303. He had started construction on a new cathedral, and he had defended and reaffirmed his feudal jurisdiction through his long struggle with the viscount.

With all this, he had amassed a large personal fortune. On 6 November 1311, a few months after his translation, Aycelin was given permission to make a will in which he endowed the College of Montaigue at the University of Paris and financed several other pious projects which had been approved by the pope.[1] So successful had he been in defending his privileges that the church of Narbonne, almost alone among the churches of France, found it unnecessary to contribute to the complaints being compiled at that time for consideration by the Council of Vienne.

In contrast to the prosperous condition of Narbonne, the condition of the church of Rouen seemed specially designed to serve as a warning against placing an important office in the hands of an incompetent prelate. Aycelin's predecessor, the nephew of

1. *Reg. Clem.* V, 7622.

Clement V, had been removed from office "because in the insolence of his youth, he could not get along with the Normans."[2] This was a complaint no one could have directed at Aycelin. He could be depended upon to soothe the ruffled feelings of his new suffragans, the Bishops of Bayeux and Coutances, with whom he had worked harmoniously in the past. The chroniclers welcomed his appointment, praising his gifts.[3]

On 29 August 1311, while in Paris to celebrate the marriage of the daughter of Charles de Valois to Philip of Taranto, he gave his oath of fidelity for his new office to the King of France.[4] In November 1312 he performed a similar ceremony, doing homage to Edward II of England for lands which the archbishopric of Rouen held in his realm.[5] Though still preoccupied with the condemnation of the Templars, he put an energetic hand to the affairs of his new diocese. A procurator from his home church of Billon was sent to collect Aycelin's pallium and receive oaths of fidelity from his new vassals. His representative was instructed to organize the administration of the church according to its customary rights.[6] On 31 December he persuaded Clement V to annul all donations made in the diocese by his nephew because the scandalous state of the finances demanded instant retrenchment.[7] In addition, he got permission to contract a loan of 5000 gold florins to cover outstanding expenses, which was arranged on 23 January with his nephew, Gilles Aycelin, Lord of Montaigue.[8]

Following the pattern established on his elevation to Narbonne, he then collected a series of bulls from Clement V, 13 July 1312, establishing his powers and liberties in his new diocese. In addition to settling questions of rights over benefices, he strengthened his jurisdictional position by obtaining a bull giving him control of absolutions from excommunications and exemption for

2. Guillaume de Nangis, Continuator, *Chronique latine*, 396.
3. *Ibid.*, 396: ". . . litterali et seculari prudentia valde peritus, multisque gaxis opulentissimus." P. 383: "He was prudent and learned in the law and a member of the king's council." Frachet (p. 35) calls him the principal member of the council.
4. *Reg. Clem. V*, 8898.
5. Rymer, *Foedera*, III, 361.
6. *Reg. Clem. V*, 7151.
7. *Ibid.*, 7652.
8. *Ibid.*, 7636 and 7674.

any but papal excommunications for himself. He obtained a completely free hand to enforce existing rights of jurisdiction against any who might challenge them except the King or Queen of France. Particularly, he got permission to proceed against the members of the cathedral chapter to force them to respect his rights, which they had formerly ignored.[9]

During his tenure of Rouen, Aycelin's policies were similar to those he had followed at Narbonne—but he never achieved the complete success there that marked his career in the south. Shortly after Aycelin's translation, Clement V undertook a full-scale investigation of conditions in the churches of France. Each province was invited to submit a list of grievances, particularly against aggressions by the secular powers, which could be used to establish guidelines for additions to canon law. The redaction of these complaints, with additional comments, was completed for submission to the Council of Vienne by a committee which combined the separate dossiers under general rubrics with an indication of their origin and proposed remedies. Those which have survived the centuries have been recovered and printed, providing some indication of Aycelin's principal concerns when he took control of the church of Rouen.[10]

Rouen apparently had little or nothing to contribute to most of the sections of the dossier. Only in the section pertaining to lay encroachments against ecclesiastical jurisdiction did it show much interest. There it provided a lengthy and interesting answer to the complaints of Pierre Dubois in 1300 on ecclesiastical aggression in the courts of Normandy.[11] With his own expertise in the law and his previous experience at the Exchequer of Normandy, Aycelin must have considered himself peculiarly well qualified to take up this problem. He complained that ecclesiastical persons were being forced to answer for personal actions before temporal courts; that they were seized without the authorization of the diocesans and put to torture and otherwise maltreated.[12] Moreover, he

---

9. *Ibid.*, 9510–23. The question of the claims of the chapter of Rouen caused a brief but unresolved flurry in the time of Boniface VIII.

10. Ehrle, "Ein Bruchstück der Acten des Concils von Vienne," *Archiv für Literatür- und Kirchengeschichte*, IV, 361–470.

11. De Wailly (ed.), *Summaria Brevis, passim.*

12. Ehrle, "Ein Bruchstück," 373.

accused the secular courts of encroaching on the ecclesiastical courts in cases concerning the distribution of confiscated goods, tenths, and other property matters pertaining to the church. In this instance, Aycelin displayed his erudition with citations from the Customs of Normandy.[13]

The church of Rouen, in addition to the complaints it shared with other provinces, supplied a unique section of the dossier, detailing the abuses of lay patrons who abused the revenues of vacant churches under their guardianship.[14] This complaint may have been intended as part of a general effort to secure a body of privileges similar to those he had gained for Narbonne. At the time of his translation he had already received a royal charter for Rouen, giving the church the exclusive right to collect royal subventions and thus keeping the ruinous officials away from church property, but no mention of the regalia was included.[15] After Aycelin's death in 1319, John XXII undertook to investigate the problem and was informed by the Bishop of Coutances that the temporal and spiritual regalia had always been held by the cathedral chapter. But in 1339 the king exercised the right without opposition.[16]

13. *Ibid.*, 396–97: ". . . quod de consuetudine regionis Normannie sunt quedam feuda laycalia, in quibus suam exercent iurisdictionem domini temporales; et alia, que in elemosinam puram et perpetuam ecclesie donata fuerunt; et quedam alia, in quibus omnum iurisdictionem habent sole persone ecclesiastice. Nunc autem cum super feudis huiusmodi vel iuribus eorum realibus agitur, pars, que dictam rem suum esse asserit feudum laycale, capere solet quandam scripturam modicam a iudice seculari, que brevium de feudo et elemosina nuncupatur; quo brevio sumpto et iudici ecclesiastico insinuato, idem iudex ecclesiasticus, licet primitus de cause cognoscere incepisset, in cognitione huiusmodi, videlicet utrum sit feudum vel elemosina, pendente lite coram seculari iudice, ulterius non procedat in causa; quia cognitio feudorum et rerum immobilium generaliter de consuetudine dicte terre spectat ad iudicem secularem."

14. *Ibid.*, 389: "Quod quamquam vacantibus beneficiis contentionis, per locorum ordinarios de yconomis, qui fructus beneficiorum ipsorum in utilitate ecclesie convertant vel successoribus futuris reservant fideliter, debeat provideri; tamen iudices seculares de iure patronatus dictorum beneficiorum cognoscentes impediunt et contradicunt quod iudices ecclesiastici ad custodiam fructuum beneficiorum huiusmodi non ponunt yconomos, sed ipsorum quandoque, quibus volunt, commitunt custodiam; et eos quandoque dissipant ac sibi retinent, in eorum, ad quos spectat, preiudicium et totius ecclesiastice libertatis. Ac super causa predicta iuris patronatus et eius cognitione per ipsos seculares iudices personis ecclesiasticis Rothomagensis provincie plura particularia gravamina sepissime sunt inflicta."

15. Artonne, "Le mouvement de 1314," 82.

16. Gaudemet, *La collation*, 61.

Nevertheless, Aycelin apparently had some success with the king during the period when the conciliar commissions were compiling their reports. In 1312 Philip ordered his officials not to interfere with the jurisdictional rights of the Archbishop of Rouen.[17] As he had done in Narbonne, Aycelin was undertaking a general housecleaning of his diocese and used both his influence with the king and his participation in a reforming council to establish a meaningful and practical separation of civil and ecclesiastical powers. To the king's orders he could add the recommendations of the Council of Vienne in his resistance to the encroachments of lay agents, even though the decisions of the council were not incorporated into canon law in his lifetime.

Though some of these recommendations were published in the *Clementines* some years after the death of Clement V, the seriousness of the reform discussions at the Council has been questioned. The actual records of the Council have been lost and the published complaints of the clergy illustrate only the need for reform, not its achievement. The whole discussion was largely a side issue compared to the condemnation of the Templars. Moreover, if the pope recommended strong steps toward the correction of abuses, he could not depend on the support of the French clergy. The prelates of France who had deserted Boniface VIII could hardly have been expected to mobilize resistance under the leadership of Clement V.

At best the actions of the council could have provided an energetic prelate with useful support for his independent activities. Possibly his complaints had not been intended to do more. Aycelin collected as many safeguards and privileges for his church as possible; but considering the strength of the royal position in 1312 as compared to 1302, he could not have expected to repeat the spectacular gains he had made in Narbonne. As was his custom, he followed up his activities at the Council of Vienne and at court with a provincial synod in October 1313, to restate and strengthen the customary rights which investigation had proven to belong to his church. To their reassertion he added a support-

17. Fallue, *Histoire politique et religieuse de l'église métropolitaine et du diocèse de Rouen*, II, 195.

ing series of disciplinary decrees rather like those issued under his presidency at Narbonne.[18] This synod represented a recovery and reorganization of rights asserted by similar provincial decrees in the thirteenth century. Aycelin had delayed its meeting not only for purposes of investigating his own claims but because, by holding it after the Council of Vienne, he could support his position with the decrees obtained there.

During these latter years Philip the Fair seemed to be moving toward a renewal of his earlier policy of centralizing the kingdom so far as possible. Private wars and duels, prohibited in the early years of the reign by a law revoked in 1306, were again forbidden. Local complaints began to mount that royal officials, in defiance of the Grand Ordinance of 1303 and its expanded guarantees of 1307–1308, were once more disregarding local privileges and liberties. In 1314, to obtain the consent of his subjects for a new levy of taxes for a campaign in Flanders, Philip called an assembly which was to include representatives of the entire realm,[19] bypassing the local negotiations generally preferred by its various components.[20]

Discontent began to spread, particularly against the new taxes. The lords of the north and east of France began to form a series of leagues against the king especially to resist the levies. They charged that the money was not being used to the profit of the kingdom or its common defense but rather to enrich certain councillors. The king was accused of violating his coronation oath and desiring to "eat his people."[21] Philip's attempts to investigate the causes of these complaints and suppress the opposition only resulted in a more extensive demand that the king respect the liberties of his subjects. The situation was still unresolved when Philip the Fair died in November 1314.

At the accession of Louis X, lords and prelates alike demanded and got from the new king a renewal of the Grand Ordinance

18. Mansi, *Sacrorum Concilliorum*, XXV, 526ff.
19. *Grandes chroniques de France*, V, 206: "En cest an, le jour de la feste de sainte Pierre, Philippe le Biaux, roy de France, assemble a Paris pluseurs barons et evesques; et enseurquetout, il fest venire pluseurs bourgois de chascune cité du royaume que semons y estoient a venir."
20. Fawtier, "Parlement d'Angleterre et Etats Généraux de France," 277.
21. Geoffroi de Paris, *Chronique rimée*, 151.

with its promise to keep to the customs of Saint Louis, particularly in respect to local rights of justice. In addition, local groups were demanding specific charters outlining their own liberties. As Artonne[22] has shown, the movement cannot be compared with the general movement in England which produced the Magna Charta since it did not result at any point in the formulation of a common set of grievances. However, it did achieve much the same result within the framework of the greater decentralization of France and the greater independence of local powers. Unlike the situation in England, it did not arise from a discontent which embraced the entire country and, in this sense, cannot be called a feudal reaction against the policies of Philip the Fair. Many of the great lords did not join the leagues and many of the leaders of the resistance were prelates and townsmen rather than barons.

The first area to receive the desired charter of liberties was Normandy. The names of those who formulated and urged the adoption of the charter were not recorded but it seems more than likely, considering his own activities in pursuit of such a statement for his own church, that Aycelin participated in the movement. The *Charte aux Normands*[23] included articles pertaining to the rights of every class of people. It has often been praised for the juridical character that distinguished it from the more amorphous charters issued for other provinces in this period and for its more "democratic" character in comparison to contemporary charters. In fact, it was so effective a document that for nearly two centuries the *Charte aux Normands* represented the basic statement of Norman customs, and was frequently confirmed as the law of the land.[24] Once obtained, it was deposited in Aycelin's church of Rouen for safekeeping and reissued by most of the kings of the fourteenth and fifteenth centuries.

Normandy was rich in lawyers, but it is unlikely that the experience of the Archbishop of Rouen was not drawn upon in the devising of the careful legal safeguards for which the charter is justly famous. Royal officials assigned to the province were to be required to take an oath to observe its provisions on penalty of

22. "Le mouvement de 1314 et les chartes provinciales de 1315," 25.
23. *Ordonnances,* 551; reissued and expanded, p. 587.
24. Artonne, "Le mouvement de 1314," 44.

suspension from office. Heavy money fines were to be levied on those who broke the oath. These were problems and solutions with which Aycelin had had much experience through his work on the royal council and in the Parlement of Paris. It is therefore likely that his experience helped to make the Norman charter the only one of the many issued by Louis X to outlast the movement that brought it into being.[25]

Such activity from a member of Philip the Fair's inner circle did not necessarily constitute a rejection of the policies of the dead king. Cooperative as he always was in pursuing royal objectives in foreign policy, Aycelin was also consistently distinguished for his efforts to maintain his feudal and ecclesiastical rights at home. Further, his commitment to the protection of Norman liberties can be readily compared to his demands for privileges in Narbonne in 1296 and the confirmation of the liberties of the churches of Languedoc which he obtained in 1303. Thus, his participation in the movement can be seen as fully conformable with the traditions of the French monarchy and the policies previously followed by Philip the Fair.

This drive for legal reforms and the confirmation of charters of liberty, must be distinguished from the simultaneous reaction which was occuring in 1314–1315 against some of the ministers of Philip the Fair, principally Enguerrand de Marigny. Their power and influence caused great resentment among some nobles at court who felt that they had been cheated of their proper share in the government. Most particularly, the king's brother, Charles de Valois—who had spent much of his life vainly searching for a crown of his own—brooded long over the success of lesser men in filling the place with the king which he felt should have been his own. Others in France were readily persuaded that at least Marigny, who was given to ostentatious displays of wealth, had been using public funds for his own enrichment.

In particular, complaints against Marigny were coming in from the lords of Normandy, where he was constantly adding to his extensive estates.[26] Charles de Valois supported their claims and added a demand that his accounts should be examined. Aware

25. Lot and Fawtier, *Histoire des institutions,* II, 560.
26. Geoffroi de Paris, *Chronique rimée,* 158.

of this hatred, Marigny is said to have begged the dying Philip to speak to Louis on his behalf. But Philip was content to advise his son not to despoil the minister if he could be proved to have served him faithfully.[27] Louis X himself had long resented the finance minister for much the same reasons that motivated Charles de Valois. Moreover, shortly before his accession, Marigny had earned the prince's enmity by thwarting his plans for a new Flemish expedition, procuring peace there without a fight. One of his first acts was to order an examination of Marigny's accounts in January 1315.[28] Though they were found to be in good order, a new process was immediately opened against him.

It was supposed, in the first study made of the "feudal reaction" following the death of Philip the Fair,[29] that the movement against the former king's ministers was connected to the movement for the charters and that both were the product of Charles de Valois' hatred of his brother's policies. Langlois[30] reexamined the problem, and concluded that the movement for the charters of 1315 was entirely independent of Valois' agitation for revenge against Marigny and his colleagues. Likewise, Petit[31] argued that Valois was as committed as anyone in the court to the principle of royal rights, and had no part in the movement to secure the charters.

A similar distinction is easily supposed on the part of the former ministers of the dead king. Assuming that Gilles Aycelin did join in the movement of 1314 to secure the *Charte aux Normands*, it remains quite unlikely that he could have had any sympathy with the second movement, designed to destroy his companions in office. Aycelin knew Marigny well, as he knew the other famous victim of the period, Pierre de Latilly, Bishop of Châlons. He had worked with both of them in the past, but there is no way of knowing how close their aquaintanceship may have been.

When Marigny was arrested in the spring of 1315, there were

27. Baudon de Mony, "La mort et les funérailles de Philippe le Bel," 5–14.
28. Geoffroi de Paris, *Chronique rimée*, 153ff.
29. Dufayard, "La réaction féodale sous les fils de Philippe le Bel," *Revue historique*, LIV, 241–72; LV, 241–70.
30. *Saint-Louis*, 267.
31. *Charles de Valois*, 146ff.

two men in his household who were in all likelihood related to the Archbishop of Rouen. Pierre Aiscelin, a subdeacon, received a dispensation from Clement V in 1312 to become a clerk for Enguerrand de Marigny.[32] It is probable that he still held that post when Marigny fell from power.[33] Marigny had obtained several benefices and dispensations for Pierre as well as for Bertaut de Montaigue, another of his clerks who was probably related to Aycelin and who was arrested with Marigny on 21 April 1315, being listed as his chaplain.[34] Their ultimate fate is unknown, but the arrest of at least one of his relatives at this time must have helped to convince Gilles Aycelin that a firm resistance might be needed to prevent the spread of this attack on members of the council.

This mood was solidified by the arrest of the Bishop of Châlons on a preposterous charge of poisoning Philip the Fair as well as his predecessor in the bishopric.[35] Until his arrest, de Latilly had been guardian of the seals, having succeeded to the office on the death of Nogaret. He had been consecrated as Bishop of Châlons in 1313 by Aycelin himself.[36] Since de Latilly was a prelate, Louis X felt that his own jurisdiction did not extend beyond his imprisonment and deprivation of the offices he held from the king. Consequently, he urged the clergy to undertake his condemnation. The Archbishop of Rheims was persuaded to open a council for preliminary investigation of the charges in May 1316, but he had to adjourn the hearings because he lacked a sufficient number of prelates in attendance to fulfill canonical requirements. Accordingly, he wrote to Aycelin and other French prelates urging their appearance and asking that they append their seals to a copy of the letter in acknowledgement of its receipt.

Since the requisite quorum was never obtained and de Latilly was finally acquitted by Philip V,[37] the French prelates were apparently united in their refusal to countenance the process. More than one of them must have thought that if such a proceed-

32. *Reg. Clem. V*, 8651.
33. This is the view of Favier, *Enguerran de Marigny*, 21.
34. *Ibid.*, 21. The privileges for these two are listed in *Reg. Clem. V*, 7794–95.
35. Guillaume de Nangis, Cont., *Chronique latine* 612.
36. *Ibid.*, 609.
37. Lehugeur, *Histoire de Philippe le Long*, 107.

ing succeeded, any of them might be the next victim. Moreover, de Latilly was no Bernard Saisset. The official charges against him have been lost, but the accusation that he poisoned Philip the Fair is patently ridiculous. Philip had just rewarded his loyalty with the highest office on his council. Where Saisset had been unpopular, a troublemaker, and easily convicted at least of talking treason—whether or not he undertook the singularly inept plots charged against him—de Latilly was a loyal and valuable servant of the king he was accused of murdering. Moreover, in the Saisset case, Philip had taken every care to disavow the charges that he had behaved tyranically against the person of the bishop. Now the bishop had been unceremoniously flung into prison and his fellow prelates summoned to try him, although there was little or no proof of his guilt. It is small wonder that the prelates, who had taken such care not to involve themselves in the proceedings against Saisset, refused altogether to join de Latilly's enemies. They could behave in no other way if they put any value on their own immunities.

After the failure of the Archbishop of Rheims, Louis X himself undertook to urge the attendance of the clergy and, fortuitously, the reply of Gilles Aycelin has been preserved. He refused in the most uncertain terms, alleging secret reasons which he said he had explained in person before the council and did not wish to repeat in writing. He concluded that he would consider himself but an evildoer and prevaricator if he were to act against his honor and conscience.[38]

Exactly what secret reasons Aycelin had for his refusal will never, and can never, be known. His refusal to become a liar in this case is probably a reference to his own conviction that the Bishop of Châlons was an innocent victim of his enemies. Pegues bases an entire interpretation of Aycelin's character on this letter, claiming that the "awful secret which Aicelin knew" threatened

38. D'Achéry, *Spicilegium*, III, 708: "Verum, Carissime Domine, scitis quod diebus assignatis in dicto negotio non potui interesse propter causas secretas quae non sunt literis inserendae, quae in vestri praesentia et consilii vestri secrete apud nemus Viceniarum possem, nec potero aliquo modo propter causas easdem, nisi velim esse malus homo et praevaricator et id facere contra meam conscientiam et honorem; quod non libenter facerem quovismodo; nec vestra clementia, sicut suppono, id vellet."

to "tear the fraudulent facade" from the secret trials of Philip the Fair's time.[39] Because of this particular show of resistance, Pegues argues that the prelate had throughout his career represented an opposition force to Philip's acts of aggression against Saisset, the Templars, and even Boniface VIII. Favier has recently concurred in this argument.[40] Aycelin's actions in these cases have been examined and do not support this contention. It is not very fruitful to speculate about the secret he mentions in his letter to any great length. There is, however, one possibility which should be noted. Assuming that Aycelin's real interest was to prevent what seemed to him an outrageous act of aggression against his former colleague that would endanger all of Philip's councillors, he may have reminded the council that de Latilly had been privy to a number of dubious dealings in the past which they could not afford to have revealed in an open court. Specifically, he may have reminded them that de Latilly had participated in Aycelin's secret discussions of 1306 with Clement V, which could have opened the proceedings against the Templars.

Aycelin was far from representing a conservative force in opposition to Philip the Fair and his fellow lawyers. He had supported the king energetically in most of the affairs that now seem shocking to us, but he had never acquiesced in royal aggressions against the traditional rights and liberties of his subjects. In Narbonne he steadily refused to abandon his claims against the viscount and actively opposed the royal effort to encroach on their mutual rights in the case of the Jewish property. In Rouen he was still seeking the establishment of his rights and probably interesting himself in the local movement to secure a charter. The charges against de Latilly and the effort to force the clergy to condemn him represented a dangerous attack on legal rights and the immunities of clergymen. Additionally, it appears to have been based on a totally unjustified set of accusations. The man who had so deftly used the law to dispose of Saisset and destroy the Templars could not approve the abuse of the law against one of his fellow prelates in France.

The available evidence certainly does not appear to support

39. *Lawyers of the Last Capetians,* 72.
40. Favier, "Les Légistes," 99.

Favier's contention that Aycelin's refusal to participate in this case lost him the favor of Louis X.[41] Throughout the reign and during the early years of the reign of Philip V, Aycelin continued to act as a leading member of the council until his death in 1318, a position which was becoming increasingly endowed with strict legal definitions.[42] The development of the leagues of 1314–1315 gave the body still greater importance, as it was generally intended by the leaguers to represent a check on the royal power.[43] Under Louis X and during the regency of Philip V, it enjoyed a brief moment of success in reserving decisions on certain crucial questions to its own authority.[44] During the period between the death of Louis X in June 1316 and the arrival of his brother in Paris to assume the regency, the business of government was carried on by the council and the name of Gilles Aycelin was prominent among those of the councillors who officially recognized the regency in exchange for Philip's agreement to give the council power to appoint his officials and distribute ecclesiastical benefices in his name.[45]

These controls were discarded when Philip V became king in 1317. At that time Aycelin was dispatched to undertake a settlement of the claims of Jeanne of Burgundy, daughter of Louis X, whose claim to the throne had been set aside. The Archbishop of Rouen had already participated in the meeting which proclaimed Philip V and was therefore familiar with her case. Her uncle, the Duke of Burgundy, bowing to the decision of the meeting, still laid claim to her independent right to the duchy. Aycelin headed

41. *Ibid.*, 94: "Gilles Aiscelin, professor and jurisconsult, diplomat and master of the Parlement, was distinguished by his moral rectitude, his independent spirit, his acute sense of honor and justice, which forced him to oppose the king in the Saisset affair and to preside with impartiality over the pontifical commission charged with the interrogation of the Templars; the Archbishop of Narbonne was a legist before he was a servant of the king and with him *raison d'état* gave way before respect for the rules of procedure; his refusal to assist in the prosecution of Latilly lost him the favor of Louis X."

42. Luchaire, *Manuel des institutions*, 539, has shown that the title *concilium* was beginning to be used exclusively to distinguish a body of advisors distinct from the judges of the Parlement of Paris. Boutaric, *La France sous Philippe le Bel*, 164, cited examples of letters to show that the rank of councillor was being transformed into a specific title conferred by special royal appointment.

43. Cazelles, *La société politique*, 36.

44. Lehugeur, *Histoire de Philippe le Long*, II, 115–36.

45. Cazelles, *La société politique*, 37.

a board of arbiters in the summer and again in November 1317. On 27 March 1318 they completed their work, ceding Burgundy to the heiress but holding Champagne and Brie for Philip V, with the provise that they would revert to Jeanne if the king should die without a male heir.[46]

In April 1318 the Archbishop of Rouen was one of a group of French prelates who threatened Robert of Bethune with excommunication according to the terms of the Treaty of Athis, as part of the organization of a new Flemish campaign. Aycelin died a month later, having had the final satisfaction of striking a parting blow at this old adversary who had once called him a crafty lawyer who twisted and perverted the honorable men ranged against him, thus securing that very "Treaty of Iniquity" with whose enforcement he ended his official career.

46. Fisquet, *La France Pontificale,* 143.

XVI

Conclusion

The life of Gilles Aycelin is the story of great achievements attained through intelligent application of the broad policies of Philip the Fair. At court he played his part in the formulations of programs which he then helped to carry out as a diplomat, a feudal lord, a lawyer, and a prelate. For a complete appreciation of the interrelationship of the various problems that commanded the archbishop's attention, it must never be forgotten that through most of his life he was pursuing several ends simultaneously. While the affair of Bernard Saisset was at its height, he was still occupied with negotiating the king's objectives in Flanders. Likewise, during the months of his involvement with the quarrel with Boniface VIII, he was deeply occupied in the royal efforts to organize a program of legal and administrative reforms within France. While presiding over the investigation of the Templars, he was working as the chief officer of the royal council.

As a diplomat, his principal accomplishment was to bring the long struggle with the King of England over Aquitaine and Flanders to a successful, if temporary, conclusion. The treaties of Montreuil and Athis gave renewed strength to the lordship of the King of France over his mighty and rebellious vassals. This domination was continually buttressed by the decisions of their peers in the Parlement of Paris over which Aycelin so frequently presided. But as a feudal lord in his own right in Narbonne and in Rouen, he displayed inexhaustible energy in defense of his own privileges and in obtaining charters from the king restating and reinforcing those liberties. His position was in no way contradictory. He labored hard to establish the ultimate sovereignty of the king over his realm. He put equal effort into ensuring that this sovereignty would be exercised in strict conformity with the

ancient custom which protected the liberties and privileges of the
king's subjects.

Aycelin's motives are known to us only obliquely, though his
actions speak fairly clearly. His record obliges us to agree with his
contemporaries that he was wise, learned in the law, and one of
king's most valuable councillors. When he died in 1318, he had
passed unscathed through the orgy of vengeance that overtook so
many of his companions at the court of Philip the Fair. Indeed,
he assisted in blunting the force of that attack by his refusal to
act in the case against Pierre de Latilly. To the end, he did his
duty to his church of Rouen and continued to play an important
part in the service of two of the sons of his dead master.

The only profound conflict in his career in the service of both
the temporal and spiritual lords of France occurred in 1302 when
he was forced to make a definite and public choice between Boniface VIII and Philip the Fair. He chose the king—as did the over-
whelming majority of his fellow prelates. There is no need to
suppose that the choice was dictated by fear, or even by unre-
lieved self-interest. His is one of the first voices of the emerging
"Gallican spirit," which would make itself felt for centuries to
come in the ecclesiastical history of France. Aycelin's choice is
proof only that Philip the Fair had succeeded in making the
nationalist appeal to the loyalties of the people stronger than the
internationalist appeal of the papacy.

The question was never raised again in Aycelin's lifetime.
Clement V had neither the courage nor the strength to renew the
demands of Boniface VIII. That Aycelin never regretted his
original decision, however, is implicit in his pursuit of the
Templars. He showed no concern with the question of whether or
not the order was guilty as charged. He appears to have cared
little for the prestige or the jurisdictional power of the papacy,
which he had been appointed to represent in the work of his commission. Instead, he single-mindedly pursued the interests of the
King of France who was irretrievably committed to the dissolution of the order.

Wholeheartedly as he pursued all his assignments in the service of Philip the Fair, his loyalty was defined by a clear concept
of the limitations which bound the king. He failed to protect his

suffragan, Bernard Saisset, from the king's agents; despite his lengthy protests to Boniface VIII, he made no apparent effort to do so. But Saisset was accused of treason, which Aycelin was not the man to tolerate. In more normal circumstances, his efforts as a prelate to clarify and strengthen the independent position of the Church cannot be faulted. He supported the king in the dispute over *Clericis Laicos*, but he never recognized his right to tax the clergy. He and his suffragans contributed generously to the royal coffers, but never failed to demand new privileges for their churches in return. Even in 1302–1303 his stand was limited to specific charges against the ruling pope. It did not extend, nor was it expected to extend, to a challenge to the papal office itself.

Of all the brilliant men who served Philip the Fair, Aycelin was the most versatile. No other councillor appears so often, in so many capacities, in the records of the time as the Archbishop of Narbonne. The history of his private life, the record of his inner cares and motivations, was never recorded. But the bare record of his service alone more than justified his claim to greater attention than he has ever received.

Gilles Aycelin's history is most valuable for the light it sheds on hitherto obscure aspects of the reign of Philip the Fair. The most important aspect of his career is the extent to which it is typical of the royal councillors. Nogaret and Flote have too often filled the eyes of those who have studied the reign. Even they have been discussed primarily in the light of their public and radical responses to the great challenges of the period. The statements of less influential propagandists like Dubois have been given an overinflated value to support the common belief in a growing secular spirit among the lawyers of Philip the Fair. Yet there were few laymen who could rival in importance the great prelates like Aycelin. They were the men who filled the council— who as lawyers framed the great ordinances and manned the courts where they were executed, and as lords and prelates, held the balance between local and central power in France.

These ecclesiastics fail to display any purely religious sensibility and in that respect might be called "secular." The great ideals of their forefathers seem to have lost their power over these men. Boniface VIII's appeals for a renewal of the crusades were greeted in France with a profound indifference. His attempt to revive the ideal of the primacy of the international Church fell on deaf ears. But though the heart of Gilles Aycelin has never been opened to us, what has been recorded of his life shows that he was not a man without ideals. Every aspect of his variegated career seems to illustrate a vision which must have guided him, his fellow councillors, and perhaps even his silent master: a vision of France, united under a king who held his rights from God alone and exercised them in a spirit of equity and profound respect for the liberties and privileges of his subjects.

Bibliography

d'Achéry, Luke, *Spicilegium sive Collectio Veterum Aliquot Scriptorum*. Paris: Montalant, 1723.

Acta Sanctorum, IV (May), 418–537. Paris and Rome: Victor Palmé, 1866.

Alberic, *Compendium of the History of the Cistercian Order*. Abbey of Gethsemane: 1944.

Père Anselme, *Histoire généalogique de la maison royale de France*. Paris: 1730.

Arquillière, H. X., "Boniface VIII," *Dictionnaire de droit canonique*, II, 940–48.

———, "L'appel au concile sous Philippe le Bel et la génèse des théories conciliares," *Revue des questions historiques*, LXXXIX, 23–55.

Artonne, A., "Le mouvement de 1314 et les chartes provinciales de 1315," *Bibliothèque de la Faculté des Lettres de l'Université de Paris*, XXIX (1912).

Aubert, Félix, *Histoire du Parlement de Paris (1250–1515)* Paris: Librairie Alphonse Picard et Fils, 1894.

Auw, Lidia von, "Da Celestino V a Bonifacio VIII," *Ricerche Religiose*, IX (1933), 424–40.

Baethgen, Friedrich, *Beiträge zur Geschichte Cölestins V*. Königsberger Gelehrten Gesellschaft: Niemeyer Verlag, 1934.

———, *Der Engelpapst; Idee und Erscheinung*. Leipzig: Hoehler und Anelang, 1949.

Baillet, Adrien, *Histoire des démeslez du pape Boniface VIII avec Philippe le Bel, roy de France*. Paris: 1718.

Baluze, Etienne, *Histoire généalogique de la maison d'Auvergne*, 2 vols. Paris: A. Dezallier, 1708.

———, *Miscellanea Novo Ordine Digesta*, I. Lucca: 1761.

———, *Vitae Paparum Avenionensium*, 4 vols., new edition by G. Mollat, Paris: 1927.

Baudon de Mony, Charles, "La mort et les funérailles de Philippe le Bel," *Bibliothèque de l'Ecole des Chartes*, LVIII, 5–14.

Baudouin, A. (ed.), *Lettres inédites de Philippe le Bel*. Paris: H. Champion, 1887.

Baumgarten, Paul M., *Untersuchungen und Urkunden über die Camera Colegii Cardinalium für die Zeit von 1295–1437*. Leipzig: Geisecke und Devrient, 1898.

Baumhauer, August, *Philipp der Schöne und Bonifaz VIII in ihrer Stellung zur franz. Kirche mit besonderer Berücksichtigung der Bischofswahlen.* Freiburg: Karl Henn, 1920.

Bernard Gui, *Historia.* See Martène and Durand, *Veterum Scriptorum et Monumentorum.*

Beugnot, Le Comte (ed.), *Les Olim ou registres des arrets, rendue par la cour du roi. Collection de documents inédits,* III. Paris: 1842–1844.

Black, J. G., "Edward I and Gascony in 1300," *English Historical Review,* XVII (1902), 518–27.

Boase, T. S. R., *Boniface VIII,* London: Constable and Co., 1933.

Bonassieux, Pierre, *De la réunion de Lyon à la France.* Lyon: 1874.

Bossuat, A. In Lot and Fawtier, *Institutions seigneuriales,* ch. IV, "L'Auvergne," 101–22.

Boulainvilliers, Henri de, *Histoire de l'ancien gouvernement de la France.* La Haye and Amsterdam: 1727.

Boutaric, Edgar, *Actes du Parlement de Paris,* I–II. Paris: 1863.

———, "Clément V, Philippe le Bel et les Templiers," *Revue des questions historiques,* X (1871), 301–42; XI (1872), 5–40.

———, *La France sous Philippe le Bel,* Paris: Plon, 1861.

———, "Notices et extraits de documents inédits relatifs à l'histoire de France sous Philippe le Bel," *Notices et extraits des manuscrits de la Bibliothèque Impériale,* XX, 83–237.

Bréquigny, M., *Tables chronologiques des diplômes, chartes, titres et actes imprimés concernant l'histoire de France,* VII, VIII. Paris: 1863.

Carbonel, Paul, *Histoire de Narbonne.* Narbonne: Brille and Gautier, 1956.

Carolus-Barré, Louis, "Les baillis de Philippe III le Hardi. Recherches sur le milieu social et la carrière des agents du pouvoir royal dans la seconde moitié de la société du XIIIᵉ siècle," *Annuaire-bulletin de la Société de l'Histoire de France* (1969), 109–244.

Carrière, Victor, *Introduction aux études d'histoire écclésiastique locale,* 3 vols. Paris: Letouzey, 1934–1940.

Cazelles, Raymond, *La Société politique et la crise de la royauté sous Philippe de Valois.* Paris: Librairie d'Argences, 1958.

Chaplais, Pierre, "Règlement des conflits internationaux franco-anglais au XIVᵉ siècle," *Le moyen age,* LVII (1951), 269–302.

Chapotin, Marie-Dominique, *Histoire des dominicains de la Province de France.* Rouen: Imprimerie Cagniard, 1898.

Chassaing, Augustin, *Spicilegium Brivatense.* Paris: Imprimerie Nationale, 1886.

Chenu, M-D., "Dogme et théologie dans la bulle Unam Sanctam," *Recherches de science religieuse,* XL (1952), 307–17.

Chevalier, Ulysse, *Régeste dauphinois,* III. Valence: Imprimerie Valentinoise, 1914.

Chronica Rotomagensis, cont. *Recueil des historiens des Gaules et de la France,* XXIII, 343–48. Paris: Imprimerie Nationale, 1876.

Chronique attribué à Jean Desnouelles. Recueil des historiens des Gaules et de la France, 181–98. Paris: Imprimerie Nationale, 1875.

Chronique parisienne anonyme. Mémoires de la Société de l'histoire de Paris, XI. Paris: H. Champion, 1885.

Ciaconius, Alphonse, *Vitae et Res Gestae Pontificum Romanorum et S. R. E. Cardinalium*, II. Rome: 1677.

Corvi, Antonio, *Il Processo di Bonifacio VIII. Studio Critico*. Rome: 1940.

Creytens, Raymond, "Le 'Studium Romanae Curiae' et le Maître du Sacré Palais," *Archivum Fratrum Praedicatorum*, XII (1942), 5–83.

Davis, Georgene W., *The Inquisition at Albi*. New York: Columbia University Press, 1948.

Delisle, Léopold, "Gilles Aicelin, Archevêque de Narbonne et de Rouen," *Histoire littéraire de la France*, XXXII, 474–502. Paris: 1898.

———, *Recueil de jugements de l'Echiquier de Normandie*. Paris: 1864.

Denifle, Heinrich (ed.), "Die Denkschriften der Colonna gegen Bonifaz VIII," *Archiv für Literatür- und Kirchengeschichte*, V, 493–529.

Denifle, Heinrich, and Chatelain, E. (eds.), *Chartularium Universitatis Parisiensis*. Paris: Delelaine, 1891.

De Vic, Claude, and Vaissette, J., *Histoire générale de Languedoc*, IX, X. Toulouse: E. Privat, 1885.

Digard, Georges, *Philippe le Bel et le Saint Siège de 1285 à 1304*, 2 vols. Paris: Librairie de Recueil Sirey, 1936.

Digard, Georges, *et al.* (eds.), *Les registres de Boniface VIII*, 4 vols. Paris: Bibliothèque des Ecoles Françaises d'Athènes et de Rome, 1907.

Douie, Decima, *The Nature and Effect of the Heresy of the Fraticelli*. Manchester University Press, 1932.

Drumann, W., *Geschichte Bonifacius des Achten*, 2 vols. Königsberg: Gebrüder Bornträger, 1852.

Duchesne, François, *Histoire des cardinaux français*. Paris: 1660.

———, *Histoire des chanceliers et gardes des sceaux de France*. Paris: 1680.

Ducoudray, Gustave, *Les origines du Parlement de Paris et la justice*. Paris: Librairie Hachette, 1902.

Dufayard, Charles, "La réaction féodale sous les fils de Philippe le Bel," *Revue historique*, LIV (1894), 241–72; LV (1895), 241–90.

Dumont, J., *Corps universel diplomatique du droit des gens*. Amsterdam: 1726.

Dupuy, P., *Histoire du différend d'entre le pape Boniface VIII et Philippe le Bel Roy de France*. Paris: 1655.

Ehrle, Franz, "Ein Bruchstück der Acten des Concils von Vienne," *Archiv für Literatür- und Kirchengeschichte*, IV (1888), 361–470.

Emery, Richard W., *Heresy and Inquisition in Narbonne*. New York: Columbia University Press, 1941.

Fallue, L., *Histoire politique et religieuse de l'église métropolitaine et du diocèse de Rouen*, II. Rouen: 1850.

Favier, Jean, "Les légistes et le gouvernement de Philippe le Bel," *Journal des Savants* (1969), 92–108.

———, *Un conseiller de Philippe le Bel: Enguerran de Marigny. Mémoires et documents publiée par la Société de l'École des Chartes*, no. 16. Paris: 1963.

Fawtier, Robert, *Comptes royaux (1285–1314). Recueil des historiens de la France*, III. Paris: 1953.

———, "Parlement d'Angleterre et Etats Généraux de France au moyen-age," *Comptes rendus de l'Académie des Inscriptions et Belles-Lettres* (1953), 275–84.

Fiamma, Galvano, "La Cronaca Maggiore." *See* Odetto, Gundisalvo.

Finke, Heinrich, *Acta Aragonensia*, 3 vols. Berlin and Leipzig: Rothschild, 1908.

———, *Aus den Tagen Bonifaz VIII. Vorreformationsgeschichtliche Forschungen*, II. Münster: Ashendorffschen, 1902.

———, *Pappstum und Untergang des Templerordens. Vorreformationsgeschichtliche Forschungen*, III, IV. Münster: Ashendorffschen, 1907.

Fisquet, M. H., *La France pontificale. Métropole de Rouen*, V, pt. 3. Paris: E. Repos.

Floquet, A., *Histoire du Parlement de Normandie*. Rouen: Edouard Frère, 1840.

Forte, Stephen L., "A Late Thirteenth Century Collection of Questions in ms. Vat. Lat. 14013," *Archivum Fratrum Praedicatorum*, XVIII (1948), 95–121.

Fournier, Paul, "Les conflits de jurisdiction entre l'église et le pouvoir séculier de 1180 à 1328," *Revue des questions historiques*, XXVII (1880), 432–64.

Fragment d'une chronique anonyme, finissant en MCCCXXVIII. Recueils des historiens des Gaules et de la France, XXI, 146–58. Paris: Imprimerie Nationale (1875).

Funck-Brentano, Frantz, *Additions au codex diplomaticus Flandriae. Bibliothèque de l'Ecole des Chartes*, LVII, 1896.

———, "Mémoire sur la bataille de Courtrai (1302, 11 Juillet) et les chroniqueurs qui en ont traité," *Mémoires de l'Academie des Inscriptions et Belles-Lettres*, ser. 1, vol. X, pt. 1 (1893), 293–327.

———, *Philippe le Bel en Flandre*, Paris: H. Champion, 1896.

———, (ed.), *Chronique artésienne (1295–1304) et Chronique tournaisienne (1296–1314). Collection des textes*, XXIV. Paris: Librairie Alphonse Picard et Fils, 1899.

Gaignard, Romain, "Le gouvernement pontifical au travail: l'exemple des dernières années du règne de Clement V: 1 Août 1311–20 Avril 1314," *Annales du Midi*, LXXII (1960), 169–214.

Galabert, Fr., "Le Toulousain Anselme Ysalquier est-il allé au Niger au XV° siècle?" *Mémoires de l'Academie des Sciences, Inscriptions et Belles-Lettres de Toulouse,* ser. 12, vol. XI (1933), 2–45.

Gallia Christiana in provincias ecclesiastica distributa, VI, XIII. Paris: 1739.

Gaudemet, Jean, *La collation par le roi de France des bénéfices vacants en régale des origines à la fin du XIV° siècle. Bibliothèque de l'école des Hautes Etudes,* LI. Paris: 1935.

Génestal, R., *Le Privilegium Fori en France,* 2 vols. *Bibliothèque de l'école des Hautes Etudes,* XXXV, XXXIX. Paris: 1921, 1924.

Geoffroi de Paris, *Chronique rimée. Recueils des historiens des Gaules et de la France,* XXII, 87–166. Paris: Imprimerie Nationale, 1876.

Girardi de Fracheto, *Chronicon. Recueils des historiens des Gaules et de la France,* XXI, 5–70. Paris: Imprimerie Nationale, 1875.

Glorieux, Palémon, *Repertoire des maîtres en théologie de Paris au XIII° siècle. Etudes de philosophie médievale,* XIII, XIV. Paris: Vrin, 1933, 1934.

Gramain, Monique, "La composition de la cour vicomtale de Narbonne aux XII° et XIII° siècles," *Annales du Midi,* LXXXI (April 1969), 121–39.

Grandes chroniques de France, P. Paris, ed., V. Paris: Librairie Techener. 1837.

Grandjean, C. (ed.), *Le Registre de Benoît XI. Bibliothèque des Ecoles Françaises d'Athènes et de Rome.* Paris: 1905.

Gregorovius, Ferdinand, *History of the City of Rome in the Middle Ages.* Translated from the German, 14th ed. London: 1897.

Guigue, M-C., *Cartulaire municipal de la ville de Lyon.* Lyon: Auguste Brun, 1876.

Guillaume de Nangis, *Chronique latine.* Paris: Jules Renouard, 1843.

Hauréau, Barthélemy, *Bernard Délicieux et l'inquisition albigeoise, 1300–1321.* Paris: Librairie Hachette, 1877.

———, "Richard Leneveu, Evêque de Béziers," *Histoire littéraire de la France,* XXVI, 539–51.

Hefele, C-H., and Leclercq, H., *Histoire des Conciles,* VI, pt. 1. Paris, 1914.

Hervieu, Henri, *Recherches sur les premiers Etats Généraux.* Paris: Ernest Thorin, 1879.

Höfler, Constantin, "Rückblick auf P. Bonifacius VIII und die Literatür seiner Geschichte," *Abhandlungen der Historischen Classe der Königlich Bayerischen Akademie der Wissenschaften,* III, pt. 3 (1843).

Hofman, Herbert, *Kardinalat und kuriale Politik in der ersten Halfte des 14. Jahrhunderts.* Bleicherode: C. Nieft, 1935.

Holtzmann, R. "War Bonifaz VIII ein Ketzer?" *Mitteilungen des Instituts für österreichische Geschichtsforschung,* XXVI (1906).

———, *Wilhelm von Nogaret,* Freiburg: 1898.

Johannes Victoriensis [or Victring], *Chronicle*, J. F. Boehmer, ed., *Fontes Rerum Germanicarum*, I. Stuttgart: J. G. Cotta'scher, 271–450.

John of Saint Victor, *Excerpta e memoriali historiarum. Recueil des historiens des Gaules et de la France*, XXI, 630–76. Paris: Imprimerie Nationale, 1875.

Journal du trésor. See Viard.

Kervyn de Lettenhove, "Etudes sur l'histoire du XIIIᵉ siècle de la part que l'ordre de Cîteaux et le Comte de Flandres prirent à la lutte de Boniface VIII et de Philippe le Bel," *Mémoires de l'Academie des Sciences et Belles-Lettres de Bruxelles*, XXVIII (1854), 1–105.

———, *Histoire de Flandres*, II, III. Brussels: Vandale, 1847.

Kirsch, Johann P., *Die Finanzverwaltung des Kardinalkollegiums im XIII und XIV Jahrhundert*. Münster: Heinrich Schoningh, 1895.

de Lagarde, Georges, *La naissance de l'esprit laïque au déclin du moyen age*, 3d ed., I. Paris: B. Nauwelaerts, 1956.

Lajard, Félix, "Le Cardinal Hugues Aycelin de Billiom," *Histoire littéraire de la France*, XXI, 71–79.

Langlois, Charles-Victor, "Documents relatifs à Bertrand de Got (Clement V)," *Revue historique*, XL (1889), 48–54.

———, "Geoffroi du Plessis, protonotaire de France," *Revue Historique*, LXVII (1899).

———, *Le règne de Philippe III, le Hardi*. Paris: Librairie Hachette, 1887.

———, "Les doléances du clergé de France au temps de Philippe le Bel," *Revue bleue*, ser. 5, vol. IV (1905), 329–33; 486–90.

———, "Les origines du Parlement de Paris," *Revue historique*, LXII, 74–114.

———, *Saint-Louis–Philippe le Bel–Les derniers Capétiens directs*, III, pt. 2, *Histoire de France*, E. Lavisse, ed. Paris: Librairie Hachette, 1919.

———, *Textes relatifs à l'histoire du Parlement depuis les origines jusqu'en 1314*. Paris: Alphonse Picard et Fils, 1888.

———, "Une réunion publique à Paris sous Philippe le Bel, 24 Juin 1303," *Bulletin de la Société de l'histoire de Paris et de l'Ile de France*, XV (1888), 130–34.

———, (ed.), "Les papiers de Guillaume de Nogaret," *Notices et extraits des manuscrits de la Bibliothèque Nationale*, XXXIV (1909).

Langlois, Ernest (ed.), *Les registres de Nicholas IV*. Paris: 1886.

Langlois, Monique, "Le Parlement de Paris," *Guide de recherches dans le fonds judiciaires de l'ancien régime*, M. Antoine, ed. Paris: Ministère de l'Education Nationale (1958), 67–160.

Lavocat, *Procès des frères et de l'ordre du Temple*. Paris: Plon, Nourrit et Cie., 1888.

LeBras, G., Lefebvre, Ch., and Rambaud, J., *L'age classique, 1140–1378. Sources et théories du droit*. Vol. VII of *Histoire de droit et des institu-*

tions de l'église en occident, G. LeBras, ed. Paris: Librairie de Recueil Sirey, 1965.

Lehugeur, Paul, Histoire de Philippe le Long. Paris: Librairie Hachette, 1897.

Lemarignier, J. F., Gaudemet, J., and Mollat, G., Institutions écclésiatiques. Vol. III of Histoire des institutions francaises au moyen age, F. Lot and R. Fawtier, eds. Paris: Presses Universitaires de France, 1962.

Leroux, Alfred, Recherches critiques sur les relations politiques de la France avec l'Allemagne, 1292–1378. Bibliothèque de l'école des Hautes Etudes, L. Paris: Viewege, 1882.

Levis-Mirepoix, Philippe le Bel. Paris: Les Editions de France, 1936.

Limburg-Stirum, Thierry, Codex Diplomaticus Flandriae, 2 vols. Bruges: 1879.

Lizérand, Georges, Clement V et Philippe le Bel. Paris: Librairie Hachette, 1910.

Lodge, Eleanor C., Gascony under English Rule. London: Methuen, 1926.

Loenertz, R., "Saint Dominique, écrivain, maître en théologie, professeur à Rome et Maître du Sacré Palais, d'après quelques auteurs du XIVᵉ et XVᵉ siècles," Archivum Fratrum Praedicatorum, XII (1942), 84–97.

Lot, Ferdinand, and Fawtier, Robert (eds.), Institutions seigneuriales, Vol. I of Histoire des institutions françaises au moyen age. Paris: Presses Universitaires de France, 1957.

———, Institutions Royales. Vol. II of Histoire des institutions françaises au moyen age. Paris: Presses Universitaires de France, 1958.

Luchaire, Achille, Manuel des institutions françaises. Paris: Librairie Hachette, 1892.

Maier, Anneliese, "Due sermoni del Card. Nicola di Nonancour relativi alla lotta dei cardinali Colonna contro Bonifacio VIII," Rivista di Storia della Chiesa in Italia, III (1944), 344–64.

Mandonnet, P., "Premiers travaux de polémique Thomiste," Revue des sciences philosophiques et théologiques, VII (1913), 46–70; 245–62.

Manselli, Raoul, "Arnaldo de Villanova e i Papi del suo tempo," Studi Romani, VII (1959), 146–61.

Mansi, Joannes D., Sacrorum Conciliorum Nova et Amplissima Collectio, XXIV, XXV. Venice: 1780.

Martène Edmond, and Durand, Ursini, Thesaurus Novus Anecdotorum, I, IV. Paris: Bibliopolarum Parisiensium, 1717.

———, Veterum Scriptorum et Monumentorum, VI. Paris: 1729.

Martin, Henri, Histoire de France, V. Paris: 1839.

Martin, Victor, Les cardinaux et la curie. Bibliothèque catholique des sciences religieuses, LXXVIII, 1930.

———, Les origines du gallicanisme. Paris: Bloud and Gay, 1939.

Martin-Chabot, M. E., "Contribution à l'histoire de la famille Colonna de

Rome dans ses rapports avec la France," *Annuaire-bulletin de la Société de l'Histoire de France,* LVII (1920), 137–90.

Matthew of Westminster, *Flores Historiarum. Rerum Britannicarum Medii Aevi Scriptores,* XCV, pt. 3. London: 1890.

Maugis, Edouard, *Histoire du Parlement de Paris de l'avènement des rois Valois à la mort d'Henri IV.* Paris: Librairie Alphonse Picard et Fils, 1913.

Mayer, *Des Etats Généraux et autres assemblées nationales,* I. Paris, 1788.

McNamara, J., "Simon de Beaulieu and *Clericis Laicos,*" *Traditio,* XXV (1969), 155–70.

Ménard, *Histoire civile, écclésiastique et littéraire de la ville de Nismes,* I. Paris: Chaubert, 1750.

Menestrier, Claude F., *Histoire civile ou consiliaire de la ville de Lyon.* Lyon: 1696.

Michelet, Jules, *Histoire de France,* III. Paris: Ernest Flamarion, 1830.

———, *Procès des templiers,* 2 vols. *Collection des documents inédits,* VII. Paris: 1841–1851.

Möhler, Ludwig, *Die Kardinäle Jakob und Peter Colonna. Quellen und Forschungen aus dem Gebiete des Geschichte,* XVII, 1914.

Molinier, Auguste (ed.), *Correspondence administrative d'Alphonse de Poitiers. Collection des documents inédits,* V². Paris: Imprimerie Nationale, 1900.

———, *Les sources de l'histoire de France,* III. *Les Capétiens, 1180–1328.* Paris: Librairie Alphonse Picard et Fils, 1903.

Mollat, Guy, *Les Papes d'Avignon (1305–1378),* 2d ed. Paris: Librairie Victor Lecoffre, 1912.

Morel, Octave, *La grande chancellerie royale.* Paris: 1900.

Mortier, R. P., *Histoire des Maîtres Généraux de l'Ordre des Frères Prêcheurs,* II. Paris: Librairie Alphonse Picard et Fils, 1905.

Mouynès, Germain, *Ville de Narbonne. Inventaire des archives communales antérieures à 1790.* Narbonne: 1871–1879.

Müller, Ewald, *Das Konzil von Vienne, 1311–1312; seine Quellen und seine Geschichte. Vorreformationgeschichtliche Forschungen,* XII. Münster: 1934.

Odetto, Gundisalvo (ed.), "La Cronaca Maggiore dell'Ordine Domenicano di Galvanno Fiamma," *Archivum Fratrum Praedicatorum,* X (1940), 297–373.

Ordonnances des roys de France de la troisième race, I, XII. Paris: 1723, 1777.

Parliamentary Writs and Writs of Military Summons, I. London: 1827.

Pasquier, Estienne, *Les recherches de la France.* Paris: De Varennes, 1633.

Pegues, Franklin J., *The Lawyers of the Last Capetians,* Princeton: Princeton University Press, 1962.

Perrichet, Lucien, *La grande chancellerie de France des origines à 1320.* Paris: 1912.

Petit, Joseph, *Charles de Valois (1270–1325).* Paris: Librairie Alphonse Picard et Fils, 1900.

Picot, Georges, *Documents relatifs aux Etats Généraux et assemblées réunis sous Philippe le Bel. Collection des documents inédits,* XXXV. Paris: 1901.

Port, Célestin, (ed.), *Le livre de Guillaume le Maire. Collection des documents inédits,* XI, *Mélanges historiques,* II, 187–537. Paris: 1877.

Prutz, Hans, *Entwicklung und Untergang des Tempelherrenordens.* Berlin: G. Grotesche, 1888.

Ptolemy of Lucca, *Historia Ecclesiastica. Rerum Italicarum Scriptores,* Muratori, ed., XI, 741–1307.

Quétif, Jacques, and Echard, Jacques, *Scriptores Ordinis Praedicatorum,* I, pt. 1. New York: Burt Franklin, 1959.

Rabanis, J. *Clement V et Philippe le Bel.* Paris: Durand, 1858.

Raine, James (ed.), *Historical Papers and Letters from the Northern Registers. Rerum Britannicarum Medii Aevi Scriptores,* LXI. London: 1873.

Raynaldi, Odorico, *Annales Ecclesiastici ab Anno 1198,* revised by J. D. Mansi, XXIII. Lucca: 1749.

Raynaud, Gaston, "Nouvelle charte de la 'Pais aus Englois' (1299)," *Romania,* XIV (1885), 279–80.

Regestum Clementis Papae V, 9 vols., edited by the Monks of Saint Benedict. Rome: Typographia Vaticana, 1885.

Le registre de Benoit XI. See Grandjean, C.

Les registres de Boniface VIII. See Digard *et al.*

Les registres de Nicholas IV. See Langlois, Ernest.

Regné, Jean, *Amaury II Vicomte de Narbonne, 1260(?)–1328.* Narbonne: Caillard, 1910.

Renan, Ernest, "Diverses pièces relatives aux différends de Philippe le Bel avec la Papauté," *Histoire littéraire de France,* XXVII, 371–81.

———, *Etudes sur la politique religieuse du règne de Philippe le Bel.* Paris: Calmann Levy, 1899.

Renouard, Yves, "Les papes et le conflit franco-anglais en Aquitaine de 1259 à 1337," in *Etudes d'histoire mediéval* (1968), II, 911–34.

Rigault, Abel, *Le procès de Guichard, Evêque de Troyes (1308–1313).* Paris: Calmann Levy, 1899.

Rishanger, William, *Chronica et Annales. Rerum Britannicarum Medii Aevi Scriptores,* XXVIII, pt. 2. London: Longmans Green.

Rivière, A. F., *Histoire des institutions de l'Auvergne,* 2 vols. Paris: 1874.

Rivière, Jean, *Le problème de l'église et de l'état au temps de Philippe le Bel.* Louvain and Paris: 1926.

Rochet, Charles, *Les rapports de l'église du Puy avec la ville de Girone en Espagne et le comté de Bigorre.* Le Puy: Perard, 1873.

Rocquain, Félix, "Philippe le Bel et la bulle 'Ausculta Fili,' " *Bibliothèque de l'Ecole des Chartes*, XLIV (1883), 393–418.

Rothwell, H., "The Confirmation of the Charters, 1297," *English Historical Review*, LX, LXI (1946–1947), 16–35; 177; 300.

Rymer, Thomas, *Foedera, Conventiones, Literae et cujusconque Generis Acta Publica*, I–III. London: J. Tonson, 1727.

Sägmuller, J. B., *Tätigkeit und Stellung Kardinäle bis auf Bonifaz VIII.* Freiburg: 1896.

Schelenz, Erich, *Studien zur Geschichte des Kardinalats im 13 und 14 Jahrhundert*. University of Marburg dissertation: 1913.

Schleyer, Kurt, *Die Anfange des Gallikanismus im 13 Jahrhundert. Historische Studien*, CCCXIV. Berlin: 1937.

Scholz, Richard, *Die Publizistik zur Zeit Philipps des Schönen und Bonifaz VIII. Kirchenrechtliche Abhandlungen*, VI–VIII. Stuttgart: 1903.

―――, "Zur Beurteilung Bonifaz VIII und seiner sittlichreligiosen Charakters," *Historische Vierteljahrschrift*, IX (1906), 470–515.

Schöttmüller, Konrad, *Der Untergang des Templerordens*. Berlin: Mittler, 1887.

Schulz, Hans, *Peter von Murrhone*. Berlin: W. Weber, 1894.

Seppelt, F-X., *Studien zum Pontifikat Papst Coelestins V. Abhandlungen zur Mittleren und Neueren Geschichte*, XXVII. Berlin and Leipzig: Rothschild, 1911.

Sommer, Clemens, *Die Anklage der Idolatrie gegen Papst Bonifaz VIII.* Freiburg: Kuenzer, 1920.

Souchon, Martin, *Die Papstwahlen von Boniface VIII bis Urban VI und die Enstehung des Schismas 1378.* Braunschweig: Benno Goeritz, 1888.

Soudet, Fernand, *Ordonnances de l'Eschiquier de Normandie aux XIVe et XVe siècles*. Caen: L. Jovan et R. Bigot, 1926.

Stefaneschi, J., *Opus Metricum. Monumenta Coelestiniana*, F-X. Seppelt, ed., 1–146. Paderborn: F. Schoningh, 1921.

Strayer, Joseph R., "Consent to Taxation under Philip the Fair," *Studies in Early French Taxation*, pt. 1. Cambridge, Mass.: Harvard University Press, 1939.

―――, "Normandy and Languedoc," *Medieval Statecraft and the Perspectives of History*, 44–59. Princeton: Princeton University Press, 1971.

―――, "Philip the Fair—A 'Constitutional King," *Medieval Statecraft and the Perspectives of History*, 195–212. Princeton: Princeton University Press, 1971.

Tessier, Georges, "L'enregistrement à la chancellerie royale française," *Le moyen age*, XXVI (1956), 41–62.

Tout, T. F., *Edward the First*. London: Macmillan, 1932.

Trivet, Nicholas, *Annales Sex Regum Angliae*, Th. Hog, ed. London: English Historical Society, 1845.

"Une satire contre Philippe le Bel, 1290," *Bulletin de la Société de l'histoire de France* (1857–1858), 197–201.

Valbonnais, *Histoire des dauphins de la troisième race.* Geneva: 1718.

Viard, Jules (ed.), *Les journaux du trésor de Charles IV le Bel.* Paris: Imprimerie Nationale, 1917.

———, *Les journaux du trésor de Philippe le Bel.* Paris: Imprimerie Nationale, 1940.

de Vidaillon, M., *Histoire des conseils du roi.* Paris: Amyot, 1856.

Vidal, J-M., *Bernard Saisset (1232–1311).* Toulouse and Paris: Librairie Alphonse Picard et Fils, 1926.

Villani, Giovanni, *Istorie Fiorentine,* IV–V. Milan: Bocchetto, 1802.

de Wailly, Natalis (ed.), "Mémoire sur un opuscule anonyme intitulé: Summaria brevis et compendiosa doctrina felicis expeditionis et abbreviationis guerrarum ac litium regni Francorum," *Mémoires de l'Academie des Inscriptions et Belles-Lettres,* XVIII (1899), 435–94.

Walter of Gisburne [or Hemingburgh], *Cronica de Gestis Regum Angliae. Monumenta Germaniae Historica,* XXVIII, 644–46.

Waquet, Henri, *Les sources de l'histoire religieuse de la France dans les archives departmentales.* Paris: Occitania, 1925.

Wenck, Karl, *Philipp der Schöne von Frankreich, seine Persönlichkeit und das Urteil der Zeitgenossen.* Marburg: 1905.

———, "War Bonifaz VIII ein Ketzer?" *Historische Zeitschrift,* XCIV (1905), 1–66.

Index